As We Recall

As We Recall

Reminiscences of the
Naval Academy Class of 1952

Edited by

Vice Admiral James A. Sagerholm, USN (Ret.)

NAVAL INSTITUTE PRESS
ANNAPOLIS, MARYLAND

**This book was made possible by a generous donation of the
Naval Academy Class of 1952**

Naval Institute Press
291 Wood Road
Annapolis, MD 21402

Library of Congress Cataloging-in-Publication Data
United States Naval Academy. Class of 1952.
  As we recall : reminiscences of the Naval Academy class of 1952 / edited by
James A. Sagerholm.
    pages cm
  Summary: "As We Recall is the first book of its kind. A collection of
reminiscences written by members of the U.S. Naval Academy class of 1952, it
is a testament to the value of a Naval Academy education. Some stories are of
combat in Korea, exploits in space, aerial combat over Vietnam, or development
of major weapons systems. Others are stories of life at sea or of the challenges
faced by the families supporting their husbands and fathers. It is safe to say, this
book is an edifying, intimate, and inspiring history"— Provided by publisher.
  ISBN 978-1-61251-899-2 (hardback)
  1. United States Naval Academy. Class of 1952—Biography. I. Sagerholm,
James A., editor. II. Title.
  V415.K4 1952b
  359.0071'173—dc23
                          2015022084

∞ Print editions meet the requirements of ANSI/NISO z39.48–1992
(Permanence of Paper).
Printed in the United States of America.

23 22 21 20 19 18 17 16 15   9 8 7 6 5 4 3 2 1
First printing

Contents

Foreword

T he United States Naval Academy has been producing outstanding leaders for well over a century and a half. Some of them command battle fleets in the nation's wars, others go on to important government and corporate leadership positions, and still others quietly but effectively man the ramparts in times of national crisis and of relative stability, ensuring the continued safety and security of this great nation. The vast majority of these unusual alumni carry out these vital missions in virtual anonymity, most of their contributions unsung and rarely recognized.

In the pages of this unique book, fortunate readers are given a glimpse into that vast universe of national service and sacrifice by focusing on one of the many classes that have marched to the thunder of drums on Worden Field and hurried along the ancient path of Stribling Walk, headed for the transformational classes that prepared them for the "dangers of the sea and the violence of the enemy" as described in the Sailor's prayer.

Every Naval Academy class emerges from its four years by the Severn River with a certain desirable uniformity that relies on steadfast traditions to meet the challenges of an ever-changing and hostile world. Yet each class also takes on its own "personality," born of a composite of the hundreds of individuals that come together from all corners of the nation The Class of 1952 is no exception. They stood out in many ways, beginning with a famous (some would say "infamous") incident on the parade field, and continuing on through adventures on and under the high seas and in the silent realms of outer space. They donned the uniforms of the Navy and Marine Corps and (yes) the Air Force, and distinguished themselves by acts of courage on the field of battle, saving lives in operating rooms, using humor as an antidote to fear and tension, and proving that service comes in many shapes and sizes.

Many suns have set since the Naval Academy Class of 1952 tossed their caps to the sky and left the shores of Chesapeake Bay to venture out to distant lands and uncharted waters. And though they "scattered far and wide" as mandated in their alma mater, they remain bound together by shared experiences of their fledgling youth and by the unbreakable bond of their honor, their courage, and their commitment to serve the greatest nation on earth.

This is their story . . . in their words.

LCDR Thomas J. Cutler, USN (Ret.)
Author of *A Sailor's History*

As We Recall

Introduction

I t was a typical day in February 2014. A group of United States Naval Academy classmates were on the class e-mail circuit, exchanging reminiscences of their days on active duty. Some had been naval aviators, some submariners, and some tin-can sailors. There were also those who had served in the Marine Corps and those who had worn Air Force blue. All were members of the Naval Academy Class of 1952.

As I read some of the "sea stories," I was struck by the historical significance of the experiences described in our e-mail exchanges. The need to gather these stories and get them recorded prompted me to post a letter to the class asking for their recollections. I requested that individual members write articles about their achievements and experiences, giving a picture of service life, including Cold War or hot war incidents.

The result is a composite profile and history of a class that graduated under a cloud, an infamous class that was predicted to have few if any creditable achievements (the reason is explained later in this book). In any event, the reader will see a class that attained significant and indeed historical achievements, produced research and development critical to America's success in the Cold War, produced more flag officers than any Naval Academy class to date, made exceptional contributions to aviation, produced more astronauts than any single class of any institution, and includes college professors and academic deans, clergymen and medical doctors. In short, a remarkable class of which I am truly privileged to be a member, the Naval Academy Class of 1952.

I

THE NAVAL ACADEMY

The United States Naval Academy was sort of a strange place. It was an engineering school with a composite of entries from every state, and quite a few foreign countries, . . . rich boys, poor boys, dull boys, interesting boys, smart boys, and really smart boys. It was designed to forge normal boys into men who served their country with honor, integrity, and competence. But it did much more than that; it forged a tight band of brothers who truly cared about one another, and those they served.

W. J. Ryan, Class of 1952, U.S. Naval Academy

From Plebes to Warriors and Heroes

Frank Hannegan

Each entering class at the United States Naval Academy relies on the usual variety of appointments to fill its roster. It is no secret that these "tickets to admission" produce a random sample of committed and not-so-committed, ambitious and not-so-ambitious, and eager and not-so-eager young men and women at the time they are sworn in. While academics and discipline help bring focus to those not identified as "committed," "ambitious," and "eager," the evolution of class uniqueness helps foster the esprit so important in the military. This uniqueness starts with the differing geographic and demographic sources of applicants and how those disparate applicants evolve and mature.

In that hot and humid summer of 1948, inductees arrived over the course of a number of weeks. Each group had the opportunity to make an unholy mess of stenciling, make a proper bed, and come up with a passable dress-shoe spit shine. Some of us were lucky enough to be mentored by someone from the Naval Academy Preparatory School (NAPS) who was experienced in such things. Classes, labs, p-rades, rifle range, sailing yawls, and competitions, specifically cutter races and battalion boxing, created camaraderie and appreciation of teamwork. The inevitable derelictions and extra duty running the "grinder" led to new acquaintances. By the end of that long-ago plebe summer, we were well bonded with our fellow cutter-crew mates and to a lesser extent those in our battalion. Over the course of the next four years, company and battalion assignments, varsity and intramural sports, and summer cruises expanded friendships and an overall sense of identity and pride in our class.

Following a memorable graduation, the members of our twenty-four "tribes" were scattered, often worldwide. You might say we experienced a diaspora. Air Force, Marine Corps, naval air, submarine, and surface ship commitments, and in time civilian pursuits, often broke previous lines of personal and class communication. The focus on Cold War operations, the space race, and the hot wars in Korea and Vietnam challenged our attention. Nonetheless, it was Korea and Vietnam where many served valiantly, risked their lives, and in some cases never received the recognition they deserved. Still, the valor of four in the Class of 1952 was recognized. In the case of these four, exceptional heroism led to the award of our nation's second-highest combat award. The details of their exploits were not widely publicized, nor to this day are they known to most. These warriors are Lt Gen James R. Brickel, USAF (Ret.), RADM Lowell F. "Gus" Eggert, USN (Ret.), Col Theodore J. Lutz Jr., USMC (Ret.), and CAPT Jerrold "Jerry" M. Zacharias, USN (Ret.). Being that life is getting late, we need to review what these men did because they are our friends and enjoy a special place in the Class of 1952. Their deeds are recorded in separate articles in this book.

The Honor Concept

Jim Sagerholm

During youngster year, the superintendent of the Naval Academy, RADM James L. Holloway Jr., was relieved by VADM Harry W. Hill, who was superintendent until shortly after our graduation in 1952. Admiral Hill formed the Brigade Executive Committee, consisting of the three class presidents: Chuck Dobony, Class of 1950; Bill Lawrence, Class of 1951; and me, Class of 1952. We met once a month with Admiral Hill, apprising him of our view of things in the Brigade.

As the time approached in the spring of 1950 for final exams, Chuck Dobony spoke to Bill Lawrence and me about his concern regarding a practice known as "passing the gouge," wherein the initial sections in a class to take an exam passed the substance of that exam to the sections taking it later. We all agreed that it was an unethical practice and eventually could lead to outright cheating. Since there remained but a few weeks until graduation, we agreed that Bill and I, if reelected, would follow up on the issue when we returned in September.

With the commencement of second class year, I was reelected class president, Bill Lawrence was again elected to lead the Class of 1951, and a midshipman named Ross Perot was elected president of the Class of 1953. True to our promise to Chuck Dobony, under the excellent leadership of Bill Lawrence, the three of us tackled the task of rectifying the practice of the gouge system.

Unlike West Point, the Naval Academy had no institutionalized honor code, although Academy regulations recognized "honor" offenses, such as lying, cheating, and stealing, as class A offenses, and those found guilty were subject to dismissal. It soon became apparent that something akin to an honor code was needed. However, our study of West Point's code indicated that there was no room for an honest mistake in judgment or action by a cadet. An act that could be construed as being a violation of the code was acted upon as a violation ipso facto, with no apparent leeway for reprieve. We concluded that, if justice were to be served, there had to be some provision for remediation when it was a first offense and the circumstances of the case did not clearly show dishonorable intent.

The result, after months of work, was creation of the Honor Concept (not an honor code), which required an in-depth investigation of the alleged offense, impartial adjudication based upon the results of the investigation, and remediation where warranted. We each presented the proposed Honor Concept to our respective classes and received unanimous approval. In the process, we cited the gouge system as being the initial impetus and received again unanimous agreement to stop the practice. By the time we had completed the foregoing, graduation for the Class of 1951 was drawing near, so, with the concurrence of the superintendent, it was agreed that implementation would wait until the following academic year.

In September 1951, Ross Perot and I were reelected presidents of our respective classes, and we were joined on the Brigade Executive Committee by Clyde Dean, the newly elected president of the Class of 1954. The Honor Concept having been approved just prior to the graduation of the Class of 1951, it was left to the Class of 1952 to lead in the implementation of it. Bill Lawrence had provided very strong leadership during our work the previous year in developing the concept, and it was now up to Ross Perot, Clyde Dean, and me to work on the procedures to be followed, a task that involved considerable trial and error and a great deal of discussion with the commandant, who seemed to have missed the idea of allowing remediation where warranted.

It took the entire academic year before a fairly smooth system was in place, and the following year, Ross Perot codified the procedures we had developed during my first class year. With that, the Honor Concept was firmly in place, and with some modifications from time to time, it still serves the Brigade of Midshipmen.

The Flaming "N" Caper

Ken Weir

A few days before the 1951 Naval Academy–Maryland football game, the midshipmen marched on their way to class past the Herndon monument in front of their sacred Naval Academy chapel. The entire monument had been painted purple. No one knew for certain who had done it, but there were indications that Maryland students were responsible—it read, "Go Maryland, beat Navy" or something—but it could have been mids or Hy Gurney and his cheerleaders trying to get the Brigade worked up for the big game. In fact, some mids later on even tried to take credit for having pulled it off.

At any rate, the stunt had the desired effect on several members of the Class of 1952. Dave Davison had a two-tone 1940 Buick that his grandmother had given him. She had put it up on blocks during the war, and the floorboards in the rear seat area had rusted, so there were large holes that allowed exhaust fumes to fill the back seat area. Windows had to be kept open wide so it got quite cold riding there in winter. Dave couldn't afford antifreeze for the radiator, and the brilliant solution was to drain the radiator and cooling system at the end of a day's use so it would not freeze up. When the time came to restart, Dave would make a quick run to the nearby gas station and fill the radiator with water before it overheated. It worked every time.

Ken Weir had a 1939 Plymouth four-door parked up on a hill at the top of Green Street. It was a cold winter. Weir's car had a very weak battery. He would coast down the hill, let the clutch out, start the engine, and away he would go—usually. So back to the Maryland game.

A few torqued-off mids were going to get even. Ken Weir, Bill Jacobson, and Jimmy King went out in town and bought paint and brushes after class before evening meal. *[Editor's note: Weir couldn't afford to buy a new battery, but he had no problem buying paint and brushes for an escapade. Go figure.]* The plan was to rendezvous with Davison down by the waterfront at Dock Street, near the intersection with Green and Main streets. I'm not positive who was with Dave, but Jim Bottomly and/or Jack Blackwood might have gone along on that drill.

After taps, we went over the wall behind the sacred chapel to the car at the top of Green Street and coasted down the hill. Weir's car did not start. It was time for Davison to give Weir a push start—only the front bumper of Dave's car was too low for Weir's rear bumper. But no problem, Dave's front bumper and Weir's front bumper matched perfectly. So off they went, Dave pushing Weir's car backward at the bottom of Main Street in Annapolis at midnight. With the gear shift in reverse, Weir let the clutch out and the transmission exploded. What now?

Weir walked over to a hack daddy in a green Buick taxi and for five dollars, big money in those days, *[Editor's note: But not big enough for a new battery, apparently.]* got him to push Weir's car forward since the Plymouth's and taxi's bumpers matched. But when Weir let out the clutch, nothing happened. After much messing around, the taxi pushed Weir a second time, no extra charge, only that time Weir used second gear and let the clutch out, and after going a block or so, the engine started. Weir went back to the waterfront circle, and Bill Jacobson and Jimmy King jumped in. With only first and second gear, away they went at zero dark thirty, mission bound, no third gear or reverse. No sweat. Those guys were always living on the edge!

It was past midnight and they were ready for the journey to College Park, Maryland. Weir could not keep up with Davison in any case, but more so without third gear. Davison had the five-gallon cans of gasoline and the smoking cigarettes inside his car, all the windows up tight, and the heater going full blast. He got way ahead of Weir and went straight for the half circle lawn at the entrance to Maryland University. Jimmy King, Bill Jacobson, and Weir proceeded to the girls' dorms with the paint. Dave spread the gasoline, lit the flaming N, and smoked off out of there. Jacobson, King, and Weir got the columns to the dorms painted with letter Ns and "Navy Wives" and hopped back into the Plymouth with the engine running all the time for fear it would not crank if he shut it down. They never did see Dave's fireworks, so they left by way of the half-circle entrance, stopped, hopped out to see what Dave had done, and there it was, a big perfect N right in the middle of the lawn. Weir got back in the broken-down Plymouth and headed back to Annapolis, all the while laboring in second gear with no heater. He parked the sedan on the hill at the top of Green Street ready for the next coast start.

Back inside Bancroft about 3:00 a.m., Weir went straight to a pay phone and called the *Baltimore Sun* to tell them they should run over to

College Park and check out what had happened. That day's evening edition had pictures of both the N burned on the lawn and the painted-up dorms. The USNA Executive Department was in a state of total disarray.

On game day, as the midcoolies marched into Byrd Stadium, the Maryland student body threw every piece of trash, eggs, fruit, tomatoes and what all at them. The white cap covers and uniforms were a disaster. And Navy lost the game badly.

It was time to repair the 1939 Plymouth so Jimmy King could borrow the car and drive his girlfriend home to West Virginia for Christmas leave. Weir rented a garage on Saint George Street. *[Editor's note: See what I mean about Weir and money?]* He coasted down the Green Street hill in second gear, let the clutch out, and taxied into the garage. He pulled the transmission out of the car and discovered that the idler gear shaft had disintegrated when Dave had tried to push start Weir backward with the gear shift in reverse. Jimmy King and Weir hopped on a bus, went far out on West Street to a junk yard, purchased a used transmission for twelve dollars, and went back to the bus stop.

Standing there freezing at the bus stop in their blues and overcoats, with a greasy, dirty, rusty transmission, our two heroes saw a red-headed Navy lieutenant, an instructor in the Seamanship and Navigation Department, pull up and stop. He asked King and Weir if they wanted a ride. Cold as hell, they thanked him and said they would wait for the bus. "Put the transmission in the car and get in, I'll take you into town," he replied. So they got in. Not a word was said the whole trip back to town. They got out at the corner of Randall and Saint George streets near Weir's garage (it's still there). A week or two later, the red-headed lieutenant walked up to one of the navigation plotting desks and asked Weir, "Get your car fixed?" Sweating bullets, Weir replied, "Yes, sir!" and thanked him again for the lift.

Off Yankee Station during the war in Vietnam in 1965, a red-headed lieutenant commander and president of the mess on board USS *Mount McKinley* asked Weir one day, "Didn't I give you and another first classman with a junk automobile transmission a ride back to Annapolis in 1951?"

Walter Gragg and Navy Football

Dick Denfeld

A mong all our classmates' stories, Walt's is truly unique. Recalling what he and I experienced together and what we shared during nearly sixty-six years of friendship, I will try to describe why I feel as I do and why he is my hero.

Walt and I entered the Naval Academy in the summer of 1948, having spent the prior year attending different universities, Walt at North Carolina State and I at Oklahoma. Walt had knocked on congressional doors in Washington until he found a congressman who had a nomination to spare. Perseverance was one of his characteristics, and he succeeded against seemingly impossible odds. We each came to Annapolis with the desire to play varsity football and compete in the Army-Navy football games. Getting a good education was also a factor, of course, but it was on the football practice field that we became friends, bumping heads, so to speak. National Collegiate Athletic Association rules at that time did not permit freshmen to play varsity sports, thus our plebe team competed against freshman teams from nearby colleges—and defeated them all.

Plebe teams as well as varsity teams enjoyed the privilege of dining at special training tables, so while our classmates were enduring square meals and endless professional questions from the first classmen at their tables, we were free of all that. When the winless 1948 football season ended with a 21–21 tie against Army, the euphoria that swept over the Brigade resulted in plebes being given "carry on" until the return from Christmas leave. In addition, in the 4th Company, where I was, deference was accorded members of the plebe football team, perhaps because of our winning record, and our second semester was as easy as the first. Come spring, we were back on the training tables, again out of the clutches of the upper classes. To accusations that we on the plebe football team did not have a plebe year, I say right— and I'm not at all sorry.

During our four years at the Academy, the Class of 1952 never had a winning football season, the three wins in our youngster (sophomore) and second class (junior) years being the most experienced. In addition, we suffered a 38–0 loss to Army in our youngster season finale, probably the worst defeat Navy ever suffered against Army. We played a tough schedule, competing against teams like Notre Dame, the University of Southern California, and similarly big teams, but I never felt we were in over our heads. We always gave them a run for their money and enjoyed the competition despite the losses. It was admittedly painful for me, a 180-pound lineman. During the 1950 season, I started nine games and was carried out of eight.

The Army game is always special, and the 1950 game was particularly so. Army came into the game with a twenty-eight-game win streak, whereas Navy had won only two out of eight games that season. But against all odds, Navy won, 14–2, quarterbacked by a 1952 classmate, Zug Zastrow. We who played for Navy that day have an indelible memory of something that ranks near the top of all our lifetime experiences. The famous sports columnist, Red Smith, said this in the next day's issue of the *New York Herald Tribune*:

> A stranger, looking the scene over, would have understood. He would have known that once again, the quality that makes football the game that it is—and which makes the Army-Navy game, especially, the delight it is—had been demonstrated. Once again, a team that had been conceded no chance at all on the record had made a mockery of the records. Once again it had been proved that no matter what happens during any football season, the Army-Navy game is a new season, a different season.

Walt and I were both commissioned second lieutenants in the Air Force, he in electronics and I to flight training as a navigator. Walt later left the Air Force and began a civilian career that reflected his broad interests and remarkable talents. He initially worked for Hughes Aircraft as an engineer while also running his own rug-cleaning business and raising two children in Los Angeles. Nearby Hollywood undoubtedly drew him into the acting field, where, as Steve London, he appeared in movies and television and on stage. His most notable role was Agent Jack Rossman in the original television series *The Untouchables*. Of the more than eight hundred different actors who were on the show from time to time, only five had more appearances than Walt in the five seasons in which it aired. When the series ended and other acting jobs became scarce, Walt began studying law in night school while continuing his rug-cleaning business. He passed the bar exam on the first attempt, and in 1979 he started his own law practice in Pasadena.

What set Walt Gragg apart from most of us is how he willingly, skill-fully, and successfully undertook a multifaceted business, acting, and legal career while contending with serious heart and other health conditions. Beginning in May 1979, Walt was guided by his dedication to a "higher power," his firm belief in God. It was at this time that he met Judy, the love of his life. They were married in 1982, and among other benefits of their life together, they enjoyed the company of various lovable dogs. As far as I am concerned, the best result of their marriage was bringing them into contact with many of us classmates and our wives; we have been inspired by their example and have enjoyed many wonderful times together. The bond made on the football field at the Naval Academy remained intact.

Walt Gragg died of heart failure on 9 June 2014. He lives on in memory.

The Rest of the Story

Jim Sagerholm

The Naval Academy Class of 1952 remembers well the events of Thursday, 5 June 1952, our day of infamy. But how many know the "rest of the story"?

At the color parade that afternoon, all went according to the rules until it was time to pass in review. The reviewing stand was occupied by the superintendent, VADM Harry W. Hill, by the Chief of Naval Operations, ADM William Fechteler, by the former Chief of Naval Operations, ADM Louis Denfeld, by the secretary of the navy, and by several other three- and four-star admirals. At the order to pass in review, it appeared as if the entire 1st Battalion left their shoes in formation as they swung into column for the march off. Prank after prank followed, including gloves tossed into the air at the command "Eyes right!" in front of the reviewing stand. Standing in front of the 6th Battalion, the last to march off, Lou Lambert, the battalion commander, and I, the deputy battalion commander, viewed all this with a great deal of surprise. Remarking that the pranks were getting out of hand, Lambert passed the word back to our ranks that there were to be no such activities by the 6th Battalion, except for the traditional red lanterns carried by the rear rank of the last company.

There had been some pranks at the color parades of previous years, but nothing like this, and it seemed to me that the youthful exuberance of some was indeed getting out of hand. As we marched past the reviewing stand, we had to dodge not only the stuff left on the field but also the youngsters who were darting around the field, collecting souvenirs.

The next morning, at six o'clock, I was awakened by the mate of the deck, who informed me that I was to report immediately to the commandant in his office. I jumped into my white works and chopped down to the office. When I entered, I was immediately greeted with "What are you going to do about that disgraceful episode yesterday?"

Standing there at rigid attention in service dress khaki were the brigade commander and deputy commander. I glanced at them to see what they had to say since they were responsible for parades, not the class president. My attention was rapidly engaged, however, when Captain Buchanan said, "Sagerholm, do you want to graduate?" Why was the commandant placing

14

the onus for the events at the color parade on me? What follows is my speculation, and it requires going back to the fall of 1951.

I was the brigade commander in the fall set, and as such, I stood duty periodically as the midshipman officer of the watch (MOOW). One afternoon, while on duty as the MOOW, I approved a dental appointment chit, a routine part of the MOOW duties. In less than a minute after I had forwarded the chit to the officer of the watch, Lieutenant H—, he came striding into the office, loudly proclaiming that I had overlooked an error on the chit and was therefore guilty of improper performance of duty. He slammed the report chit down on the desk and ordered me to sign it. When I requested to see the dental chit, he held it up and pointed to a red circle around the date at the bottom of the chit, which was one number different from the date at the top. So I received fifteen demerits and was restricted for the weekend. Those fifteen demerits were more than I had received over the previous three years.

In February 1952, Captain Pirie was relieved as commandant by Captain Buchanan. On a day in mid-March, the final set of stripers was to be announced at the noon meal. Fifteen minutes prior to noon meal formation, I was called down to the commandant's office. Captain Buchanan informed me that I was not going to be the six striper, or the five striper, or even a four striper: "You are going to be the battalion subcommander of the Sixth Battalion." I acknowledged all, attributing the news to the debacle with the dental chit. Then Captain Buchanan said, "Sagerholm, as class president, you can cause a lot of trouble if you want to."

Until then, I was taking what was said as just the way the cards had been dealt, but his last comment I took as an insult. "Sir," I replied, "I came here to get only one stripe, that of an ensign, and you need have no worry that I would stoop to any kind of retaliation." With that, I requested permission to be dismissed.

Back to the morning of 6 June 1952 and the question "Do you want to graduate?"

"Yes, sir!" I answered.

"Well, what are you going to do about this?"

It being obvious that the onus was on me rather than the brigade commander, the wheels in my head started spinning, and somehow the thought came to me to make an "impromptu" speech just before I led the midshipmen in the traditional three cheers "for those we leave behind." I said I would speak of the leadership given us by Admiral Hill, whom I now knew was retiring shortly after our graduation, mention that the Brigade would remember his example of integrity in his many duties over the years, and wish him well in retirement. Captain Buchanan pondered this proposal for a minute or so and then told me in a very firm tone of voice that I had better make it good.

I called a meeting of the first class company representatives, told them what was transpiring, and then told them that when I was finished speaking, I would turn to shake Admiral Hill's hand, at which time they were to ensure that the mids erupted in loud cheers.

Having been a member of the Brigade Executive Committee for the past three years, I had come to know Admiral Hill better than most in the Brigade, and I deeply respected him as a leader and as a gentleman who was firm but courteous and fair, one who had listened to our comments with due regard. When the time came for me to go up on the stage there in Dahlgren Hall to lead the three cheers, I surprised Hill by speaking at the lectern, where I began by noting that we were not the only ones about to leave the hallowed halls of the Academy, that he too was leaving, going into retirement after forty-two years of exemplary service in the Navy. I then praised his leadership and example as superintendent, and after similar comments, all of which I sincerely meant, I wished him and Mrs. Hill the traditional fair winds and following seas. When I turned to shake his hand, the hall was filled with cheers, as tears coursed down the admiral's cheeks. On seeing that, I realized how deeply he had felt those pranks of the day before.

Over the years, I had thought that the entire class was being threatened with delayed graduation, but about fifty-some years later, I learned that the authorities had to let the class graduate because those going into the Air Force had been sworn in as second lieutenants on Wednesday, 4 June 1952. It now appears that I was the only one being threatened, and after my agreeing to "do something," Captain Buchanan recommended I be permitted to graduate. If so, then obviously he had thought I instigated the pranks at the color parade as a parting shot for not having been selected as the six striper.

Several years after I had retired, I attended a lacrosse game at the Navy–Marine Corps Memorial Stadium in Annapolis. After taking my seat, I noticed that the seat in front of and below mine was occupied by (retired) Rear Admiral Buchanan. I leaned forward and touched him on the shoulder. When he turned, I said, "Good afternoon, Admiral, I'm Jim Sagerholm."

"I remember you, Sagerholm." With that, he turned around and said no more throughout the game. As he stood to leave, he turned, shook my hand, and said, "Good luck, Sagerholm." I guess I had finally been forgiven for those long-ago pranks of which I was innocent.

And that's the rest of the story.

Shoes Aftermath

Jack Young

In 1954 I was enjoying submarine life on the *Tilefish* (SS 307). We managed with six officers and an interesting crew that specialized in raising hell. Our skipper was a World War II sub patrol wizard who seemed to handle things well.

Then a new commanding officer (CO) came on board—LCDR A. A. Vaughn (not the Hank Vaughn of our midshipman days). The new captain was in the Class of 1944 and had just come from duty as a company officer at the Naval Academy. We were introduced in the wardroom to the new CO by the executive officer (XO), Al (Ace) Davis, Class of 1946. First he introduced Bob Thomas, not USNA but from Altus, Oklahoma, home of A. A. Vaughn. Next he introduced Blackie Wise, Class of 1950. Then he introduced Paul Tomb (rhymes with atomic "bomb"), Class of 1951. Everything was going fine.

Then he introduced Jack Young, Class of 1952. The captain was standing in the door. He paused and backed into the passageway. He said, "52." The guys looked at me to figure out what was going on. It seemed Company Officer Vaughn had been taught the evils of the 1952 parade—and now he had one of them in his own submarine.

I told the guys I thought it had something to do with shoes and went into the passageway to shake the CO's hand and assure him it would be all right. The fame of our class had reached the Submarine Force, Pacific Fleet.

Courtesy of Dave Davison, Class of 1952

II

THE CORPS

The safest place in Korea was right behind a platoon of Marines. Lord, how they could fight!

MG Frank E. Lowe, USA, Korea, 26 January 1952

1stLt Theodore J. Lutz Jr., USMC

Frank Hannegan

L t Ted Lutz was a very young platoon commander as the Korean War armistice loomed in the summer of 1953. The potential end to hostilities didn't deter the Chinese from trying to kill our Marines, however, as evidenced by a firefight in which Ted engaged. The following citation for his actions in that firefight makes clear why he was awarded the Navy Cross:

> The President of the United States takes pleasure in presenting the Navy Cross to First Lieutenant Theodore Joseph Lutz, Jr., United States Marine Corps, for extraordinary heroism in connection with military operations against an armed enemy of the United Nations while serving as a Platoon Leader of Company H, Third Battalion, First Marines, First Marine Division (Reinforced), in action against enemy aggressor forces in the Republic of Korea on 25 July 1953. Subjected to a devastating mortar and artillery barrage while leading his platoon to the main line of resistance in order to effect the relief of a bitterly contested sector, Second Lieutenant Lutz fearlessly remained in an exposed position and quickly directed his troops into positions of safety. Assured that all of his men were under cover, he gallantly moved forward into the trench line to investigate the situation. Informed that the left flank of his platoon's sector had been overrun by hostile troops, he immediately organized a small detail of Marines to reestablish contact with friendly elements on the flank and proceeded to lead the group towards the enemy. Although seriously wounded by hostile small arms fire which knocked his helmet and gun to the ground, he directed his men to safe positions and personally engaged the enemy, killing one and wounding several others with hand grenades. Sustaining additional wounds during this action, he refused to be evacuated and reorganized his platoon, leading it in three successive counterattacks in the face of extremely heavy mortar, artillery and small arms fire to rout the enemy from the trenches. After placing his men in defensive positions in the newly regained area, he remained with his platoon for over forty-eight hours submitting to medical treatment only after the

cease-fire agreement brought the fighting to an end. By his marked fortitude, courageous leadership and indomitable fighting spirit, Second Lieutenant Lutz served to inspire all who observed him. His personal valor reflects the highest credit upon himself and the United States Naval Service.

Col T. J. Lutz Jr., USMC (Ret.), died on 14 November 2013.

2ndLt Mort Cox, USMC

Lee Holmes

A fter graduation and Basic School at Quantico, Virginia, we Class of 1952 Marines mostly proceeded to the 1st Marine Division in Korea or the expanding 3rd Marine Division at Camp Pendleton in California. Mort Cox and I had been in the 5th Company at the Naval Academy. Mort went straight to Korea. I arrived in Korea in May 1953, two months before the shooting stopped. Mort and I were both platoon commanders in the 1st Marines, he in the 2nd Battalion and I in the 1st Battalion.

On Sunday, 12 July, the 1st Marines were in reserve. When Mort came over to our battalion for lunch, we talked over old times and he told me a story. When the 1st Marines had last been "on the line," his company was on the regiment's left flank, a few hundred meters from the Panmunjom–Freedom Gate Bridge "Peace Road," which was considered demilitarized. One night, the Chinese occupied a small hill, which the Marines had named the Molar, between the Marines and the road. From the Molar, they could fire at the Marines, but the Marines could not fire back without shooting into the road. Naturally, that wouldn't do, so the Marines built a position right against the road, which they had named the Toothache. For the troops on the Toothache, it was great duty. They could fire at the Molar, but the Chinese on the Molar couldn't return the fire. The mess sergeant could drive up the road with hot chow, and the troops could eat out in the open.

One day the Marines heard music and saw a small Chinese band come down the road with a dancing girl. The band stopped at the Toothache, proceeded to give a show, and handed out candy. Cameras were broken out on both sides. As soon as the affair began, the company commander called up the chain of command for instructions. Meanwhile, everyone was having a blast. Two hours later, the word came down: "Ignore them." End of story.

The Korean War cease-fire started Monday, 27 July 1953. The next day, the twenty-eighth, our battalion exec told me, "Your friend who came for lunch two weeks ago was killed Saturday." I drove a jeep over to Mort's company position and asked a Basic School classmate, Bobby Haydock, what had happened.

On Friday night, 24 July, the Chinese had hit the 2nd Battalion position in a mass attack. Mort's and Bobby's platoons were out front. The Marines had two bulldozer tanks that had dug in, so they were in hull defilade, with only their turrets above ground. All through the night, the Chinese would attack along the front, firing, shelling, and running up to the tanks to blow them up with satchel charges. Mort and Bobby called in illumination and had positioned machine guns to protect the tanks, firing at the attacking Chinese and shooting right at the tanks as the Chinese tried to climb the turrets. The Marines won; the Chinese withdrew. The next day, Mort, Bobby, and their platoon sergeants met on the reverse slope of their position to decide where to tie in for the night.

From time to time, both we and the Chinese would fire blindly where the enemy might be. It was called harassment and interdiction fire. That day, the Chinese got lucky, and an 81-mm mortar shell landed right among the four Marines. Bobby's platoon sergeant and Mort were both hit. Bobby told me that a shard of the mortar shell went right up under Mort's flak jacket. Mort said, "Get me out of here, Bobby!" and died moments later.

The cease-fire started two days later.

[Editor's note: The last two years of the Korean War were fought while the North Koreans and the Chinese stubbornly insisted on more and more concessions from the United Nations side, resulting in the needless loss of thousands of lives on both sides. In the end, the Chinese and the North Koreans grudgingly agreed to a cease-fire truce. The Korean War has still not been officially ended. Mort Cox was the first member of the Class of 1952 to be killed in combat and was the only member killed in the Korean War.]

Korea
The Last Battle

Cy Blanton

In July 1953, as the truce in Korea was about to begin, the Chinese made a last push on a hill known as Boulder City. The complex was tenuously held by the 1st Marine Division. The terms of the cease-fire provided for each side to withdraw the lines four thousand meters from the line of contact. Boulder City was critical because if we were dislodged by the Chinese, the NATO line would have to go south of the Imjin River, placing the NATO defensive line at a disadvantage. Therefore, Boulder City had to be held at all cost.

I was the platoon leader of the 1st Platoon, Charlie Company, 1st Battalion, 1st Marines. We were in a reserve area behind the battle site. I was summoned by my company commander, Capt Henry Armstrong (former captain of the 1948 Rice University football team that won the Sugar Bowl that year). He told me that my platoon was to reinforce the company defending Boulder City. I had a total of fifty-five men, including a machine-gun squad, and I was told to report to the commanding officer, 3rd Battalion, 1st Marines.

At the battalion headquarters, the CO explained the situation to me and dispatched my platoon to report to the senior officer on Boulder City. We were taken by Army personnel carriers to the bottom of Boulder City and disembarked. About that time, a tremendous explosion occurred. The Chinese had hit the ammunition dump. Fortunately, we were not in the vicinity of the explosion, but it got our attention. I made my way to the company commander, reported to him, and received orders as to what I was to do. I was given a portion of the line that included a tank to defend and hold.

The next day was the day of the truce and cease-fire, which was to begin at ten o'clock p.m. on 27 July 1953. The Chinese really wanted to kick us off the hill, and we were just as determined to hold it. We were under relentless mortar and artillery fire, but we succeeded in our mission and we held the hill called Boulder City. (This was during the same action in which Ted Lutz was awarded the Navy Cross.)

At 10:00 p.m. on the twenty-seventh, all units on the front lines fired a white star cluster signifying a cease-fire. Quite a sight. Not knowing how much trust to have in the Chinese, we stayed in our fighting holes all night, remaining on the alert. The Chinese started moving from their positions toward us across no-man's-land. They started picking up their dead and wounded, while recovering their discarded weapons and equipment. By daybreak, after a sleepless night, they were at our trench line. Other than the fighting, the thing I remember most vividly was the stench. Two weeks after the truce I still could smell the stench of death.

Shortly after dawn, a photographer from *Life* magazine told my platoon sergeant, Sergeant Windom, that he wanted to talk with me. I didn't want to talk with him and told him so. He took photos of the battle area and, without my knowledge, took a picture of me talking to a Chinese officer. It appeared in the 18 August 1953 issue of *Life*. Ted Lutz's picture is in the same story. About a month later, I got a letter from my plebe, Carl Strang, with the picture from *Life* with the annotation "I'd recognize that nose anywhere." My platoon is also depicted in *Life* magazine, walking down the road back to the rear. The war was over for us, and we were thankful to be alive.

My First and Last Tours of Duty as a Marine Officer

Robert E. Elmwood

I submit these two recollections as the bookends of my twenty years of service as an officer in the United States Marine Corps. The first recounts my very first combat experience in Korea. The second describes one of my experiences in my last tour of duty, during the Vietnam War, as inspector-instructor with the 2nd Military Police Battalion, Fleet Marine Force in New Orleans, Louisiana.

Prior to entering the United States Naval Academy, I had enlisted in the Marine Corps at age seventeen. Three years later, by the time I entered the Naval Academy Prep School, I had become an aircraft electrician and had achieved the rank of corporal.

My Baptism by Fire

After graduation from the United States Naval Academy in 1952, those of us who chose to enter the Marine Corps attended the 15th Special Basic Class. Then we were sent to any special training necessary to prepare us for combat. In my case, I attended the chemical, biological, and radiation defense course at Eta Jima, Japan. Eta Jima was the site of the pre–World War II Japanese Naval Academy.

From there, I was transferred to Korea, where I was assigned to Company D, 2nd Battalion, 5th Marines. The year was 1953. Upon arrival at company headquarters, I was directed to the 2nd Platoon command post on the other side of a ridge, about two hundred yards away. Walking on the open trail between the two units, I could see in the valley to the northwest, the village of Panmunjom, where negotiations to end the Korean conflict had been in progress for two years. It was located in what was to become the DMZ—the demilitarized zone.

Suddenly, I heard something explode about twenty feet behind me. That's when I realized that the whizzing sound that had gone past my ear only a second before had been a round from a 76-mm Russian antitank gun, located where 1000 Meter Road (which ran from north to south) intersected with the two-thousand-meter Panmunjom circle. This area had been designated a no-fire zone. Unfortunately I was not in a no-fire zone.

I had just been shot at for the first time in my life. Although I had trained for six years for this moment, nothing had truly prepared me for it. The North Koreans were firing at me! I took it very personally. Fortunately, they missed. After my baptism by fire, I dived into the brush and crawled the rest of the way to the platoon command post, where I assumed my duties. Welcome to combat!

As a postscript to this episode, by 1966 I was back at the Academy, teaching plebe steam in the Marine Engineering Department. Outside, at the end of my classroom, next to Weems Creek, was a small monument of captured equipment from the Korean War. It was a 76-mm antitank gun, and it was aimed right at my classroom window. Could it be that that very same antitank gun had followed me from Panmunjom?

Recollection of a Casualty Assistance Call

My last duty station was as inspector-instructor with the 2nd Military Police Battalion, Fleet Marine Force in New Orleans. One of my less-pleasant responsibilities was making casualty calls to the next of kin of Marines killed in action. While serving in the battalion, I made more than a dozen of these calls to families of all walks of life, from the very rich to the very poor. One of them stands out in my memory because of the unique cultural identity of the next of kin.

PFC Rudolph John Billiot had been killed in action on 21 December 1967. His family lived on Bayou du Large, a small community in south-central Louisiana about twenty-five swampy miles from the Gulf of Mexico.

It was common knowledge at that time that folks who lived deep in the swamps did not always welcome the intrusion of strangers, so I called my Reserve chief medical corpsman, Charles Page, who lived in nearby Houma, Louisiana, and gave him the details. His response was that I should not go down there without a state police escort. I asked him if he knew the Billiots; he indicated that he and the state police knew them well. He cautioned that the Billiots were Sabine Indians and that there was no way of knowing how they would react to an outsider bearing such tragic news.

I arranged for a state trooper vehicle to meet me at the bridge leading to the Bayou du Large community and to escort my car in. At the very end of the bayou, the Billiot home was an unpainted weatherboard house that bespoke the poverty of those who lived within it. When the Marine sedan in which I was riding pulled up front, a woman came out the door and approached the car as I got out. After verifying she was the deceased Marine's mother, I asked where her husband was. She answered that he was a mile back up the bayou at their daughter's home.

I delivered the grim news: "I have come to tell you that your son has been killed in Vietnam." These words are always cruel, and those Marine officers who made the casualty calls took carefully counted turns. The call only counted for the officer who actually spoke the words, not for any other personnel who accompanied or assisted him.

"Take me to where your husband is," I said. "I have to tell him this terrible news." I asked Mrs. Billiot to sit with me in the back of the Marine sedan while the driver took us to her daughter's house. As soon as she got in, she threw herself onto the floor of the back seat and began to cry loudly over and over in Cajun French, "Char bon Dieu! Char bon Dieu!" (Cher bon Dieu, "dear good God"). I wept with her.

When the sedan pulled into the daughter's yard, the family all came out of the house. It was easy to identify the rather tall next of kin, the Marine's father. After I spoke the words to him, he said sadly, "He was my best son, he always went hunting with me." Then he turned and walked quietly around to the back of the house; no one followed him. He returned in about ten minutes. I was curious as to why he had done that, but it was not until later that I realized he did not want anyone to see him cry.

My visit also elicited hostility from the Marine's brother. He asked me why I wasn't in Vietnam and why I hadn't been killed (the insinuation being instead of his brother). I simply replied that I had just been luckier than his brother when I was over there. He replied bitterly, "Now *I* have to go to replace him." As isolated as the Sabine Indians are, they still honor the custom of replacing a fallen warrior with his brother.

On my last trip to Bayou du Large, after the funeral, the brother gave me a large crock of molasses. I suppose he realized that I had just been trying to help the family in their time of bereavement, and this was his way of apologizing for his earlier confrontation. To this day, the taste of molasses makes me feel sad, although I never got to eat any from that crock. I accidentally dropped it on my kitchen floor and it broke, molasses flowing everywhere. I scooped up the thick brown syrup and poured it down the drain. I guess God didn't intend for anyone to enjoy anything from a casualty call.

Courtesy of Dave Davison, Class of 1952

III

THE WILD BLUE YONDER

A little-known fact is that the Air Force did not immediately have its own academy when the service was first created in 1947. West Point and Annapolis were required to send 25 percent of their graduates to the Air Force each year until the new Air Force Academy graduated its first class in 1959.

When SAC Was Young (And So Was I)

Joseph Pidkowicz

It's a cool night in November 1956 at Barksdale Air Force Base in Mississippi. I am awakened by the ear-piercing siren signaling all 10,000 personnel to report to their units immediately. It is 1:40 a.m. I jump on my bike and race to the main road leading to a 1930s-vintage hangar. At the hangar, lockers contained our flight gear and B-4 bags filled with all the necessities for a prolonged stay away from base.

In the ready room, operational briefings start, covering en route weather (heavy snow storms, strong winds at refueling altitudes, turbulence, and lightning), aircraft status, tanker rendezvous data, tanker codes, and signing for top secret documents for emergency use. I am the pilot of a B-47 assigned to the 376th Bomb Wing, the electronic countermeasures (ECM) wing that leads our bombers carrying nuclear weapons into enemy territory. We can cause a total blackout of all radios, radar, and airborne communications. We pave the way for those following us.

The base is lit up like Times Square. I see our flight line of B-47s, nearly two miles long, guarded by Air Force sentries with submachine guns and large German shepherds. The atmosphere is electrified, people shouting, equipment being loaded, crews manning their aircraft. After the sentry at our plane checks our identification, the crew chief opens the crew compartment hatch and we climb aboard with parachutes, survival gear, and brief cases. Preflight inspections are carefully done, both externally and internally. Time to start engines.

As the leader of the first wave of six ECM planes, we are first to taxi to the runway, where we perform engine run-ups and wait for our controlled takeoff time. Number 2 is right behind us, followed by numbers 3, 4, 5, and 6. All ninety B-47 jet bombers of the Second Air Force are proceeding toward takeoff for the Arctic, where we will receive our final orders from Strategic Air Command Headquarters.

At the end of runway 320, we take the far-right position on the 500-foot-wide, 12,500-foot-long strip. Number 2 takes the center with 3 on his left; numbers 4, 5, and 6 are ready to move rapidly into position. I see the line of B-47s proceeding down the taxiway, a sight that fills me with pride.

"Bearcat 27, thirty seconds to controlled takeoff. Acknowledge."

"Roger, Bearcat 27."

I advance power. All engines are running smoothly at 104 percent (full military power).

"Bearcat 27, fifteen seconds to roll."

Time to start water-alcohol injection, which provides the additional power needed to rapidly reach a thousand feet in altitude, after which we will gradually accelerate to 325 knots and rapidly climb to cruising altitude.

"Bearcat 27, five seconds to roll. Four, three, two, one, *roll*!"

The radar celestial navigator (RCN) calls out speed as we pass the four-thousand-foot marker, the go–no go acceleration checkpoint. We are go. At 237 knots, we lift off the runway. Number 2 is halfway down the runway and number 3 is starting to roll. Numbers 4, 5, and 6 are already in position. Precision. With gear and nose up, entering the climb corridor, I accelerate to 325 knots and maintain military power. Climb, baby, climb. Every thirty seconds a B-47 lifts off, all headed to the Arctic like angry hornets swarming from their nest.

We head for our first refueling, which will be over the St. Lawrence River, cruising at 29,000 feet. I set autopilot and adjust speed to .86 Mach. All systems are OK. Approaching New York State, there are storm clouds ahead. Snow. Lightning. The RCN reports tankers showing on radar. Codes show they are our tankers.

We are rapidly closing on the tanker. "Commence descent, now!" Power back, drag gear down. I descend at 6,000 feet per minute. Dense snow, heavy turbulence, lightning, pitching, tossing. Steady up on course to tanker and hold it. I level out at 15,000 feet. The RCN is directing: "Steer 025 degrees, down 50 feet, slow to 250 knots for contact."

Our six-engine jet bomber refuels from a four-engine propeller tanker, a serious mismatch that causes difficulties. Weather's nasty. Watch altitude—we're down fifty feet. Down twenty feet. We are three hundred feet behind the tanker. I pull power back. Turbulence is a problem.

RCN: "250 feet. 200 feet. 150 feet. 100 feet. Down 20 feet, steady, closing nicely, 50 feet. See 'em?"

Me: "No. Wait! Opening refueling door. Light is on at refueling door. I see the tanker's green light but not the plane."

RCN: "You're lined up. Speed is matched. 20 feet."

Me: "I see the green light. We're in the slot."

Bam! The refueling boom is in the B-47 receptacle. We have contact. The boom operator on the tanker says, "Commencing fuel flow now." Pitching and tossing in the turbulence, tanker and bomber descend at three hundred feet per minute to avoid stalling as our weight from the added fuel increases. Dense snow again. I must hold formation. I need that 40,000 pounds of fuel. I tell myself to stay alert and concentrate on controlling the plane. Power up, power down, steady, steady. Now left a bit, hold on to the green light—just a few more minutes but seems like forever. Six minutes, we should be nearing full. Eight minutes—power up. No, power back!

At last I hear, "Fuel transfer complete, sir. We'll get your credit card number later. Ready for breakaway."

"Disconnect on my count of three," I reply. Pause. "Three, two, one, disconnect!"

I drop below the tanker, full military power, then clear the tanker, accelerate to 325 knots, and climb back to cruising altitude, heading for second refueling area. I am beat, but on we fly.

The second and third refuelings are also in heavy weather, but now we are in our designated Arctic area and the weather is clear. The sky is filled with B-47s from horizon to horizon. What an awesome sight! All those strobe lights look like a million fireflies. Millions of man-hours of work and billions of dollars were spent to put us here. Thousands of hours in classrooms across the country and thousands of flying hours were expended to make this happen. We are ready to protect the United States and the free world. I am proud to be a part of the most powerful aerial armada the world has ever seen.

The Strategic Air Command had over two thousand B-47s, of which about half were lost between 1951 and 1965, testimony to the hazardous duty. God bless their crews and their families.

It Might Have Been War

Wendell Stockdale

I t isn't often that one is in a situation to start, or prevent, a war. In 1956 I found myself in that unenviable position. Well, sort of. The following is based upon my recollections.

The mission of the 45th Fighter Day Squadron stationed at Sidi Slimane, French Morocco, was to protect several U.S. bases, radar stations, and aircraft stationed in Morocco. The 45th Squadron consisted of twenty F-86-E and F-86-F jet fighters with the attendant operational and maintenance personnel. In 1955, the 45th was co-located with a squadron of B-36s. Early in 1956, the B-36s were replaced with B-47s.

The "lush" quarters for the 45th pilots consisted of plywood huts approximately twenty-five by twenty-five feet. The heating system was an oil stove in the middle of the hut; the air conditioning system was a fan. Each hut could accommodate four pilots. The toilet facilities and showers were in a Quonset building located twenty to two hundred feet from the huts, depending on where your hut was located. The married pilots who had arrived at Sidi Slimane before December 1955 had the privilege of living off base in relatively luxurious, local-economy housing. Although I arrived in September 1955, because my wife was pregnant, I was advised not to bring her to Morocco. It was a wise decision as she had a difficult time giving birth to our first child.

The sum of the pilots' recreation on base consisted of a baseball field and an Officers' Club. Some of the more exciting events occurred when outside squadrons, either United States Air Forces in Europe or foreign, came on temporary duty (TDY) to Sidi for gunnery practice. After a hard day, it was not unusual for a group of 45th and guest pilots to gather at the club for a bit of camaraderie.

The most "energetic" guests were the Canadians. They enjoyed competitive endeavors such as beer chug-a-lug contests, which were usually weekend events. The winner's prize—you guessed it—was another round of drinks paid for by the losers. (I usually won due to my "trick" of putting two holes in the top rim.) The Canadians had an unusual custom. If they liked your tie, and sometimes even if they didn't, they bit it off. Honestly!

Of course, this fascinating event usually occurred rather late in the evening so no one noticed who might be out of uniform.

Weekends, when not on alert, were often spent in Casablanca, Rabat, Tangiers, Fez, and Meknes touring area attractions, shopping for local "treasures," or just sunning on the Atlantic beaches. That was about as exciting as it got. Several guys in the squadron had cars, so transportation was not a problem.

Maintaining flying proficiency, gunnery practice, and alert status took up most of our time. Occasionally we transported VIPs in the squadron's T-33s. I recall one mission when I picked up Maj Gen Frederic Glantzberg, 17th Air Force commander, in Rabat to bring him to Sidi Slimane. As I turned onto final, I ran into a wall of fog. These vertical fog banks came off the Atlantic Ocean and were unique in size, speed of travel, and density. I experienced vertigo for a moment while I transferred from flying visual flight rules (VFR) to instrument flight rules (IFR). Just as fast as it came up, I was through it, broke out at the end of the runway, and landed without incident. I do not think the general knew what had happened—at least his "Nice landing, Stockdale" gave no clue that he was aware (or maybe he was just his usual gracious self).

The regular operations schedule required each pilot to stand alert on a rotating basis. This involved having your aircraft preflighted and ready to go at a moment's notice. Upon sounding of the alert alarm, we ran out of our "lush" alert shack (one similar to our living quarters) to our aircraft about a hundred feet away, jumped in, started up, and took off. Sometimes we went up single, other times we had a wingman.

One particularly beautiful afternoon, I was on single alert. The call came in from our radar site that an unidentified aircraft was incoming. I took the vector, climbed to around 30,000 feet, and was ordered to intercept. The standing order was that if an unidentified or "enemy" aircraft crossed what today would be called the "red line," we were to prepare to attack. After making visual contact, I identified the incoming as a TU-95 Bear, a Soviet long-range bomber. It ignored me while I maneuvered into attack position, high and behind the Bear, following it and waiting for the controller's message that it had crossed the line and the authenticated order to attack. This was not the first time that the Soviets had sent aircraft, seemingly to test our defenses. Their incursions were common, and just as every time before, this Bear started a lazy right turn just short of the line. It then headed back toward Russia.

The possible implications of their foray didn't hit me until I returned to base. All I had been concerned about was staying in position to attack if it became necessary. At the time, the fact that the Bear had more powerful cannons than my F-86s 50-caliber machine guns did not cross my mind. Later, however, I appreciated the Bear's wise decision to retreat. As I recall, that was the last day the Soviets came that close to French Morocco.

And it was the first time that I had come close to starting World War III.

Stealth and More

Tom Stafford

Approximately three weeks before I flew the Apollo-Soyuz mission in July 1975, Gen Sam Phillips, commander of the Air Force System Command and former Apollo program manager, called me and said that he wanted me to take command of the Air Force Flight Test Center (AFFTC) after completing the mission. Accordingly, I assumed command of the Air Force Flight Test Center at Edwards Air Force Base in November 1975.

The AFFTC consisted of the headquarters and central test facilities at Edwards AFB, the Aircraft Operations Control of Area 51 in the Nevada Department of Energy test area, and the parachute test facility at El Centro, California. Activity was at its high point at the center, with the flight testing of the F-15, YF-16, YF-17, YC-14, and YC-15 prototypes, the B-1A, the C-141B, and the air launched cruise missile as well as many aircraft modification tests.

Gen David Jones, the chief of staff, called me in the summer of 1976 and said that he was sending a colonel to me for a special briefing. The colonel arrived at my headquarters with a large briefcase bearing two locks and requested we move into a secure compartmented information facility (SCIF) room. He had me sign numerous documents, then he unlocked the briefcase. Inside it was a model of a weird-shaped aircraft and a series of charts—the Have Blue project being worked by the Air Force and the Defense Advanced Research Projects Agency. Have Blue was the first experimental, all-stealth aircraft, built by Lockheed's Skunk Works in Burbank, California.

There were to be two aircraft built. The first would be for typical flight testing to determine the performance, stability, and control characteristics of the aircraft. The second aircraft would be covered with different types of radar energy absorbing material that would render it, via low observable technology, nearly invisible to the transmitting radar. This second aircraft was called "Stealth" and was classified at the time. I was assigned the overall responsibility of testing both aircraft and assigning a chief test pilot, a flight test engineer, and a project officer to flight test the two aircraft.

Have Blue was a top secret SAR (special access required) program, and I immediately chose Maj Ken Dyson, the F-15 joint test force commander and chief test pilot, to conduct the tests. Within a week, Dyson and I were flying to Burbank to meet Ben Rich, head of the Skunk Works, and Kelly Johnson, who although retired was the chief consultant in design. Johnson had been involved with designing the P-38, the Constellation, the U-2, the F-104, and the SR-71 Blackbird. He was one of the premier aircraft designers in the world. I was briefed by them on the theory of low observable technology and how it would work, with reduction due to no ninety-degree angles on the aircraft so that the radar energy would be bounced away from the originating source and the special absorbent material on the aircraft, which would further reduce any reflection of electromagnetic energy that otherwise would be reflected back to the source radar.

The two aircraft were disassembled and flown in a C-5A to Area 51 to be reassembled and tested there. I made numerous trips to the Skunk Works to see the progress and to the Pentagon, where only a very few knew of the program, including Bill Perry, the undersecretary of defense for research and engineering (R&E). The chief of staff knew a little, but the vice chief and the commander of the Tactical Air Command knew nothing. Perry's executive assistant for the program was Lt Col Paul Kominski, USAF. The USAF Headquarters program manager was Maj Joe Ralston, who would later become vice chairman of the Joint Chiefs of Staff.

The first aircraft progressed in construction, and on 1 December 1977, at the Groom Lake Area 51 facility, Bill Parks, the Lockheed test pilot, made the first flight. Major Dyson made the second. As the aircraft rolled down the runway and got airborne, I turned and said to Dyson that this technology, if it worked, would change air warfare forever. Following the successful first flight, Kelly Johnson, Ben Rich, Bill Parks, Ken Dyson, the Lockheed program manager, I had a great celebration in an adjacent empty hangar—with Cuban cigars supplied by a certain agency and champagne.

Within two months, the second aircraft had arrived with the radar absorbent material applied. I was interested to see if the radar return would be reduced as much as had been theorized. Lockheed had made a full-scale mock-up with the radar absorbent material applied and put it on a V-shaped steel pole covered with the radar absorbent material as well. The material was so good that the radar could not find the steel pole until a sparrow landed on top of it.

In perfecting low observable technology, attention to minute details is absolutely essential. I was anxious to see the radar return, or lack thereof, from the aircraft as it flew against our potential hostile radar systems. Once I saw the lack of return data, I thought, Eureka! I knew that it would change air warfare forever. I envisioned that every new fighter and bomber aircraft would include stealth in its design. I continued to be fascinated by this area of technology, and in my trips to the Skunk Works I continued to talk to Kelly Johnson and Ben Rich about this new potential. However, I never expected to have the opportunity to participate in its development,

In early March 1978, I was called to Washington for a personal meeting with General Jones, who told me that he was promoting me to lieutenant general and that I would be the deputy chief of staff for research, development, and acquisition, replacing Lt Gen Alton Slay, who was being promoted to general and commander of the Air Force Systems Command. He told me he wanted me to put to work all the knowledge that I had learned at NASA on the Gemini and Apollo programs. I was elated about the promotion but also knew I had a chance to potentially enhance the future Air Force capability of stealth technology. At that time, this position was responsible for the acquisition, research, and development of all new systems and the generation of requirements for all new systems.

Immediately within a week of assuming my new position in March 1978, I met with Major Ralston and Maj Ken Staten, who were heading the management of the low observable program. I told them that if we could use the Have Blue concept for an attack plane to counter command and control systems, it would greatly reduce enemy war-fighting capability. Ralston and Staten were already thinking along the same lines, and we came up with the A and B models, but the one had to be scrapped since it required a nearly 10,000-foot takeoff roll.

I was still in frequent touch with Ben Rich and Kelly Johnson and was ready to push them, but it did not take much pushing as they were already thinking of similar ideas; thus began the Senior Trend program, which became the F-117A. The contract for Senior Trend was signed in January 1979, and the first aircraft flew in two years and eight months, which is a modern record from time of contract until the first flight of the aircraft. It was operational in a total of four years, which is also a modern record. The aircraft remained secret until 1988.

During its first test in combat, Desert Storm, the F-117A flew 1.9 percent of the air-ground missions that attacked approximately 40 percent of the strategic targets and did not suffer a scratch. Indeed, air warfare had been changed forever.

At the time of the contract for the F-117A, I made a speech in Chicago and met with the chairman of Northrop, Tom Jones, who was working on the only other stealth program, a program that Perry had started so that there would be competition in designing stealth. The Northrop program was called Tacit Blue and consisted of a lot of curved surfaces with different types of material. He asked me if they should think of any other applications for this. I was extremely frustrated with President Carter, whose administration had reduced our armed forces and canceled or delayed our major strategic programs. He had canceled the B-1 bomber, and for two years in a row he had delayed the MX missile, which we thought he might trade away in some future arms negotiation. The Trident submarine was also being delayed at the time and was encountering technical difficulties. To say I was frustrated is to put it mildly. I took a piece of hotel stationery, and saying, "See what you can do with your technology on a strategic bomber," I wrote the initial specifications for the range, payload, radar cross section, and maximum gross takeoff weight. I told him that I did not have any money at that time but to use his own resources to make studies and come back to me in two months with his assessment.

A week later, I flew to Burbank and met with Johnson and Rich. On a different piece of paper, I wrote the same specs and asked if they could come up with designs using these criteria. Within two months, both companies came back to me with their designs, which I took to Perry. The Northrop design of a flying wing required a fly-by-wire flight control system. This system had been developed for the F-16, and it was obvious that it would work on a bomber as well. I then obtained $2 million to further enhance each company's efforts. We termed the aircraft the advanced technology bomber, which would later be renamed the B-2.

At this time, I was briefed by the intelligence agencies that the Soviets were developing a look-down/shoot-down Doppler radar for their interceptors. This would be bad news for the Tomahawk and the air launched cruise missile. The horizontal and vertical control services on the tail and straight wings of the missiles would make ideal radar reflectors. I knew that we had to go high and go stealth for long-range cruise missiles.

I then told the chairman of Williams International that I needed him to build a small, more powerful turbo-fan engine to replace the one in the Tomahawk and ALCM. I had him sign papers that cleared him for stealth.

I told him we needed a high-altitude, stealth, nuclear cruise missile that required an engine with twice the thrust of the Tomahawk/ALCM engine and with a reduction of 25 percent in specific fuel consumption. We needed this engine performance in order to get well over the fifteen-hundred-nautical-mile range. As a result, the AGM-129 was born even though there was no statement of need or requirement, just as there was none for the F-117A and B-2. The Air Force ultimately procured 460 AGM-129 missiles. A B-52H bomber could carry twenty of these missiles, giving our strategic air arm an increased flexibility in weapon employment. The standoff delivery of these missiles, combined with their ability to attack the enemy command and control system, significantly complicated the defense problem for a potential enemy.

Two able deputies, classmates from the Naval Academy Class of 1952, helped me a lot during this time: Maj Gen Jim Brickel, who was assistant deputy chief of staff for research, development, and acquisition, and Maj Gen Bill Maxson, who was deputy for operational requirements. I had seven general officers who worked for me in various deputy positions. It was great to have two classmates who did an outstanding job in helping me on various issues. At that time, however, neither one was briefed on the Stealth program, but I made them aware that I was working on some very large SAR programs and fighting the Carter administration to keep the B-1 alive under the table after Carter had canceled it. I was also pushing the MX missile into full-scale development despite the delays that the Carter administration continued to impose.

Jim Brickel had extensive experience in the Pentagon in various positions and was well versed in the operations that go on within the Defense Department. At times, I turned much of the internal operations over to Jim while I worked on the Stealth, B-1, and MX programs. In addition, I started the F-110 engine development in competition with the F-100 since we were losing F-16s at an alarming rate and new F-15 aircraft were parked beside the McDonnell Douglas hangar in St. Louis with empty holes in their engine bays. After we lost an F-15 over England due to both engines failing, I went through the overhead and called Secretary of the Air Force Hans Mark (Stetson had left for civilian life) and told him that I was going to see Perry. Hans told me to press ahead. I briefed Perry about the high loss rate of the F-16 and now the F-15 due to engine failure. I informed him that we needed competition and warranties. The F-100 had no warranties, and the Air Force spent $1.5 billion per year for spare parts. Furthermore, the aircraft in-commission rate was horrible, mostly due to engine problems.

The Navy had some money to reengine the F-14, which was under-powered with the TF-30 engine. The engine also had major problems, but the Navy was not moving aggressively on a program to replace it. I told Perry that I needed to move out right away with the F-110, which would take the core of a B1 engine, which had the most advanced engine tech-nology, and use that with a new fan and low-pressure turbine. We would put that in competition for the F-16's engine and possibly for the F-15; it could also replace the TF-30 in the Navy F-14A. The GE F-110 would have nearly 30,000 pounds more thrust than the F-100, and 50 percent more than the TF-30. Perry gave me the go-ahead, and we started a pro-gram with an Air Force colonel as program manager and a Navy captain as deputy then rotated between Air Force and Navy for program managers and deputy program managers.

United Technology/Pratt & Whitney fought this by using lobbyists and the media. The *Washington Post* termed it the "Great Engine Wars." In the end, the F-110 program survived and Pratt & Whitney had to greatly improve their engine and give warranties. Today they have to decide each year which engine to provide for the F-16, and each year, the F-110 has received the highest percentage. The F-110 also made the F-14 a real fight-ing machine. The F-16 losses dropped drastically, and today, the Air Force has 4,000 cycle warranties on each engine from the companies. The engine core that I described was so advanced that GE teamed with SCENMA of France to produce the CFM-56, which is used in all Boeing 737 series and Airbus A320 aircraft, and is the most successful engine program in the his-tory of commercial aviation.

With all of the stealth activity, it became obvious to me that we also needed a new stealth air superiority fighter to replace the F-15. However, with all the other programs going, there was not funding available to do another SAR program. So I directed that a roadmap be started for the advanced tactical fighter (ATF) that would take the normal program requirements and demonstration/validation concepts. My few require-ments were to start with a super-cruise like the Concord (i.e., Mach 1.5+ without using after burner) and have super-stealth characteristics and great maneuverability. It would be the replacement for the F-15.

Following my retirement in 1979 due to my wife's serious illness, a request for proposal was issued within eighteen months for the ATF demonstration/validation competition. This resulted in the YF-22 versus YF-23 flyoff competition. The YF-22 was chosen, and today the F-22 is the most capable fighter in the world.

How I Survived

John Haaren

One of the jobs I had at 15th Air Force was senior controller for the 15th Air Force Command Post. This was a kind of extra-duty job. When the command-post people were overwhelmed, or if they needed extra help, a certain few of us who were qualified as Strategic Air Command controllers were pulled in to assist in the mission. This was relatively routine until the Cuban Missile Crisis.

Cuban Missile Crisis

The CIA, with their U2 capabilities, had over flown Cuba and discovered that there were strategic intercontinental ballistic missiles on the island that were capable of reaching the United States. If you look at the map, Florida is not far from Cuba—certainly well within the range of the missiles that were embedded there. The president of the United States, John F. Kennedy, had been to Russia, and Khrushchev apparently thought he was young and inexperienced and could be bullied, particularly after the fiasco of the Bay of Pigs. The confrontation became very serious, and within the armed forces, including the SAC, there was a series of what were called defense conditions, or DEFCONs. DEFCON 5 was a day-to-day thing, and if you got to DEFCON 1, you were on the brink of a strategic nuclear exchange. The crisis deepened and both countries started to take serious steps toward the beginnings of nuclear war.

The potential conflict progressed to the point where SAC deployed numerous B-47s to county airfields all over the southern part of the United States. A crew would go to an airfield that had never been used before by the military with the intent to disperse the B-47 fleet as widely as possible in case the Soviet Union actually launched some of their missiles from Cuba or utilized some of their submarines. In any event, if there was to be a nuclear attack on the United States, we wanted to have our weapons as widely dispersed as possible and as safe as we could make them. In the same mold, the airborne alert that was usually in a semiactive phase went into full-blown effort: B-52s were circulating on airborne alert, fully fueled, right on the perimeter of the Soviet Union. In addition, we counted down all of our missiles to a minimum response time. At that point we just had the beginnings of the Minuteman system. I think we had one squadron at Malstrom Air Force Base. We had taken some launch control panels and could have launched ten Minuteman, but there were hundreds of Atlas Ds and Es and Fs that were on alert.

The Atlas Ds were erected and loaded, as were the Es and Fs. The Fs were silo mounted and had a one-minute countdown. In addition, there were the Titan 1s and the Titan 2s, all of which were ready to go on essentially a minute or less notice. The Minuteman could launch in thirty-two seconds. This was, needless to say, a very serious confrontation. I had grown up in the B-47 business and had taken numerous courses on nuclear effects. We were carrying multiple warhead H-bombs, and the testing that we had done was not at high yields, and not multiples, so my opinion was that if there had been a nuclear exchange, there was a high probability that the majority of the world would have died. Nobody really knew what effects multiple warheads would have, and we certainly didn't understand what would happen if both sides launched nuclear weapons. If you weren't scared, you sure as hell should have been.

I was pressed into duty at the 15th Air Force Command Post because when the crisis started, it was on a twenty-four-hour basis. With the alerts, and the participation of the intelligence people, the SAC Go Code was available at SAC Headquarters down through the individual weapons. Each crewmember wore a badge and the envelope that had those magic codes in it around his neck. If the Go Code was issued, each crewmember would open up his envelope and read his code. If the codes matched, that was the authority to go to war and utilize their weapons. This was a well-guarded capability. As a controller in the Command Center, I had the messages but not the authentication. The message that would have launched all of this was called the Red Dot 4, which according to SAC Manual 55-2A was classified "Secret."

So the procedures and process were at the secret level but the absolute availability of the Go Code itself was highly classified and highly compartmented. The intelligence people had to bring that particular code release into the command post so it could be broadcast as an authentication. Essentially you would have a message that was something like this: "This is 15th Air Force Command Post with a Red Dot 4 message. The time is 1200 Zulu. The authentication is Victor Victor." Then you would issue the release code, and they would open it up and weapons would be launched.

The crisis intensified when commercial radio broadcast that a Russian freighter carrying missiles was approaching Cuba. There were U.S. Navy ships on station blockading the island of Cuba from any further deliveries from the Soviet Union. At that point I can remember thinking that if this exchange was authorized and the systems were used, the likelihood that anybody would survive was pretty small. The crisis ended with the Russians backing down, and one of the president's advisers said, "Well, we were eyeball to eyeball when the other person blinked"—meaning the Russians finally gave in.

This was a very serious and explosive confrontation. The possibility of all those nuclear systems being used is just appalling. and many of those same nuclear systems are still available. Later I was involved at SAC Headquarters as the person who assigned the nuclear missile warheads to targets according to a document called the National Strategic Targeting Attack Policy, or NSTAP. The president supposedly approved this, but actually the secretary of defense signed it. The number of warheads was something over one thousand, and you essentially run out of targets to use them on because of some of the hard targets underground in tunnels and the rest of it. Nonetheless, if you take a look at having the ability to destroy, just take the top one hundred cities of any country that you want to attack, or if you think about one hundred cities in the United States being obliterated, the ability for survivors to carry on is obviously pretty small. Those of us who went through that time have an appreciation of the horrors and hazards of a nuclear exchange. I'm not sure if that is or isn't true in the current world, but it sure as hell should be.

The Global Positioning System

The global positioning system (GPS) program was one of the most efficient and well-run programs in the history of Air Force acquisition. The original program manager was a colonel named Brad Parkinson, a brilliant individual who had a PhD and was a superb manager. I had been involved in the program because at Air Force Systems Command Headquarters I was the officer having primary responsibility for the budget. This was a highly politicized program in many ways. For example, the United States Navy saw the GPS system as a threat. It had its own satellite system called 612B, which was a system of two satellites that were in orbit for the use of Polaris submarines. The Polaris ships inertial navigation system, or SINS, had to have an update from time to time, requiring them to go to periscope depth, put up an antenna, and grab a signal off of their satellites, updating the SINS with a very accurate position. They also had to do this if they were going to launch. Obviously if you don't know where you are, sending a missile to a target is not too accurate. So the Navy liked its system and didn't want to change.

Nevertheless, it did in fact become part of the triservice program office and eventually participated in GPS. The system was unique in that it was fielded faster than scheduled, it was under budget, and it provided more capability than the original specifications asked for. It was a unique system in another way, in that most of the testing was between the satellite in orbit and the station on the ground. The preliminary bugs were worked out and maybe another satellite was launched, but that was the normal process.

Brad Parkinson discovered an ingenious way to carry out testing on the GPS. He took the satellite system and, rather than put it up in orbit, put it on the ground and then put what would have been the earth station on board an airplane and used the ground satellite simulation to test the earth station equipment that was now in an aircraft. That let us quickly work out whatever bugs there were. Then when we came to the testing phase, we launched a few test birds and reversed the process to the way it should have been. In any event, the testing initially was a few hours a day in certain areas of the world. The eventual constellation was six orbit-inclined planes with four satellites in each orbit. One of the satellites had to be a timing satellite because essentially GPS works with three intersecting spheres—and you know if you cross two lines you get a point—but doing it with spheres, you wind up with a point in two places. The GPS software figures which is the right one, and that gives you the accuracy of the position.

In point of fact, the early tests were giving us roughly ten feet in accuracy, which was much better than we expected. The system was tested in various ways. For example, in the early testing I talked about, we flew helicopters to represent the earth station and cargo planes and jeeps. In fact, one test we did in Long Beach used a Navy cruiser with GPS gear on board. On the day of the test, the fog rolled in while the cruiser was going out the channel and they were searching for a particular buoy. The fog was so bad you couldn't see the bow of the ship from the bridge. When the system told them to stop, they stopped at what they hoped was the buoy. The captain was on the bridge, and he asked the lookouts to see if they could see the buoy. The lookout looked over the bow and saw they were right on top of the buoy, which was indicative of the excellence of this particular system.

After all the testing and all the money and the readiness to have the system deployed, it went before the DSARC, the Defense Systems Acquisition Review Council, chaired by the defense director of research and engineering (DDR&E). I had retired after many years of being involved with GPS on active duty and I was working for a company called ASEC, Analytical Systems Engineering Corporation. We had negotiated contracts with the GPS program office in Los Angeles and we were also working for the Air Staff GPS office and the Department of Defense.

This became a highly political fight because the Federal Aviation Administration was concerned with the FAA radars, the Coast Guard was involved because of Loran C, and the Defense Department was involved in GPS. The system demanded a first-ever radio navigation system architecture, which meant the Air Force was now representing DOD in suggesting that we eliminate some of the FAA control systems and the Loran A and C. The politics became pretty involved at the same time GPS was coming up for final approval. Since the system had performed so well, the people who were in favor of it were bringing it to the review cycle, but the people who didn't like the system were saying things like "Well, the enemy could use it as well if it's international and worldwide and so we better figure out a way to keep it out of enemy hands." Their notion of doing that was to degrade the accuracy to perhaps one hundred yards. This would then prevent the bad guys from using the system. Despite the complaints, the system went to reviews.

Because the review sequence was determined by when each service was founded, Army was first. The Army had what was known as ASARC, the Army Systems Acquisition Review Council, and it looked at GPS and said no, we don't want it, we don't need it, and we'd rather have some more tanks or artillery or whatever, but we don't want to spend any money on GPS. The next in line was the Navy, and the Navy didn't like GPS because it thought the Navy should keep its own satellites, the 612B system. Of all things, the Air Force, which had invented it and had done all the testing and was running the program office, said it didn't want GPS either. Well, as the people under contract, we were responsible for writing the development concept paper, the document that would go to the review council. It had schedules, test results, costs, and anything you could think of, and it was about two inches thick.

The DSARC was chaired by the DDR&E, and strangely enough, this was Dick Delauer, an old friend of mine who was a naval officer when I was at the Naval Academy. He was a commander and the baseball officer representative at the academy. He was also a nuclear physicist and later went on to work for TRW, where he became an executive vice president. When it was TRW's turn to have someone in the government, they offered up Dick Delauer, who became the number three man in the entire Pentagon.

Delauer was running this conference to decide about GPS. In addition to him, people on this council were the vice chiefs of the Army and Air Force, both four stars, and the deputy chief of naval operations for R&D, a three star. They all got to vote on this. Delauer polled the delegation. The Army said no, the Air Force said no, and the Navy said no. What they didn't know was there was a secret group that had already decided that GPS was absolutely mandatory.

One night Dick Delauer, the DDR&E and the decision maker, Larry Skantze, a Naval Academy classmate from the Class of 1952 who was the four-star general in charge of Air Force Systems Command, and me, the contractor who was supposed to be providing the data and information for this decision process, met for dinner. We decided that GPS should go through, no matter what. It wasn't just for the navigation side, it was tied back into the Strategic Integrated Operation Plan (SIOP) because GPS had a Bhang Meter. The Bhang Meter could detect and measure a nuclear blast, and since GPS would cover the world, you could know when and where the SIOP was effective. If there were three weapons destined for the same target and the first one was exactly on target with the yield that it had, you could measure that and save the other two weapons, which would increase the efficiency of the SIOP execution.

The three of us felt this was even more important than the excellent navigation, so it was in the documentation but not to the extent that it really mattered. In any event, when the meeting was underway and everyone said, "No, we don't need it," Dick Delauer said, "Thank you, gentlemen, for coming. This system is approved and will be bought and fielded, and by the way, the price tag for the Navy [known as the total obligation authority] is X millions, and the Army is Y millions, and the Air Force is Z millions. The program is now approved and will now go through. Thank you very much for attending the meeting."

When you fast forward to the current day, it's interesting that the whole world loves GPS and everybody's using it, down to the local fisherman who's using it to backtrack to where his latest catch was, and we've invented differential GPS, which allows you to land airplanes with remote control with GPS equipment based on the runways. Loran-C, Decca, hi-fix, and other radio navigation systems have all gone. GPS has replaced them for navigation, and something not mentioned very often, the capability to analyze nuclear explosions is also flying in orbit today.

Cold War Saga

Richard E. Kersteen

U pon graduation from the Naval Academy in June 1952, I was commissioned a second lieutenant in the United States Air Force. I was assigned to the Malden Air Base (a civilian contract base) in Malden, Missouri, where I received primary pilot training consisting of 125 hours of flight training in the T-6. Upon completion of primary flight training, I was assigned to Reese Air Force Base in Lubbock, Texas, to participate in advanced flight training consisting of approximately forty hours in the T-28 and approximately eighty hours in the B-25.

I received my "wings" in December 1953, and since the Korean conflict had ended in July 1953 and there was no longer a need for new pilots in the Far East Air Force, I was assigned to the 376th Air Refueling Squadron (ARS) at Barksdale Air Force Base in Bossier City, Louisiana. The ARS was a part of the 376th Medium Bomb Wing, which consisted of three squadrons of B-47s, the medium bomber force at the time in the Strategic Air Command. I was assigned as a copilot on a KC-97 aerial tanker combat crew.

Air Force KC-97 Aerial Tanker (U.S. Air Force Official Photo)

The tanker crew consisted of the aircraft commander, copilot, navigator, flight engineer, radio operator, refueling boom operator, and scanner. We flew many different types of missions, such as air refueling B-47s, navigation training, transition training (shooting landings), and electronic countermeasure tests, to mention a few.

A typical air refueling mission required a heavy weight takeoff (185,000 pounds). It usually took approximately forty-five minutes to get to the refueling altitude of 15,000 feet. Our rendezvous with the B-47 was accomplished by starting from an initial planned position (a radio station, VOR) and radar surveillance to initiate the hook-up. The B-47 was required to descend to our altitude for the transfer of fuel. Our typical transfer of 40,000 pounds of JP-4 took six to ten minutes, depending on flight conditions.

We flew training missions to all corners of the United States and usually spent one deployment a year at a forward operating base. My first deployment in 1955 was to Ben Guerir Air Base in central Morocco, where we spent three months supporting operations around the Mediterranean. In early 1956, I was promoted to aircraft commander of a KC-97 combat crew and spent my second deployment at Gander Air Base in Labrador.

In addition to the annual long-term deployments at forward operating bases, we also participated in short-term deployments (seven to ten days) to support SAC World Wide Simulated Combat Missions (UCSM). These exercises were dress rehearsals for the ultimate mission, if ever necessary. Deployment locations varied depending on the planning. We flew refueling missions in support of these plans from Bermuda, the Azores and Loring AFB in Limestone, Maine. During my tour of duty with the ARS, the Strategic Air Command was one of the three legs of the nuclear triad that was keeping peace in the world through a powerful military. Believe me, SAC was ready to fly the "ultimate" mission if it ever became necessary.

I left the Air Force in December 1956 and went to work for the Westinghouse Electric Corporation in Lester, Pennsylvania, as a marine engineer. In 1964 I was transferred to Sunnyvale, California, where Westinghouse established their Marine Division. During my years in engineering, I worked on propulsion equipment for the DE-1052–class destroyer escort, ballistic missile nuclear submarines, and amphibious force supply ships, as well as ship service turbine generator sets for nuclear aircraft carriers. In 1973, during a marketing assignment in Boston, Massachusetts, I became involved with the ship service turbine generator sets for the new Trident submarine program and spent eight years as the Westinghouse program manager for this very important Navy nuclear program.

In 1983 I was reassigned to the Missile Launching and Handling Department at the Marine Division of Westinghouse and managed the field engineering organization that supported the missile-launching capabilities of the ballistic missile submarines wherever they were assigned in the world. In the early 1990s, I was reassigned by the ML&H Department to be the capsule launching system program manager. This program provided the Tomahawk missile launching capability to the nuclear attack submarine fleet.

I retired in December 1994 and have enjoyed my leisure time trying to stay in good physical and mental health by keeping active physically and mentally—as we were taught as midshipmen at the Naval Academy. I count my blessings every day for the excellent education we received at the academy, which prepared us well to proceed down the road of life.

My Short Stint in Air Force Blue

Jim Burch

hortly after graduation, I drove to Lynnville, Tennessee, to pick up John Paulk on the way to our first duty station, Sandia Base in Albuquerque, New Mexico, where we were to be trained as nuclear weapons officers along with many of our classmates. John was not ready to travel, reluctant to leave his girlfriend Mary Alice, whom he married three months later.

The nuclear portion of the training course was from the Los Alamos National Laboratory at the University of California in Berkeley. I never understood why quantum mechanics was necessary to become a nuclear weapons officer, but I was thankful for the insight it gave me. The electronics/mechanical portion of the course was structured by Sandia Labs, a subsidiary of Western Electric. After finishing this training, we spent about a month with Dow Chemical outside Boulder, Colorado, observing plutonium-239 processing and the shaping of nuclear weapons parts. I witnessed a plutonium fire while there.

On a mid-June weekend, five of us went back to Albuquerque. As we were leaving Denver, the snow started to come down. Andy LeMoal was driving his car, and the other four of us were playing bridge. Andy could not stay out of the bridge game even with all the encouragement we were providing. About four miles north of Colorado Springs, we went into a spin, backing into a recently plowed and softened ditch bank. Luckily none of us were hurt. We limped into Albuquerque on a warped car frame, and I had to drive us back to Boulder. After the plutonium exposure, each of us had to spend a month working at a national nuclear weapons stockpile site. My time was at the Navy-operated Clarksville Base in Tennessee.

Shortly after classmate Bill Kirk completed the training described above, he was entrusted with "mother henning" to Okinawa the nuclear weapon with which President Eisenhower threatened the North Koreans to get them back to the negotiation table in 1953. Bill quit the Air Force as soon as he could and worked in one of the Los Alamos holes until he retired.

Next I was assigned to an Air Force depot squadron training for deployment to Anchorage, Alaska. Fortunately, perhaps, someone decided we were not needed, so back to the twice-a-day bulletin board assignment, where I noticed captains and lieutenants were invited to a lecture several days hence. I failed to attend as my first son was being born at the hospital and standing orders said I was OK. I went to the executive officer and told him why I missed the meeting. He said I would be punished by being assigned officer of the day duty Christmas and New Year's Day, which sort of ticked me off, especially after I found out the meeting was held to tell captains and lieutenants, "Don't go sit on the colonel's desk, ask for a cigarette and a light and then chew him out for running such a shoddy operation." The commanding general's aide was a friend; I asked him to get me transfer orders without the "officer assignment pool" officials knowing. He did, and I cleared the base totally, except my assigned squadron then gave the clearance papers to the executive officer. I said good-bye and headed to the national nuclear stockpile at Bossier Base near Shreveport, Louisiana (Barksdale Air Force Base), where I was greeted by classmate Jack Williams. I spent over a year there before heading back to Sandia Base to train with a tactical depot squadron.

At Bitburg Air Base in Germany, my ringing phone got me out of bed one night and my commanding officer told me to bring several changes of clothes and come to HQ as quickly as possible, I'd be away three to four days. The weather was bad, but it didn't stop the trains. I was given a top secret, restricted data operations order that had to be hand carried to our detachment at the Italian air base at Aviano, a Colt 45, a pad of NATO trip tickets, a briefcase, and a ride to the train station in Koblenz, a three-hour drive. The hand carrying had to be done because the Russians were on the way to Budapest and the crypto facility at Aviano could not yet handle top secret material.

I got to Koblenz and boarded the Rome–Amsterdam express. All sleeping accommodations had been sold out. The conductor told me there were some first-class compartments with no passengers and I could sleep in one of those. I asked if he could lock me in and others out, and he laughed. I was afraid of what might happen if I did go to sleep, so I went to a third-class car, found a seat at a "bier" drinking table, and sat on my brief case and .45 with my clothes bag at my feet. The car was jammed with Dutch college students on holiday as the schools had closed for a week. The singing and chatter in the car could have waked the dead.

In Basel the train stopped long enough for conductors to collect tickets. My NATO pass, the conductor said, was not acceptable, even though the Swiss section on the ticket said it was. The conductor said I must detrain or pay him. I asked him to write his name and employment register number in my notebook and tell me how to get to the U.S. consulate. He took the NATO pass, but I still had no lockable sleeping accommodations. It was a long trip across Switzerland to Chiaso/Como and on to Milan to change trains for Venice (Maestre). In Milan a very kind Italian gentleman said he would walk me to my Venice connection. As we walked past several second- and third-class cars, a man hanging out an aisle window invited me to share his compartment, where he took my bag, hat, and briefcase and occupied half of the compartment's seats. His belongings secured the other seats. He was looking for feminine company; several refused his kind invitations. He turned away three nuns, saying there were no vacant seats. Finally, a couple on their honeymoon sat with us, and were annoyed all the way to Verona.

At the Venice railroad station I was picked up by our squadron's weapons detachment leader, who worked for me. His name was Benvenutti, and he had relatives living up toward the Brenner Pass near Cortina d'Ampezzo. His nine-and-a-half-months pregnant wife was lolling around in his car's back seat. As we left the parking, I noticed Ben was driving very slowly, but I paid no attention until Lou said from the back seat, "Ben, quit staring and get us on home." Ben was traveling at the walking speed of a very attractive Italiana. A man approaching her turned around to look at the rear view as he passed, staggered off the sidewalk, and we ran over him. He jumped up, brushed himself off, said, "Excuse me" twice, and walked on.

We went on to the air base at Aviano, where I got rid of the top secret operations order. The next day I ran into an officer who worked for me who had been recalled from leave. He suggested I ride to Germany with him as the trip would be faster by car than by train. So we went to the PX and bought food for the return "nonstop" trip to Bitburg, Germany. We were going to eat lunch in the car when I discovered we had neglected to buy bread. I went into a bakery and asked for *panne* from a group of derelict-appearing old men. One of them got up and said to me, "What the hell do you want? Bread? I drove a cab in Chicago for twenty-five years. We used to drive the pregnant women over the tracks until they started labor, then to the hospital. We don't have bread, sold out, don't cook again until tomorrow morning." He was kind enough to raid someone's kitchen for a partial loaf, which he then gave us. He said he was sorry he had left Chicago but could not go back. We drove all night through the Brenner Pass, Austria, Garmisch, Germany, and on into Bitburg.

The alert in response to Russian entry into Hungary turned out to be a good training exercise with considerable loss of sleep. We went through a similar exercise when the French and British went into Egypt, with deployment to Adana, Turkey. Shortly after that a "wee small voice" told me we were never going to use these bombs and I decided to get out. Six weeks after my separation, I went to work for the Atomic Energy Commission and experienced a much different, more varied, and more complicated nuclear weapon and weapon material production field. Life in civvies was a bit different from life in Air Force blue.

Talking Nuclear

Charles J. (Jim) Bridgman

I accepted an Air Force commission in 1952, primarily on the veiled promise of a technical assignment. True to that promise, I was posted to Sandia Base in Albuquerque, New Mexico, as a part of the Armed Forces Special Weapons Project, which was the joint service follow-on to the Army's Manhattan Project. At Sandia I found myself one of many freshly arrived 1952 graduates from both the Naval Academy and West Point, some of whom I am still in contact with today. Although I didn't realize it until decades later, we were all part of a grand design by GEN Leslie Groves, USA, the then recently departed director of the Manhattan Project.

Groves was maneuvering to countercheck the widespread bias by the civilian scientists at Los Alamos that the military should not be trusted with the awesome power of atomic weapons. They believed that this new weapon should be kept in the hands of the civilian scientists who developed it. Groves' plan was to staff the Armed Forces Special Weapons Project with Academy graduates who stood in the top ranks of their class and were varsity athletes. He later relaxed his screen to include regular officers from top ROTC programs. Groves' strategy was successful in that the Atomic Energy Act of 1946—and later 1954—dictated that atomic weapon design would be the province of a civilian Atomic Energy Commission (now the Department of Energy) with design specifications set by a joint military-civilian committee and the storage, logistics and deployment would be the sole responsibility of the Department of Defense. The actual delivery would also be carried out by the military under control of the president. In 1952, as a too-smart-for-his-own-good second lieutenant, I appreciated very little of this high-level policy debate.

At Sandia we went through college-level courses in vacuum tube electronics (fusing and firing) and nuclear physics (the "physics package"). After a year and a half, I was posted to the Strategic Air Command B-47 Wing at Davis-Monthan Air Force Base in Tucson, Arizona, where we didn't use much nuclear physics but did continuously load and unload a lot of the early atomic weapons on B-47s for training purposes. I also met and courted a young Air Force nurse from the base hospital. We were married in the base chapel in May 1954. As I write this, Lucy and I, together with three generations of our children, recently celebrated our sixtieth wedding anniversary. Shortly after our wedding, I received emergency orders to return to Albuquerque, this time to Kirtland Air Force Base, where I joined a handful of my earlier Sandia classmates and others as members of the first military team to assemble and load the first operational hydrogen bomb, the Mk-17, on the B-36. Lucy joined me shortly after as a nurse assigned to the Kirtland infirmary. Our team was trained by civilian scientists from Los Alamos and Sandia Laboratories. As soon as we were certified, we began training other Air Force teams and were then transferred as a unit to Lowry Air Force Base in Denver to charter the Air Force Nuclear Weapons School to continue training other units on the Mk-17 as well as earlier atomic weapons.

After a year and a half at Lowry, I was selected to attend graduate school at North Carolina State College (now University) in the then new academic discipline of nuclear engineering. At North Carolina, I worked for Raymond L. Murray, one of the pioneers in nuclear reactor education. Ray Murray and a handful of his colleagues came to North Carolina State from Oak Ridge National Laboratory. At the college they designed and built the first nuclear reactor on a college campus. Murray was first a teacher and second a researcher. There is no question that he had a tremendous influence on my subsequent academic career. Because I had taken high school graduate courses at the University of Arizona, University of New Mexico, and University of Colorado, I arrived at North Carolina State with transcripts listing nearly a year's work in mathematics. As a result I was able to complete both a master of science and the course work and exams for a PhD within the time allotted by the Air Force for a full-time school tour.

In the last months of that tour, I learned of a faculty vacancy in the nuclear engineering program at the Air Force Institute of Technology (AFIT). I visited Wright Patterson Air Force Base and was able to talk my way into the position. The fellow I convinced was William L. Lehmann, head of the AFIT Department of Physics. He later went on to become the first civilian director of the Air Force Weapons Laboratory and still later an undersecretary of the Air Force. Bill was another person who influenced my academic career greatly.

As a young military faculty member at AFIT, I found myself teaching courses and supervising student research in reactor technology in support of the nascent nuclear powered aircraft, or ANP. The concept was that a very large plane powered by a nuclear reactor could stay aloft for a month or more, ready to retaliate in the event of a nuclear attack on the United States. The Achilles' heel of that system was safety. If the public objects to a nuclear power reactor next door, how about one overhead? Aircraft, nuclear or otherwise, crash! Those crashes can be statistically predicted on the basis of miles flown or on the number of takeoffs or landings. The joke among insiders was "With a system like that, we might not need the Russians." Fortunately for all of us, the intercontinental ballistic missile (ICBM) was born and quickly after it the submarine-launched ballistic missile (SLBM). The ICBM does its loitering in a missile silo and the SLBM under deep water, not at 20,000 feet overhead.

With the demise of ANP, the AFIT nuclear program turned its attention to small semiportable, remotely located reactors and space nuclear propulsion. However, at about the same time, graduates came back to us with the message that their assignments had little to do with nuclear reactors and everything to do with nuclear weapons effects such as the effect of x-rays on reentry vehicle heat shields and high-altitude electromagnetic pulse. Both Bill Lehmann and I started a series of visits to the Air Force Weapons Laboratory in Albuquerque to find out what they were talking about. In my case, the visits continued for decades. I still run into people who thought that I was assigned there. Back at AFIT I created a course and then a sequence of courses on nuclear weapons effects.

After four years of faculty duty, the Air Force Military Personnel Center informed me that I was ready for a transfer and that transfer could not be to another instructional position such as the Air Force Academy because I was a Naval Academy graduate. More than two instructional tours in a career would be bad for that career. (They counted my brief tour at Lowry as an instructional tour.) This ban was indefinite. I did some serious soul searching and decided that I might be of more value to the Air Force doing what I was doing (and besides I really enjoyed being a professor). Therefore I resigned my commission after eleven and a half years and accepted a civil service appointment into essentially the same job that I held as an active duty officer. I continued at AFIT teaching in the nuclear engineering program with a heavy emphasis on nuclear weapon effects with a research concentration on nuclear fallout. In 1968 the faculty approved my promotion to full professor and I became chairman of the AFIT nuclear engineering program. I headed the program for the next twenty years, continuing to develop courses in nuclear effects and related nuclear subjects. Over that time I chaired 115 master of science theses and 15 doctoral dissertations in nuclear technology. In 1986 a group of AFIT graduates nominated me as a fellow in the American Nuclear Society. One of those distinguished graduates was Bill Anders, *Apollo 8* astronaut and USNA graduate (1955).

In 1988 I competed in a national search for the position of associate dean for research at AFIT and was selected. In that position, with the support of a small but hardworking staff, we were able to find ways to attract and justify—within existing DOD regulations—outside funds for faculty research (that is, funds outside of the normal AFIT operations and maintenance stream of funds). That was somewhat unprecedented at the time and led to today's robustly funded faculty and student research program. This success notwithstanding, I found that I missed direct contact with students both in the classroom and in one-on-one research, and direct interaction with fellow faculty. Again, after some soul searching, I retired from active civil service in 1997 and was fortunate enough to be named an emeritus professor. That position entitled me to an office, some clerical and computer support, and the right to do pretty much as I pleased.

One of the first projects that pleased me to do was to collate and edit my course notes from the three nuclear effects courses that I had developed before taking on the position of associate dean. The result was a hardbound textbook published in 2001 by the Defense Threat Reduction Agency, the successor organization to the Armed Forces Special Weapons Project that I joined in 1952. The book replaced my notes for the three AFIT effects courses that I had created thirty years before, much enriched by things I learned in the intervening years. To my surprise, the book also came into great demand in DOD agencies supporting the nuclear field and even by select DOE offices (the book is not available to the public).

The second project was a graduate nuclear weapons certificate program offered by distance education to officers and senior NCOs in nuclear operations. Some background is in order about this program. In 2007 six nuclear armed cruise missiles were mistakenly loaded on a B-52 at Minot Air Force Base in North Dakota and flown without authorization to Barksdale Air Force Base in Louisiana. This mistake, and a few others of lesser seriousness, ultimately cost the Air Force secretary and chief of staff their jobs. A general officer investigative committee concluded that personnel in the two Air Force legs of the nuclear triad had lost the dedication and professionalism necessary for the job. I would say that we had lost General Groves' vision of the 1950s. The Air Force responded with several corrective actions, including the establishment of the Global Strike Command (some called it "SAC reborn") as well as several training programs.

One of these training programs was the AFIT nuclear weapons certificate program. Much of the early liaison on this program between AFIT and Global Strike Command was carried out by a very talented colleague of mine, Jim Petrosky. Jim came to us as an active duty Army officer from the West Point faculty. He retired in place to become head of the AFIT graduate nuclear program (my old job). I hope that I have mentored Jim as others earlier mentored me. Jim was one of a long line of Army officers who came to the AFIT nuclear engineering program both as graduate students and faculty over the past two decades. Over that span of time, I think I may have had more Army officer graduate students than Air Force. I always found this puzzling since Army has had no nukes since 1987 when tactical nukes were outlawed by the Intermediate Nuclear Forces Treaty. I have always enjoyed my association with the Army students. They come to AFIT a little more mature than our younger Air Force officers and certainly with a strong sense of professionalism.

The certificate program that Jim Petrosky negotiated with Global Strike consists of three entry-level graduate programs, nuclear weapon effects, international nonproliferation, and national nuclear policy. The nuclear effects course was adapted from my textbook and the nonproliferation course was adapted from an advanced graduate course that I had developed over the preceding several years. I wrote textbook-like notes for the first two of these courses as well as instructor notes. I also put together a detailed syllabus and instructor notes for the nuclear policy course. However we were concerned about credibility on the policy course. (How could a bunch of engineers presume to teach a course on policy?) Fortunately I had maintained contact with our classmate, Tom Julian. Tom holds a PhD in history, served two tours as faculty at the Air Force Academy, and had assignments in policy positions both at Supreme Headquarters Allied Powers, Europe and the Pentagon. We invited Tom to be a visiting professor focused on the policy course. He not only offered credibility but turned out to be a magnificent addition to the faculty team teaching the policy course. Tom continues to contribute to the course, while I have stepped back to deal with some health problems, both my wife's and my own.

Another classmate I have maintained close contact with is my four-year roommate, John P. Derr. Jack accepted a Navy line position in 1952, and we have met nearly yearly since then to trade experiences about our respective careers and reminisce about our midshipmen days, the latter with some chagrin. The only advice I might offer to the present Academy administration is this: be patient with young midshipmen; they may grow up.

I truly enjoyed working with students enrolled in the nuclear certificate program, bomber crews and missile men and women. They are a different breed than the nuclear science students in the graduate degree program with whom I have been deeply involved for over fifty years. In many ways the association with these operational officers brought me back to the early years of my career in nuclear weapons operations. The experience completed the cycle for me.

In late 2013 I was notified by the commander of the Air Force Nuclear Weapons Center at Albuquerque that I had been selected for the Order of the Nucleus for "lifetime contributions to nuclear weapons education." I suspect that the nomination was engineered by some of my former students, but I am nonetheless honored.

Turkey and the Cyprus Crisis

Bill Evans

[Editor's note: At the time of Bill Evans' arrival in Turkey, the simmering dispute between Turkey and Greece as to how each country provided security for its citizens living on the island of Cyprus was beginning to heat up, threatening to reach the boiling point. This posed a major problem for the United States and NATO because both nations were members of NATO. This is Bill's story of his firsthand experience with that situation.]

In 1974 I was transferred from a job as base commander of Torrejon Air Force Base just outside Madrid to vice commander of TUSLOG, the USAF Command of one hundred USAF units spread over the country of Turkey. (The acronym TUSLOG had no specific meaning and was used as a cover for various USAF detachments in Turkey.) No one had a vision of this command getting involved with combat operations because all assumed that either NATO or CENTO, the Central Treaty Organization, would conduct any such operations. There was no command post or anything even looking like one.

My immediate boss was Major General Braswell. A few days after I arrived, I concluded that this assignment had more complications than I had assumed. First, in day-to-day conversations, I immediately realized that my knowledge of Turkish geography was inadequate. Every entity under this command was referred to by either a TUSLOG detachment number or a geographical location. All detachment numbers were no longer occupied because many units had been deactivated and the number provided no clue as to the size, location, or purpose of the unit. TUSLOG Det 11 could be a three-man postal unit in Ankara, and TUSLOG Det 10 could be a five-thousand-man Air Force wing elsewhere in Turkey. If I asked a question, I would typically receive an answer that the unit in question was at a location defined by its Turkish name. Almost none of these names meant anything to me at that time. To say I had a lot to learn in a hurry is a big understatement.

After about one week in country, I went over to pay what I thought would be a five-minute courtesy call on the U.S. ambassador at about 1:00 p.m. He was very gracious but did ask a few pointed questions. First he asked if I spoke fluent Turkish. I said I knew not a word of Turkish. Next he asked if I was very familiar with Turkish history, and I said I knew very little of Turkish history. Then he asked what possible usefulness I would have in this assignment. I responded that I was good at straightening out screwed-up Air Force bases. He had served in the Marines and seemed to like that answer. He then told his office secretary to cancel the rest of the day's appointments, escorted me into his inner sanctum, and spent hours going over things Turkish that he thought I needed to understand. This extended conversation consumed the rest of the day. I also figured out that he had a respect for commanders and people who had held command positions, but not so much for staff types. I could have spent a semester studying Turkey and learned a lot less. His insight into Turkish thinking was phenomenal. His wife had been the secretary to John Foster Dulles, so this was a diplomatic dream team.

Trouble had been brewing over events in Cyprus since before my arrival. Deputy Secretary of State Joseph Sisco had been sent to mediate the situation between Turkey and Greece and had been shown Turkish forces marshalling on the south coast while he was flying in a C-130 with General Braswell. The Turkish government wanted Henry Kissinger to mediate and was not at all satisfied with the results being achieved by the ongoing mediation.

A few weeks later, General Braswell went off on leave and was out of touch on a small Greek sailing vessel in the Aegean Sea. Then the Turkish prime minister decided that his armed forces should invade Cyprus to protect Turkish peasants living there. He had reason to believe villagers were being slaughtered by Greek forces on Cyprus. He directed the invasion to be conducted the next morning. The Turkish army chief of staff protested that they had no plan whatsoever for such an invasion. They had lots of plans, but the invasion of Cyprus was not one of them. The prime minister said that the lack of plans did not matter because "we are on Cyprus tomorrow or you will lose your head and I don't mean figuratively." The word "tense" does not begin to capture the situation. My personal knowledge of what was going on was very little at that point. The political issues and interwoven loyalties on Cyprus would take a few pages to describe. I will just say they were complex and bewildering.

The next morning, I received a phone call informing me that the ambassador wanted me to be at a building in Ankara at 9:30. I had no clue what this was about. I appeared at the appointed time and was met by someone who immediately escorted me to a plastic room inside a locked and guarded vault of a room.

The ambassador and about ten others were there. All outranked me by one to three stars, and some in civilian attire looked mature enough to have a similar status. I was directed to sit in a chair quite near the ambassador. The doors were shut and locked. The ambassador then said, "This is Colonel Evans. Do you all know him?" After some affirmative answers, he then said, "Colonel Evans is now on the Country Team and is cleared for everything. Any questions?" There were no questions. Later I learned that he had explained to his team that he needed a military commander on his team and had sent for me. This man knew how to vaporize red tape.

I then received the same series of briefings that the ambassador and the rest of the team received. It was a remarkable display of top notch intelligence briefings. Although all in country, including the Turkish armed forces, were surprised by the rapid unfolding of events, my view is that the team that received those briefings understood what was happening where and when at least as well as anyone else. The lack of any real plan on the part of the Turks led to several bad fratricide incidents—a great example of why you need a real plan for any military operation.

I spent much of the next day with a phone in each ear giving guidance to Air Force people in strange situations that no one had anticipated. My thinking was, "This is bad now, and if any of our people get killed it will become much worse quickly." In addition to any of the military actions around Cyprus, the Turks had put their attack columns on the road and they were ready to roll into Greece from a point very near to the border. This column was serious business and in alignment with existing strategic plans to invade a larger country. It reached back about 350 miles into Turkey. This blocked the major highway from Ankara to other important locations to the west of Ankara. I also thought that if this column ever started rolling, the vanguard would be in the Adriatic Sea long before the rear guard crossed the border.

I received a call from our ambassador explaining that he needed to move to a location in Turkey where he could conduct business that had the potential to end this conflict. The roads were not open, but a small jet could move him to where he needed to be. There was such a jet nearby, but it was in Greece. I learned that a simple phone call to my counterparts in Greece was not going to make this happen. I spent hours calling anyone I could think of who could solve this problem. The next morning we had a suitable small jet on the Ankara airfield. In hindsight, I doubt my phone calls were useful. I had reported to the ambassador that my efforts had not lined up the needed aircraft to that point. I suspect that he took my report and then called the State Department representative to the White House and explained the situation. With the White House now in the picture, orders were received for the Air Force to release the jet at sunrise, flying at night being too risky due to the difficulty to recognize friend from foe. The ambassador and the other State Department experts were then able to bring the active fighting part of the conflict to a gradual halt after the usual negotiations. It was a close-run thing for all involved.

In the aftermath, both the Greek and Turkish governments fell and the heads of the armed forces also lost their jobs. Our newly elected president replaced our excellent ambassador to Turkey. There are times when things in which we are involved have a direct impact on our families; such was the case in this instance.

My ninth-grade son had been on a camping trip on the south coast when the Turkish prime minister decided to invade Cyprus. The camp was located near one of the Turkish army's departure points for the invasion, and their security efforts caused him to be pinned down there, with inadequate potable water and no sanitary facilities. He lost one-third of his body weight. My sixteen-year-old daughter, Kim, departed for Duke University on a C-130 in which she was the only person not receiving combat pay, hardly the best circumstances for any civilian to travel in, let alone a sixteen-year-old girl. Few parents would expect or desire to encounter this sort of situation. But all's well that ends well, and both children went on to significant success.

Because of the wise counsel I received from the ambassador, I got on well with the Turks, and some time later, after I had returned to the United States, I was invited to a party being given in Colorado Springs for a group of Turkish officers who were touring military installations in the country. It seems they had requested that Colonel Evans be invited, even though I had never met any of them. Subsequent to my return to the United States, our relations with Turkey had declined considerably, but I could not remember ever receiving such lavish attention as I received at that party. Apparently, they had been briefed to seek out those whom they believed to be friends of Turkey who could influence our president to come to better terms with Turkey. They overestimated my influence by at least 1,000 percent. I enjoyed the attention, but I was not going to get into any kind of diplomatic bind, especially in view of my lack of any significant influence with the administration. That party was my last contact with the Turks.

The effects of the damage inflicted on U.S.-Turkish relations by this conflict continue to this day.

A Look Back in Time

Dick Saxer

I assumed all during my years at Annapolis that I would become a naval officer. But life happens, people talk, and things change. When the time came to choose a service, I selected the Air Force. After graduation, my first assignment was as an electronics and mechanical officer with the Tactical Air Command at Sandia Base, New Mexico, submerged in special weapons and unit training. After two years, I was deployed to French Morocco with the Strategic Air Command, where our task was to load aircraft for designated missions.

When I returned stateside in 1955, I spent two years earning a master's degree in aeromechanics from the Air Force Institute of Technology. After graduation from AFIT, I was assigned to the Air Force Special Weapons Center at Kirkland Air Force Base in New Mexico, where I designed, tested, and developed nuclear weapons loading techniques for the Tactical Air Command. In 1960 I was selected to pursue a PhD in metallurgical engineering from Ohio State University. Degree in hand, I returned to the Air Force Institute of Technology as an instructor from 1962 until 1965. A six-month program at the Armed Forces Staff College in Norfolk, Virginia, was followed by duty at the U.S. Air Force Academy, where, from 1966 to 1970, I served as an associate professor and deputy department head of the engineering mechanics department. While stationed in Colorado Springs, I was twice deployed to Vietnam to assist in assessing and solving technical problems. I later attended the Industrial College of the Armed Forces at Fort Lesley J. McNair in Washington, D.C. Apparently, academic life agreed with me—I managed to not only graduate but also earn the title of the 1971 Tiger of the Year Award for Athletic Excellence.

In July 1971, I was assigned as commander/director of the Air Force Materials Laboratory at Wright-Patterson Air Force Base in Dayton, Ohio. The main goal at that time was to provide cost and weight savings in the production of B-1, F-5, F-16, and A-10 aircraft through our composite materials program.

By 1974 I was back in the special weapons business that I had begun to tackle back in 1952. I became the commander/director of the Advanced

Ballistic Reentry Systems Program in Los Angeles, where we formulated various reentry systems programs designed to provide new ballistic and maneuvering reentry vehicle options for M-X and Trident weapon systems. In the spring of 1977, I returned to Wright-Patterson as deputy for aeronautical equipment in the Aeronautical Systems Division. I was responsible for managing the Electronic Warfare, Reconnaissance Strike, Support Equipment and Avionics and Aircraft Accessories program offices. In 1979, I became the deputy for tactical systems, a job that included overseeing the F-15, A-10, fighter attack, Maverick, and remotely piloted vehicles. I completed my time at Wright-Patterson serving as the vice commander of the Aeronautical Systems Division from 1981 to 1983.

In 1983 I assumed my final assignment as the director of the Defense Nuclear Agency (DNA) in Washington, D.C. The DNA is the oldest of the defense agencies and began in 1942 with the creation of the Manhattan Project, which developed the first atomic bomb. The Manhattan Project was dissolved in 1946 and, after some changes, was renamed the Defense Nuclear Agency in 1971. As director of DNA, I was under the authority and control of the undersecretary of defense for research and engineering. The majority of DNA activity is associated with nuclear weapons effects, research, and testing. DNA plans, coordinates, and supervises the Department of Defense efforts in this area, including the testing, assessment, construction, and management of simulation facilities and field experiments. DNA is the central defense agency for coordination of nuclear weapons development and testing with the Department of Energy. DNA manages the nuclear weapons stockpile and its associated reporting system and conducts technical investigations and field tests to enhance the safety and security of theater nuclear forces. DNA provides advice and assistance to the Joint Chiefs of Staff and the services on all nuclear matters, including site security, tactics, vulnerability, radiation effects, and biomedical effects. To accomplish its mission, DNA is organized with its headquarters in Washington, D.C., the Field Command in Albuquerque, New Mexico, and the Armed Forces Radiobiology Research Institute in Bethesda, Maryland. DNA retains management of Johnston Atoll in the Pacific to ensure its availability as a test site.

I recall President Reagan's famous motto, "Peace through Strength," during my days at DNA, and it is as valid today as it was then. All we need to do is look at the chaos here and around the world today to understand that we must be better prepared. As one who vividly remembers the death and destruction of World War II, I pray we do not see a similar conflict come to our shores in our children's or grandchildren's lifetimes.

When I look back on my military career, I realize that none of my accomplishments compare to meeting and marrying my beautiful wife and raising four incredible children together. Marilyn and I grew up very near each other in Toledo, Ohio. We attended the same grade school and high school, and although we knew one another, we were like passing ships in the night. After a visit home from the Academy during my second year, however, our paths crossed and we began dating. Marilyn made a few visits to the Academy from Bowling Green, including one to attend our annual ring dance and another to see my graduation. The rest, as they say, is history. We married in July 1952, shortly after graduation, and headed off to start our adventure in the Air Force. Marilyn has been my anchor through the ups and downs of my military career. While I worked long hours and traveled overseas to Europe, North Africa, Vietnam, Korea, and Johnston Atoll—often for long periods of time—she kept things together at home. I credit her with raising our four great kids into smart, successful adults who are now best friends and have amazing kids of their own. I worried about my job and she worried about the children. We made an incredible team. As the kids grew older, Marilyn was able to accompany me to some of my overseas travels and see firsthand what I could only tell her about before. It was nice to finally share this aspect of my life with her after so many years left waiting at home. She has truly been my success.

Lt Col James R. Brickel, USAF,
Air Force Cross

Jim Sagerholm

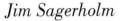

I t was November 1966, and the constant need for photo reconnaissance over North Vietnam was steadily taking a toll of the RF-101 aircraft used for that purpose. Photo runs necessarily were made at low to medium altitudes, and losses of the unarmed RF-101s were heavier than losses of strike aircraft. The pilots flying recce missions were in an extremely dangerous and rarely recognized business. Nevertheless, Lt Col James R. Brickel volunteered for RF-101 duty and arrived at Udorn Royal Thai Air Base on 30 November 1966, where he was assigned to the 20th Tactical Reconnaissance Squadron.

In February 1967, Jim was moved into the squadron operations officer billet. Losses to AAA and MiGs had made it clear that RF-101s could not continue in the recce mission, and plans were underway to replace the 101s with newer, high-performance RF-4s. But the demands for photos had to be met, regardless of the danger.

On 10 March 1967, authority was granted to the Seventh Air Force to attack the iron and steel plant at Thai Nguyen, considered by Seventh Air Force to be the most important target yet to be attacked. Only thirty miles or so from Hanoi, it was very heavily defended. The attack having been made, it was now time for photo recce to determine the damage accomplished. Brickel, with some fifty missions behind him, volunteered to make the flight through the now totally alerted ring of AAA and missiles, as well as probable MiGs.

Escorted by four F-4s, Brickel flew toward the flames and smoke coming from the damaged plant. As he entered the heavily defended area, extremely heavy flak from numerous anti-aircraft guns filled the air. Brickel continued toward the target, and rolled in for his photo run. With some ten miles to go, Brickel's aircraft was hit when an 85-mm shell exploded under his left engine. The left aileron was badly damaged, flight control hydraulics failed, oil pressure in the left engine dropped to zero, and his cockpit filled with smoke. Airspeed dropped by some fifty knots, but Brickel regained control of the plane and continued his run. Now the cameras started rolling and there was no turning back. Despite continued heavy antiaircraft fire and the imminent threat of his aircraft exploding or bursting into flames, Brickel completed his mission, acquiring complete photo coverage. In the face of heavy odds, he brought his crippled aircraft back to Udorn.

For his superb display of airmanship, courage, and exceptional heroism in the accomplishment of a critical mission, Lieutenant Colonel Brickel was awarded the Air Force Cross, second only to the Medal of Honor. Lieutenant General Brickel retired from active duty in September 1984.

We lost Jim after a valiant struggle with Parkinson's disease on 21 November 2014.

Courtesy of Dave Davison, Class of 1952

IV

THE SPELL OF SPACE

To kill time while on youngster cruise, a group of us would play the game of hearts. The object is to avoid taking any tricks containing a heart, or the queen of spades. Low score wins. The exception to avoiding hearts is to collect all of them plus the queen of spades, in which case all the other players receive twenty-six points while you get none. The latter is called "shooting the moon." Little did any of us dream at the time of the role that some of our classmates would play in fulfilling the American goal of placing men on the moon.

Ken Weir

Shooting the Moon

Ken Weir

Most of us had our first flight in a "Yellow Peril," the N3N-3 plane with biwings and two open cockpits and fitted with a single float that enabled the aircraft to use the Severn River as a runway. It was a fantastic experience, and those of us who had the flying bug would hang around the squadron ops office waiting for the opportunity to get an extra flight. Over the next four years, we also flew in the SNJ trainers as well as the Martin Mariners, the PBMs.

Following graduation, a number of our class entered flight training, either with the Navy at Pensacola or at various Air Force training fields. At Pensacola, ENS Eddie Paluso was the first to solo, despite having his bunk filled with cannon balls that Paul Gillcrist had poached from Fort Barrancas. After completion of flight training, we new aviators, called "nuggets" by the initiated, began our aviation careers, some flying from carriers, others in Marine Air Wings, while our Air Force brothers joined the Tactical Air Command or the Strategic Air Command.

One morning in October 1957, the *Washington Post* bore a startling headline about the Soviets having a satellite, *Sputnik*, that passed overhead every ninety minutes. Then they put a dog into space orbit. The United States, with the help of Werner Von Braun and other German rocket experts, attempted to equal the Soviet feat by putting a monkey into orbit. The monkey dumped into his space capsule seat on liftoff but still made the flight successfully. Not a very glamorous beginning, but the U.S. space effort was under way.

Intelligence reports indicated that the Soviet Union had its space team working feverishly to get a man into orbit as early as possible, and President Eisenhower directed the National Advisory Committee for Aeronautics (NACA) to begin work on launching an American into space.

In August 1957, John R. C. "Dimples" Mitchell was the first of our Academy class to enter the U.S. Naval Test Pilot School (TPS) in Class 19, graduating in January 1958. In 1958 Capt Ed Givens, USAF, was the first of those in powder blue to enter the Air Force Test Pilot School, in Class 58B. Ed graduated as the outstanding student, standing first in the class. Jim

Lovell and Paul Gillcrist entered Navy test pilot training in March 1958, in Class 20, with Jim Lovell snaring outstanding student honors, finishing first in the class.

In October 1958, NACA became NASA, the National Aeronautics and Space Administration, and in December of that year, President Eisenhower approved NASA's recommendation to initiate the astronaut selection process from among the military test pilot community. A total of 508 military test pilot case files were reviewed for possible selection for the initial astronaut project, Project Mercury. The thirty-two NASA finalists for the first group of astronauts included Jim Lovell, John Mitchell, and Ed Givens. Then began the grueling, tedious, and very competitive ordeal of undergoing the rigorous physical and psychological examinations and interviews dreamed up by scientists of every discipline who wanted to leave their mark on the space program. The Lovelace Clinic in New Mexico was the chosen site and the human specimens were tested to every extreme. Treadmills, electrocardiograms, breathalyzers, blood tests, rectal penetrations, Rorschach ink spot exams, centrifuge chairs, tilt tables, eye tests, hearing tests, and on and on and on. The candidates' patience and tolerance were tested to the very limit, often at the cost of their personal dignity.

About the same time in 1958, LT Bill Knutson, USN, was assigned to TPS Class 21, and Capt Tom Stafford, USAF, entered TPS Class 58C, graduating first in class in early 1959, and was named the outstanding student. In late 1958, LT Dave Davison, USN, joined TPS Class 22.

With much fanfare, on 8 April 1958, NASA announced the selection of the seven original astronauts, two of whom were Naval Academy graduates, Alan Shepard, Class of 1945, and Wally Schirra, Class of 1946. With three out of the thirty-two finalists, the Class of 1952 was indeed honored. Those three, Givens, Lovell, and Mitchell, were head and shoulders above the norm, consistently excelling in academics.

Other members of the class went through the Navy test pilot school—including Gus Eggert, 1959, John Yamnicky, 1960, and Ken Weir, 1961—while in the Air Force, it was Jimmie Honaker, Class 59B, and Roy Dickey, Class 61C. The Class of 1952 was forming a strong group of legendary test pilots in the golden years of aerospace research and development, with subsequent achievements in both aircraft and spacecraft. This exceptional group would help the Class of 1952 prove to all of the doubters and naysayers that 1952 did indeed produce some very capable and talented achievers and leaders.

Early in his term, President Kennedy declared that the United States would send men to the moon by the end of the 1960s. The race was on. Capt Tom Stafford, USAF, flew over to Patuxent River to test fly the Navy's new F4H-1F Phantom. Capt Ken Weir, USMCR, was one of the F4H-1F project pilots, and while discussing the rumored NASA second astronaut selection with Tom, the latter told Weir that "this time, NASA is going to get some really smart guys, not just red hot stick and rudder jocks!"

Easy for Tom to say, a guy who stood 50 in our Academy class and was first at test pilot school. Weir graduated near the top of the Class of 1953 and got through test pilot school only because of the late night tutoring by Gus Eggert and Dave Davison. Weir's claim to fame was that he had graduated first in his class at the Basic School, and in the late 1950s, this Marine aviator returned to Quantico to teach new second lieutenants the tactical employment of the pack animal, about which he knew absolutely nothing whatsoever. Undeterred, however, he was spectacular while giving his four-hour presentation wearing all his flight gear, complete with scarf, g-suit, parachute, swagger stick, sword, gloves, leather jacket, hard hat and sunglasses, .38-caliber revolver—all the while mounted on an old, broken-down polo pony. The latter use of the pony was used by the Basic School to justify the cost of maintaining stables on base, according to the watercooler crowd. Clearly, it was a perfect assignment for a Marine jet fighter pilot.

In the spring of 1962, NASA announced initiation of the selection process for the astronauts of Project Gemini. By the June deadline, NASA had received 253 applications that met the designated qualifications, coming from both the military and civilian test pilots. Out of those applicants, NASA picked thirty-two who were deemed best qualified to be finalists, including five from the Class of 1952: Jim Lovell, John Mitchell, Tom Stafford, Roy Dickey, and Ken Weir. Ed Givens was heavily involved in research and development projects and had not applied; if he had, he also would have been in the group.

The physical examinations were held at the U.S. Air Force School of Aerospace Medicine at Brooks Air Force Base in San Antonio, Texas. The exams included enhanced physicals and extensive psychiatric and psychological interviews. Based on skimpy rumor, Weir ran three miles a day and sat each day at home with his hands in a bucket of ice cold-water for thirty minutes. At Brooks, however, they put his *feet* in the ice bucket.

Ken Weir and one other candidate maxed out the inclined treadmill test and reportedly were the only ones to match John Glenn's record. Weir thought things were looking up. Little did he know. Now down to twenty-seven, the finalists were ordered to Houston for written tests and interviews. The exams were tedious and difficult for some of us, and included such things as trying to describe a picture of a mossy rock in a pool of water.

Then came the interviews. Alan Shepard, Deke Slayton, and Warren North sat on a dais high above the victim, who sat on a chair with the lower half of its legs sawed off. Weir met Stafford shortly after Tom's interview and was told it was a piece of cake. When it was Weir's turn, with his eyes burning from the cigar smoke in the room and his mouth dry from anxiety, it began poorly and only got worse.

"What was your class standing at the Naval Academy?"

"What was your conduct grade first class year?"

"What makes you think you could be an astronaut?"

"Were you ever drunk or disorderly in public?"

And so on. When Weir left that interview, he might as well have caught the next flight home; unless everyone else got the same grilling, he was in deep bandini as far as the astronaut program was concerned. It was the most humiliating experience of his entire life. At the dinner party that night, it was very enjoyable for some, but for others, it was dreary. Tom Stafford and Jim Lovell were among the nine selected, but Roy Dickey, John Mitchell, and Ken Weir had to swallow bitter pills of disappointment and return to their test pilot jobs.

Academy classmates Capt Donn Eisele, USAF, and LCDR John Yamnicky, USN, were among the thirty-four NASA finalists in the fall of 1963, and Eisele became the third astronaut from the Class of 1952. Ed Givens, free from his various projects, applied for selection of the fifth group of astronauts and was among the nineteen chosen. Thus the Class of 1952, with four astronauts, outmatched any other Naval Academy class. All had graduated in the top fifth of their Academy class; NASA took the best of the best.

Postscript

Ken Weir

CDR Dave Davison commanded the world famous Red Rippers of VF-11 and later commanded all Navy air assets ashore at Da Nang Air Base during the Vietnam War.

RADM Gus Eggert commanded attack squadron VA-192, Carrier Air Wing 9 during the Vietnam War and the carrier USS *Constellation*. Gus was one of the most decorated warriors of the Class of 1952, earning the Navy Cross, the Silver Star, the Legion of Merit twice with Combat "V" for valor, and two Distinguished Flying Crosses.

RADM Paul Gillcrist commanded VF-53, Carrier Air Wing 3 and Fighter Wings Pacific. He was the first flag officer to fly an F-14 fighter on and off a carrier, the USS *Kitty Hawk*. He has authored six nonfiction books as well as a TV screenplay about naval aviation.

Lt Col Jimmie Honaker became a premier rotary wing test pilot and tested numerous different types of vertical takeoff and landing aircraft.

CAPT Bill Knutson was the first commanding officer of an F4J squadron and took it into combat in Southeast Asia. He also commanded Carrier Air Wing 7. In retirement Bill served five years as president of the Navy Tailhook Association and virtually singlehandedly restored its reputation following an incident in 1991.

Col Roy Dickey shot down a MiG-17 in air-to-air combat while flying an F-105 over North Vietnam. He commanded the 44th Tactical Fighter Squadron, completing 274 combat missions without losing a single plane. He was awarded three Silver Stars and five Distinguished Flying Crosses.

CAPT John Mitchell commanded Carrier Air Wing 2, followed by command of Carrier Air Wing 9. He flew combat sorties in the A-6, A-7E, and F-4. His final command was the carrier USS *John F. Kennedy*.

MajGen Kenneth W. Weir, USMCR (Ret.), transferred to the Marine Corps Reserve and became the chief test pilot for such aerospace legends as Kelly Johnson (of Lockheed Skunk Works fame) and Willy Messerschmidt. He was the experimental test pilot for the U-2, spending nearly five thousand hours in the high-altitude reconnaissance aircraft. He performed the first flights of the TR-1A, the U-2S, and the Lockheed variant of the Douglas A-4S. He retired as the chief test pilot for high-altitude reconnaissance at the Lockheed Skunk Works at age sixty-three after performing a flight test above 70,000 feet in a single-engine U-2S. Weir had accumulated nearly twenty thousand hours of accident free total flying time when he retired, mostly in single-piloted single-engine aircraft. He commanded two Marine Reserve squadrons and was commanding general of the 65th Marine Amphibious Brigade, the 4th Marine Aircraft Wing, and deputy commanding general, Fleet Marine Force Pacific. He served two terms on the Secretary of Defense Reserve Forces Policy Board.

CAPT John D. Yamnicky, USN (Ret.), served a combat tour in amphibious ships in the Korean War before entering flight training. In his second and third combat tours, he flew attack aircraft from carriers on Yankee Station off the coast of Vietnam. John commanded an attack squadron and received the Distinguished Flying Cross for combat over North Vietnam. He became the director of the Naval Test Pilot School. Yamnicky was a passenger on the plane that was hijacked and flew into the Pentagon on September 11, 2001. He was the last member of the Class of 1952 to be killed by an enemy of the United States.

Jim Lovell, Tom Stafford, and Ken Weir were inducted into the Society of Experimental Test Pilots, of which Weir was president in 1981. Lovell and Stafford are both recipients of the Naval Academy Distinguished Graduate Award.

Gus Eggert, Paul Gillcrist, Bill Knutson, Jim Lovell, and Ken Weir were selected along with seven other members of the Class of 1952 for induction into the Golden Eagles, a limited (two-hundred-member) organization of early and pioneer naval and Marine aviators. Bill Knutson served as president of the Golden Eagles. To have twelve out of two hundred from the same class in this prestigious group is another accolade for the Class of 1952.

[Editor's note: Some space statistics for the Class of 1952:
- *A world speed record was set: 24,791 mph, Stafford in Apollo 10.*
- *A world altitude record was set: 248,791 miles, Lovell in Apollo 13.*
- *The first rendezvous in space: Stafford in Gemini 6A and Lovell in Gemini 7. During the rendezvous, Stafford held a sign saying "Beat Army" in his window, photographed by Lovell. The photo made the*

front page of the Washington Post. *The event was the world's highest football rally.*

- *In July 1975, Stafford became the first astronaut to join up with the Soviet spacecraft* Soyuz. *After hooking his Apollo spacecraft onto Soyuz, he knocked on the hatch of the Soviet craft. Back came the response: "Who's there?"*

Courtesy of Dave Davison, Class of 1952

V

NAVY BLUE

As many classes before and since, the Class of 1952 left the surreal world of "The Yard" and encountered a wide variety of real-world challenges, beginning with service in the Korean War. Many also faced the challenges of Vietnam, while others served in the seven seas and four corners of the world, keeping the Cold War from becoming hot and playing myriad roles with the common mission of defending a great nation in times of trouble.

The USS *Gray* and Soviet AGI Dogfight

Fox Johnson

The USS *Gray* (FF 1054) displaced over four thousand tons with a class-rated top speed of twenty-seven knots; however, *Gray* performed well above rated speed, with a sustained top speed of thirty-two knots during a forty-eight-hour open-sea, continuous, full-power trial run shortly after commissioning and retained her great speed throughout her life when so ordered. She was fitted with state-of-the-art sensor and weapons systems technology, including a gigantic "chin-mounted" sonar dome housing the latest acoustic sensor system and an electronic emission intercept suit of the most advanced design in the fleet. *Gray* was beautiful! Being a single-screw ship, she was, because of her a huge single propeller and large rudder, highly maneuverable and instantaneously responsive to all ordered "bells." We used to say that *Gray* could do anything with a single screw that a destroyer with twin screws could do, only better, boasting that she could maneuver on a dime and leave nine cents change.

Gray exceeded all fleet expectations and was first deployed to the Western Pacific (WESTPAC) to join the forces engaged in combat operations in the Tonkin Gulf in the spring of 1971. She conducted a variety of typical destroyer functions with recognized distinction throughout the deployment. On the occasion of her final period of operations before returning home, she was ordered to serve as the dedicated plane guard and shotgun escort for USS *Enterprise* (CVN 65) (BIG-E), then conducting combat air operations in the central Tonkin Gulf. *Gray* departed Subic Bay in the Philippines en route to join the BIG-E under total EMCON, active acoustic silent and darkened ship conditions.

Gray proceeded at top speed to rendezvous with *Enterprise* on schedule. We met the destroyer we were to relieve headed out of the gulf at high speed about ten miles southeast of the BIG-E and exchanged routine visual call signs and minor pleasantries as we proceeded onward toward our station. The outbound destroyer offered no operational data bits to us via the visual signaling process, as was the normal relieving procedure, and *Gray* asked for none. *Gray* sighted the usual Soviet intelligence collector ship then about five miles astern of *Enterprise* fishing plastic bags of garbage out of the water searching for intelligence "finds." As a matter of course and with no directions otherwise from the outbound destroyer, *Gray,* still at full power, maneuvered silently and smartly into the commonly (I thought!) used single destroyer plane guard station long designated as 2SNX (twelve hundred yards distant bearing 165 degrees relative to the guarded carrier). The initial station taking was done without any form of preliminary communications because the plane guard routine was customary and well established. When on station, *Gray* reported, "This is Sidekick, Alfa Station out," having maneuvered expeditiously into position and proceeded to maintain that position on the BIG-E without signal throughout the afternoon.

About sunset a BIG-E helicopter approached *Gray* and radioed that he intended to land on the helicopter flight deck. *Gray* had an enlarged and substantially beefed-up antisubmarine warfare (ASW) helicopter flight deck and all the warfare support items required to house, operate, and sustain a dedicated light-weight LAMPS Mk II antisubmarine warfare helo and detachment. After a slight bit of maneuvering by *Gray* to bring the relative wind over the port bow, the helo landed. Once on deck and secured, a passenger disembarked and was escorted to the ship's bridge where I was instructing the young officers of the deck in maintaining assigned station on an actively maneuvering aircraft carrier without the benefit of preparatory course and speed signals or other operational intentions. This aircraft carrier modus operandi was now standard operating procedure with most WESTPAC aircraft carriers because local area true wind conditions varied widely and momentarily, and consequently the operating carrier had to "chase the true wind" to maintain the relative wind over the deck required to launch and recover aircraft. No big deal, but the plane guard destroyer's bridge and combat information center (CIC) watch teams had to be constantly aware and prepared for the unexpected.

The visiting person just landed by the helo turned out to be CDR George Thompson, USN, then assigned as the surface operations officer on the staff of the commander, Task Force 77 (CTF-77)/commander, Attack Aircraft Carrier Division 5 (COMATKCARDIV-5) embarked in USS *Enterprise.* By chance I knew Commander Thompson from prior days, and we both were surprised to see each other. After the usual welcome greetings and such, Thompson advised me that the requirement for a destroyer-type ship to occupy the traditional 2SNX plane guard station had been superseded with the recent arrival of a detachment of specially fitted plane guard helicopters and that unless otherwise directed, *Gray* was to take shotgun station seven to ten miles distant from the BIG-E and operate independently. Fine! *Gray* would provide shotgun services willingly and respond instantaneously to such signals as CTF-77 or the BIG-E might make. Thompson departed in his helo and *Gray* vacated station 2SNX in a flash, taking flank speed to a position slightly abaft *Enterprise's* starboard beam about seven miles distant.

Those orders caused me to cease instructing my bridge watch team (officers of the deck, or OODs) on the fine points of silent station keeping on a constantly and unpredictably moving aircraft carrier. The secret we all learned years ago was to pick physical features obvious day and night that would reveal even the slightest course or speed change by visual aspect variation. Such detailed and absorbing conning officer concentration also necessitated close and continuous radar tracking by the junior officer of the watch (JOOW) and the CIC maneuvering and tracking team. The CIC was able to detect even slight speed changes made by the carrier through standard tracking procedures. It was a new but simpler world for destroyers in plane guard roles as compared with the standard fleet procedures in effect during my most recent destroyer duty in WESTPAC.

Meanwhile, the Soviet AGI continued to linger about seven miles astern of the carrier. It is interesting to recall that during the years following World War II and the Korean War, it had been standard practice to station as many as three plane guard destroyers with each carrier while conducting flight operations. One destroyer was stationed a thousand yards on the carrier's port beam as a marker for aircraft on the last downwind leg of the recovery process, the second was stationed three miles dead astern of the carrier to assist in initial approach lineup, and the third was stationed 165 degrees relative to the operating carrier at twelve hundred yards as a downed aircrew rescue destroyer. Those requirements were modified with the introduction of angled deck carriers equipped with new electronic and visual landing aids and improved night lighting, eliminating the need for stations one and two while sustaining the requirement for the 2SNX station.

The plane guard stations of yesteryear were occupied on signal whenever the operating carrier was about to commence flight ops and were vacated on signal when the carrier ceased air operations for the cycle only to be repeated before the next scheduled air ops began. Great fun! Manning and vacating plane guard stations during darkened ship conditions was a delicate, hazardous, if not sometimes dangerous maneuver, depending on the weather, visibility, and sea state conditions and formation disposition.

Use of dedicated plane guard rescue helicopters was far more timely and much safer while expediting downed aircrew recovery.

While proceeding to the traditional plane guard station, we made note of the customary Soviet intelligence ship. In those days Soviet warships were seldom encountered at sea, but AGIs were ever present. The AGIs were "civilian crew manned," large, oceangoing fishing trawler-like ships equipped with a huge array of radio-receiving antennae and a multitude of radio intercept operators (linguists). Some of those ships were three hundred feet long, displacing over three thousand tons. Usually, an AGI lingered clear but close to its "victim ship" and only occasionally maneuvered in close to harass the victim ship as it aggressively collected bags of garbage disposed over the ship's side by ship's personnel doing routine ship-keeping (housekeeping) chores. AGI functions were a long-standing, "fact-of-life" tradition in the Atlantic, Mediterranean Sea, and wide Pacific. Usually, the ships of both nations adhered to the International Rules of the Nautical Road at Sea.

Whereas U.S. Navy ships and forces complied with the rules of the road meticulously, the Soviets complied only as suited their objectives. No problem. Navy forces were aware of the Soviet practice of placing themselves in the privileged ship position with respect to the burdened victim ship and endeavored to prevent the Soviets from gaining an advantage by timely maneuvering. Most Soviet AGIs were declared to be fishing trawlers manned by civilian crews and were afforded the privileges of fishing ships when the visual signals (shapes and/or light) depicting their unmaneuverable status were displayed (seldom until needed to gain an advantage). The combination of political constraints levied by Washington, D.C., and the International Rules of the Nautical Road introduced some interesting situations for U.S. Navy warships and formations. Nevertheless, the operating forces managed to deal with the AGIs quite effectively.

For the next thirty-nine days, *Gray* lingered within seven to ten miles of *Enterprise,* varying distance and relative location according to the AGI's movements and my whims. *Gray* maneuvered randomly and frequently in the vicinity of *Enterprise,* always keeping the AGI in a "burdened" ship position (on the port bow) at all times. *Gray* exercised the ship's company at a variety of combatant readiness drills while continuing ship's material readiness work progress throughout the entire period. It was a delightful reprieve to be free of senior command oversight and to enjoy the good weather and sea conditions.

At midnight on the start of *Gray*'s fortieth day of our *Enterprise* shot-gun assignment and in anticipation of making a full-power run back to Subic, both boilers were brought up to full-power capacity slowly and were in top material condition ready for general battle problem exercises when released by competent authority. At sunrise I was on the bridge watching the AGI maneuver closer and closer to *Enterprise* and figured that the Soviet might try some different tactics this final day of *Enterprise*'s line period. (The Soviets knew the scheduled movements of all USN forces worldwide and were ever ready to capitalize on any opportunity.)

About 7:45 a.m., *Gray* was ordered to general quarters and damage control condition Zebra set in preparation for the battle problem and full-power run scheduled for the first day while en route back to Subic. Concurrently, the AGI closed position on *Enterprise*, getting very close astern of the carrier as the BIG-E conducted scheduled air-strike flight operations for her final day of the line period. I maneuvered *Gray* closer to the BIG-E and sent a flashing light message to the carrier asking whether *Gray* should intervene. In time and as the AGI moved in closer to the carrier but not yet in a harassing position, *Enterprise* responded by flashing light, "Not yet." *Gray* was about five miles distant from *Enterprise*, slightly abaft of her starboard beam in an excellent position to observe the AGI's movements and proximity to the BIG-E. For some reason I can't recall, I directed all topside weapons control systems and gun-mount crews to remain under cover within barriers and not to be seen by anyone off the ship.

About 8:15 the AGI tucked itself under the port side of the carrier, now out of my view. Still no word from the carrier. Fifteen minutes later, *Enterprise* sent a one-word flashing light message to *Gray*: "Now." I assumed the conn and ordered left full rudder and flank speed, setting a course directly for the BIG-E's number three deck-edge elevator. I adjusted course slightly to pass close under *Enterprise*'s stern, figuring that the AGI was alongside the LSO platform or near the number four deck-edge elevator, interfering with recovery operations one way or another. *Gray* had slowed and was at the standard speed of fifteen knots as we passed so closely under *Enterprise*'s port quarter that I feared that my yardarm might touch the flight deck round down. Fortunately, we cleared and emerged on *Enterprise*'s port quarter between the carrier and the AGI, then about eighty feet from the carrier much to the AGI captain's surprise and immediate concern.

I maneuvered *Gray* in between *Enterprise* and alongside of the AGI to put about forty feet between us. I slowed to match the AGI's speed and began shouldering the AGI out away from *Enterprise*. No big deal. *Gray* was supermaneuverable and could shoulder the Soviet away without doing damage to any of the three ships. *Enterprise* continued her air wing recovery as *Gray* gently shouldered the AGI away without ever making physical contact with the AGI. Close aboard was all that was needed. Aghast at our audacity, the AGI commanding officer's eyes were as big as silver dollars. I could see his face and expression as clearly as he could see mine.

Gray had and maintained the privileged ship's position with regard to the AGI and made the Soviet commence a sequence of maneuvers to regain the privileged position and force *Enterprise* to yield. The AGI commanding officer used all of the maneuvering tricks in his bag to regain his desired position. All the while *Gray* matched his moves and kept the AGI close in on *Gray*'s port bow, shouldering the AGI around and out until well clear of the carrier. This duel continued without interruption until *Gray* forced the AGI to move well clear of USS *Enterprise* as the carrier continued on its air ops course and speed on toward the south. Meanwhile, *Gray*'s ESM system detected and recorded a sudden and continuing burst of high-frequency radio traffic emissions from the AGI that continued uninterrupted thereafter until about 1:00 p.m. And all the while *Enterprise*'s island, superstructure, port catwalk, and wherever a man could stand safely without interfering with ongoing flight operations were full of "eye-ballers" watching the show!

Gray had outmaneuvered the AGI for about four hours and I was having a wonderful time "dogfighting" when, at about 12:45, the AGI stopped dead in the water as *Gray* matched its movements. We were about fifty feet apart at that time, with the AGI close aboard and slightly abaft *Gray*'s port bow. The two ships drifted dead in the water, opening the distance slowly to one hundred feet in time. Throughout this entire operation I kept the face of the AGI commanding officer focused in my binoculars so I could read his facial expressions. Periodically he would say something to one of his crew, who would leap to comply with the order. Frequently, the commanding officer's steward would bring him a cup of tea. After expressing his initial shock, the Russian's face was emotionless. Meanwhile, as we watched each other intently, one of *Gray*'s stewards would bring me a cup of coffee and a snack. *Gray*'s CIC crew had documented all operations in

their various logs and on the dead reckoning tracer as the ship's supply officer, without doubt the best officer in the ship, recorded all events on his
tape recorder, taking photographs as the event continued. Concurrently,
the quartermaster of the watch logged all events in minute detail. It was at
a standoff. But *Gray* was in complete control.

Finally the AGI commanding officer called his signalman and gave
him a message to send to *Gray* by flashing light. I read the message as it
was sent: "Good-bye I haf to go now." I instructed my signalman to reply,
"Good-bye Ivan. It was a pleasure to work with you today. Good luck going
home." The Soviet replied, "It vas a plazure," turned the AGI suddenly to
his left, increased speed, and headed out of the gulf. CIC tracked him until
his radar returns ceased and his radio transmissions terminated. He was
headed home. When scheduled air operations were completed *Enterprise*
sent *Gray* the following flashing light message: "Detached. Proceed on
duty previously assigned."

Gray was secured from battle stations and noon meal was piped down.
We steamed at full power en route to Subic with *Enterprise* ahead of us
going like blue blazes. During the night, a radio message from the commanding officer of *Enterprise* inviting the commanding officer of USS *Gray*
to join him and his executive officer for lunch at the Subic officers' club at
noon the next day was received. It was signed "Forrest Petersen, Captain,
U.S. Navy commanding officer." The invitation was humbly accepted.

I arrived on time to be met by Captain Petersen and CDR C. C.
Smith, a Naval Academy classmate, much to my surprise, who turned out
to be the BIG-E's executive officer. We had a delightful lunch, and Captain
Petersen heaped me with praise, saying that he had never seen such smart
ship handling in all of his career and complimenting me on my courageous,
daring, and skillful maneuvering while dogfighting with the Soviet AGI.
He subsequently sent a highly commendatory message to my immediate
senior in tactical command. During the course of the lunch, Smith casually mentioned that CDR Corky Lenox, USN, a classmate of ours, was the
commanding officer of Carrier Air Group 14 (CAG-14) flying from USS
Enterprise, also much to my surprise. Captain Petersen presented me a
beautifully framed and signed photograph of *Enterprise* commending me
on my professional performance of duty. That photograph remains on display among my valued service treasures to this day.

The Navy Air War over North Vietnam

Jerry Zacharias

From July 1967 to July 1968, I was the commanding officer of Attack Squadron 75, better known as VA-75 or the "Sunday Punchers." In November 1967, we embarked in USS *Kitty Hawk* (CV 63) as part of Air Wing 11 and departed San Diego for Vietnam. We were in the Gulf of Tonkin from December 1967 until June 1968 and deployed with twelve strike versions of the A-6A Intruder. The A-6A was a two-man, twin-engine, all-weather attack bomber, and in its day it was the best all-weather attack bomber in the world, bar none. VA-75 did not fly any combat sorties into South Vietnam. All VA-75 missions were to targets in North Vietnam.

A-6A Intruder with twenty-eight 500 lb bombs (Official U.S. Navy Photo)

Standard ARM Missiles

In January 1968, three special-mission A-6B aircraft arrived from the states and landed on board *Kitty Hawk* to join our squadron. These aircraft were configured to fire the long-range air-to-ground Standard ARM missile.

ARM stands for antiradiation missile. Their function was to home in on and destroy enemy radars and surface-to-air missile (SAM) sites. The advantages of the Standard ARM over previous antiradiation missiles, such as the Shrike, were that the Standard ARM had a very long range and you could fire it in a turn mode. If the SAM site was behind the aircraft, you could quickly program the missile to launch in the turn mode and it would circle back and strike the site. When fired in the forward forty-five-degree quadrant, the missile could range more than sixty-five miles.

A-6B aircraft with two Standard Arm Missiles (these aircraft could carry a maximum of four missiles) (Official U.S. Navy Photo)

On 13 February 1968, we received a message from the commander, Seventh Fleet to attend a meeting with Seventh Air Force personnel in Bangkok, Thailand, to decide on a specific date for the joint Air Force–Navy introduction of the Standard ARM missile into combat in Southeast Asia. We agreed on the date of 20 March 1968. On 6 March, we received a message from the Seventh Air Force saying that it was going to introduce the Standard ARM a week or so earlier than agreed upon. ADM Ralph

Cousins (CTF-77) responded to the Air Force with the message "We are going tonight." So on the evening of 6 March 1968, VA-75 launched four strike A-6A and two A-6B aircraft. The strike aircraft proceeded toward their individual targets and the A-6Bs, armed with ARM missiles, headed for the SAM sites. I flew one of the A-6Bs to the port city of Haiphong, which had seven active SAM sites. My bombardier-navigator (B/N) selected one and then a second SAM site, and I fired the first Standard ARM missiles used in combat in Southeast Asia. Our self-contained BDA system indicated a hit on at least one of the SAM sites.

Alpha Strikes

On good weather days, we flew alpha strikes in which twenty-five to thirty-five aircraft launched from *Kitty Hawk,* rendezvoused overhead, and proceeded to the same target as a single strike group. A-6s led every alpha strike because of their excellent navigation capabilities. Approaching the target area, we would descend to 10,000 feet and roll into a forty-five-degree visual dive-bombing run. Bomb release was at five thousand feet, and we were out of the dive by thirty-five hundred feet. Alpha strikes were unpopular because you had as much chance of having a midair collision with another aircraft as you did being shot down by a North Vietnamese antiaircraft site. Fortunately, we didn't have that much good weather and we only had about seven alpha strikes the entire deployment. Some of our fairly standard A-6A ordnance loads were five MK-84 2,000-pound bombs, thirteen MK-83 1,000-pound bombs, 22 MK-82 500-pound bombs, or various other types of ordnance.

Bad Weather and Night Flying

On bad weather days and during night operations, we flew single plane A-6 strikes and did low-level system bombing on radar. Normally there were two aircraft carriers on Yankee Station at all times, and each carrier would fly for a twelve-hour period. One carrier would fly from 10:00 a.m. to 10:00 p.m., and the other carrier would fly from 10:00 p.m. to 10:00 a.m. the next day. We much preferred the latter schedule because there was more night time, and we liked to fly at night for the following reasons:

- The A-6 was designed to fly at night and in bad weather.
- You could see SAM missiles lift off a long distance away.
- Enemy gunners couldn't see and thus shoot at you.

- We never had a problem with enemy MiG aircraft because they would never come out at night or down to our altitude, because we flew pretty low.

We flew strikes in the worst winter monsoon weather of the war, and sometimes we were the only strike aircraft flying from *Kitty Hawk*. It was a real thrill to return to the ship after a night bombing mission and find the monsoon rain so heavy that a mile astern, when you normally come visual and fly the glide slope indicator, you couldn't even see the ship. I remember telling the ship, "Keep talking to me. I can't see a thing." The ship's CATCC (Carrier Air Traffic Control Center) would then continue to give verbal glide slope and centerline alignment information to the pilot all the way to touchdown. That type of landing was far more thrilling than any bombing mission I was ever on.

Yankee Station Operations

Yankee Station was a point in the Gulf of Tonkin off the coast of Vietnam used by the U.S. Navy aircraft carriers of Task Force 77 to launch strikes into North Vietnam. It was located at 17° 30' N and 108° 30' E, just to the west of China's Hainan Island. We generally flew one or two missions a day per aircrew, and we had twenty aircrews in the squadron. Our normal cycle was twenty days on Yankee Station and then seven days off for R&R in the Philippines. However, at the end of our first twenty-day line period, our relief, the USS *Enterprise*, wasn't there. The Navy "spy ship," USS *Pueblo*, had been captured by the North Koreans and the *Enterprise* was up north in Korean waters. As a result, *Kitty Hawk* flew sixty-one continuous days of combat strikes without a break, a Navy record for the Vietnam conflict. The Hawk was awarded the Presidential Unit Citation for doing so.

Operation Rolling Thunder

Operation Rolling Thunder was the name of our air war against North Vietnam. This air war was different than any prior conflict. Why was it different? One major reason: surface-to-air missiles. This was the first conflict in which U.S. aviation forces encountered guided missiles. SAMs changed the nature of the air war, forcing our aircraft down from higher to lower altitudes, where we had better turn performance against the missiles. But coming down to lower altitude made us much more susceptible to antiaircraft fire and small-arms fire. It was antiaircraft and small arms that shot down the majority of the 2,730 U.S. Air Force, Marine Corps, and Navy aircraft.

Operation Rolling Thunder was not a full-scale bombing campaign. Rather, it was characterized by a gradual escalation. Let me explain. When we started flying combat strikes in December 1967, many of our targets were of little worth or significance (i.e., suspected truck parks, ferry crossings, cave storage, road intersections, small bridges, etc.). However, during our deployment, the target selection improved substantially (i.e., power plants, small industrial plants, rail yards, airfields, radio communication sites, port facilities, etc.). There was another departure from normal air warfare: we could not select our own targets; we could only bomb those targets on the list approved by various military and political experts in Washington.

Operation Rolling Thunder was not as effective as it could have been, and what follows are some reasons why:

- Bombing pauses. Just when we were finally getting some important night bombing targets, on 31 March 1968, Washington decreed that there would be no bombing above 20 degrees north latitude. Unfortunately, all the good targets were above 20 degrees north latitude.
- Self-imposed restrictions. Many large targets were not on the approved bombing list and many targets that were on the list were not very good targets.
- Self-designated sanctuaries. There was no attacking the dams on the Red River or the port facilities of Haiphong. We could have destroyed the dams and flooded the entire Red River valley, but Washington put them off limits. Sixty percent of the supplies coming into North Vietnam came through the port city of Haiphong. We could not touch the port facilities.
- No mining of major harbors. There was no mining of major harbors until 8 May 1972, shortly before the end of hostilities. We should have mined every harbor in North Vietnam from day one of the conflict.
- No strategic targets. There were no strategic targets on our bombing list, and that is no way to fight a war if you want to win it, which raises a question perhaps better left unasked.

I don't mean to imply that Rolling Thunder was ineffective. It was effective in many ways, but not as effective as it could have been.

Fortunately, Washington came to its senses, and in February 1972, most of the above restrictions were lifted. The United States commenced Operation Linebacker I, which was followed by Linebacker II. The unrestricted bombing of North Vietnam commenced, major harbors were mined, and our air forces did sustained bombing of most cities. The B-52s were included and did carpet-bombing of parts of Hanoi. North Vietnam fired so many missiles at our aircraft they ran out of SAMs, and the heavy bombing finally brought North Vietnam to the peace table.

In my opinion, if there is one lesson to be learned from combat in Vietnam, it is this: Don't micromanage a war. Give the military a mission, realistic rules of engagement and other constraints, and let them do the job the way they know best. That's what was done in Desert Storm/Desert Shield.

AMTI

When Washington imposed the no flying above 20 degrees north latitude rule, most of our good targets were not available. We then utilized one of the better capabilities of the A-6: the AMTI (airborne moving target

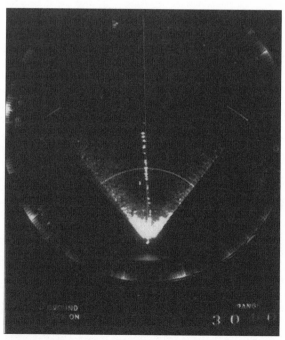

AMTI Mode on (Courtesy Capt. Jerrold Zacharias, USN)

indicator). We did lots of AMTI work in the southern part of North Vietnam, which we called "Happy Valley." When the AMTI switch was off, the radar showed extensive ground clutter, such as karst (rock outcropping), buildings, power poles, and any other objects that reflected the radar wave. When you turn the AMTI switch on, the radar cancels all radar ground returns and fixed targets except those from moving targets. With the AMTI mode on, the radar looks like a busy highway with lots of vehicle traffic. The pilot would turn the aircraft to line up on the column of vehicles, turn his track radar on to lock on one of the vehicles, and then drop a string of bombs or other ordnance. This was a very effective mission for the A-6.

Bombing Mission to Downtown Hanoi

In February 1968, I flew two bombing missions to the Hanoi area. On 10 February, my B/N (LCDR Mike Hall) and I bombed the Hanoi Radio Communications Station southeast of Hanoi. On the twenty-fourth, we bombed the Hanoi port facilities in downtown Hanoi. Both of these missions were challenging, but the Hanoi port facilities strike had some very interesting twists.

On 22 February, the USS *Enterprise* returned to Yankee Station from Korean waters and *Kitty Hawk* departed for some long overdue R&R in the Philippines. On the twenty-third, we were within sight of the Philippines and everyone was getting ready to go on liberty when a message came in from CTF-77. The message ordered a four plane A-6 aircraft strike on the Hanoi port facilities in downtown Hanoi. Because the *Enterprise* had only been on Yankee station for one day, CTF-77 ordered a joint *Enterprise–Kitty Hawk* A-6 strike. I quickly assembled my flight crews in our ready room, informed them of the mission to Hanoi, and asked, "Who wants to go with me?" My safety officer, LCDR Jerry Fink, and his B/N, LT Fred Hewitt, said they would go. We launched two of our aircraft for *Enterprise* and we landed on board that afternoon. We did mission planning for the strike with flight crews from VA-35, the *Enterprise* A-6 squadron. During flight planning, we reviewed the SAM and antiaircraft order of battle. Hanoi was the most heavily defended city in the history of air warfare, with seventeen active SAM sites and thousands of gun barrels of antiaircraft.

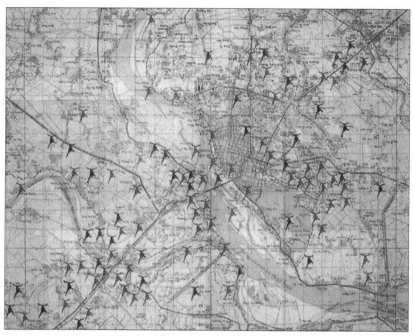

Hanoi Order of Battle, February 1968 (Courtesy Capt. Jerrold Zacharias, USN)

The gun symbols on the chart are not individual gun barrels, they are antiaircraft sites with five to seven gun barrels at each location. The Hanoi array included 105-mm, 85-mm, and 57/37-mm antiaircraft and automatic weapons all over the place. Two aircraft from VA-35 were to bomb the southern half of the port facilities complex, retire straight up the Red River until north of the city, and then head west into the mountains. The two aircraft from VA-75 were to bomb the northern section of the port facilities complex, turn hard left, fly right over the center of Hanoi at four hundred feet, and then head for the mountains.

After the mission planning, we ate dinner and hit the sack early. Reveille was at 12:30 a.m. We put on our flight gear and headed for the VA-35 ready room, where we rebriefed the mission with VA-35 flight crews. We manned aircraft at 2:00 a.m. and launched at 2:30.

I should explain a particular feature of the A-6A before I continue. When you launch from the ship and fly night missions, it is like flying into an ink well. At sea there are usually zero visual references outside the cockpit, so you have to depend 100 percent on your flight instruments to tell what the aircraft is doing. In the A-6A, the primary attitude reference is the ten-inch-wide visual display indicator (VDI) located in the center of the pilot's instrument panel.

The VDI is a computer-generated display with the lighter area with clouds (the sky) and the darker area below (the ground). In the ground area, there is a continuous stream of small elliptical dark spots that appear at the horizon, move slowly down the scope, and disappear off the bottom. This gives the pilot a sense of motion in the plane perpendicular to the VDI and completely eliminates vertigo. I occasionally got vertigo when flying other type aircraft, but never in the A-6. This is an essential requirement when dodging SAM missiles at night. The triangular shape in the center of the VDI is the "pathway in the sky" and is the means by which the B/N gives steering information to the pilot. If the B/N's radar azimuth line is on a target or a navigation checkpoint to the left, the pathway on the VDI will point to the left. When the B/N says, "Take steering," the pilot turns left and the triangle moves back into the center of the VDI. The aircraft is now heading for the next checkpoint or to the target.

Visual Display Indicator (VDI) – the primary attitude reference (Courtesy Capt. Jerrold Zacharias, USN)

Nearing the target, the B/N will switch the computer into the attack mode and the computer starts rapidly calculating bombing solutions. A black horizontal bar will then appear on the right side of the VDI. This is the signal for the pilot to squeeze a trigger on his control stick and keep squeezing. The black bar moves vertically down the scope as you close the target. When it disappears off the bottom of the VDI, the bombs come off automatically. The computer picks the right point in space to release the bombs independent of whether the pilot is climbing, descending, flying level or pulling up and tossing the bombs into the target.

One additional point: the VDI is stabilized by an inertial system (INS) in the aircraft. The INS keeps the horizon of the VDI parallel to the earth's surface at all times, even if the aircraft is in a ninety-degree bank pulling 6 g's. In VA-75, the B/N aligned the INS in the aircraft. In VA-35 on the *Enterprise,* the ground crew normally started the alignment of the INS. This practice was to have some implications for my flight to Hanoi.

When we arrived on deck of the *Enterprise* for the Hanoi strike, the A-6 INS was already aligning. We continued our preflight procedure and the B/N typed the coordinates of the entire navigation route into the computer.

I was the third of four A-6s to launch. As we moved down the catapult track, *my* VDI display turned upside down—the first time this had ever happened to me. Had I followed the roll of the VDI to the right, I would have hit the water inverted in front of the ship. Fortunately, as we moved down the catapult track, my B/N, Mike Hall, saw the warning light on the INS system illuminate and yelled, "Platform, platform!" I knew that meant the INS had a problem and I went right to a three-inch standby gyro on the instrument panel. I raised my landing gear and flaps as the aircraft accelerated and climbed out on the standby gyro.

Why did the VDI tumble? We found that the VA-35 ground crew had aligned the INS in the polar mode. You never, ever use the polar mode unless you are in the polar regions (that is, above 65 degrees north or south latitude). We were at 19 degrees north latitude. Aligning our INS in the polar mode at 19 degrees latitude created high-velocity errors in the INS, and as we moved down the catapult track, the INS platform tumbled.

I rendezvoused with the rest of the flight over *Enterprise* at 12,000 feet to top off our fuel for the long flight to Hanoi. Because of our INS problem, I was now the last aircraft to refuel from the tanker aircraft. As number 3 aircraft cleared the tanker, I moved into position to plug in and receive fuel. Suddenly, the lights on the A-3D tanker went out. The tanker had an electrical failure and could not give me any fuel. This was the second mishap in the first ten minutes of this flight and I was beginning to think it wasn't going to be my night. My B/N and I discussed the situation and decided to try an in-flight alignment of the INS (which I had never done before). That meant flying straight and level with minimal turns for about twenty minutes. After twenty-two minutes, we got a ready light on the INS. We then checked our fuel quantity. It was going to be close, but I thought we had enough fuel to complete the mission. We were now twenty-two minutes behind the rest of the flight, and we headed into the mountains southwest of Hanoi. Since we were behind the rest of the flight, which had stirred up a hornet's nest at Hanoi, I thought that when we arrived at our target everyone would be awake and shooting, and they certainly were.

I descended out of the mountains southwest of Hanoi down to two hundred feet in the flat lands of the Red River valley. During our descent, I could hear in my earphones the sounds of the SAM radars starting to track us (they sound like crickets chirping). Then it got really noisy as all of the antiaircraft radars started tracking us (they made an annoying screeching sound in our headsets). I felt fairly comfortable on a heading of 040 degrees at two hundred feet doing about 350 knots (407 mph). About half way to my next turn point, two SAM missiles lifted off about ten to twelve miles away. The loud missile warning alarm started blaring in our aircraft. I went to full throttle and told my B/N I was going down to one hundred feet (hoping to get into the ground clutter on the SAM radar operators scope). When I got down to one hundred feet, I could see objects whizzing by the left side of the cockpit. I thought they had to be farmhouses. Just then, my B/N said, "You are level at fifty-feet." I replied, "Roger, going back to one hundred feet." I watched the two missiles approach, and when I thought they were close enough, I dropped chaff, rolled the aircraft into an eighty-five-degree right bank, and pulled a 5-g turn. One missile went behind us and the second exploded under the aircraft, buffeting it violently and putting a small hole in the left wing.

My B/N then said, "Your heading is 354 degrees." We were now doing 450 knots (517 mph) and really moving along. I was level at four hundred feet and was going to release our weapons at that altitude since they had high-drag "snake-eye" fins to slow down their descent so that they would be well behind us at impact. As we approached the release point, there was so much AAA coming up, I could see the entire outline of the Red River, so I knew we were right on course to target. At 4:20 in the morning, the bombs released and I broke left over the center of Hanoi. When I rolled out on an outbound heading of about 210 degrees, I saw lots of AAA sites shooting barrage fire (straight up in the sky), hoping we would fly through it. I picked two AAA sites and flew right in between them. As soon as they passed by, I would pick two more sites and fly in between them.

I continued this until we reached the outskirts of Hanoi, where the AAA diminished. I then told my B/N, "We are home free." No sooner had those words cleared my vocal chords when the missile warning alarm sounded again. I immediately thought to myself, How am I going to know when to start an evasive maneuver since I can't see the missiles when they are behind us? Well, it didn't take long to find out. As the missiles approached the aircraft, the rocket plumes started illuminating the craft, actually lighting the cockpit. I think it's time, I thought, and I dropped chaff, rolled into a ninety-degree right bank, and pulled a 6-g turn. After ninety degrees of turn, I dropped more chaff and reversed my turn. One missile went over us and the second one exploded in a farmer's field under us in a brilliant fireball that just about wiped out my night vision. We then headed for the mountains, throttled back to a max-cruise setting, and landed on board *Enterprise* at 5:00 with fifteen minutes of fuel remaining.

After the flight we debriefed, and I found out that only two aircraft had made it to target that night. The CO of VA-35, CDR Glen Coleman, made it to target, as did I. The second aircraft from VA-75 had a radio failure and could not fly the mission. The other aircraft from VA-35 had system problems and dropped his bombs twelve miles short of the target. I regret to say that Commander Coleman was killed about a month later when his aircraft went in the water after the cat shot.

The VA-35 maintenance crew put duct tape over the holes in our left wing and we launched from *Enterprise* at noon, landing at Cubi Point at 2:30. I headed right for the officers' club at Cubi, where there was a one-thousand-stinger party going on in honor of the five guys shot down during our first line period. Everyone chipped in money and ordered a thousand stingers, which covered the bar. And I had my share.

During our deployment, we did lose some aircraft. VA-75 lost two aircraft and four flight crew members. One of the hardest things a CO has to do is write a letter to the next of kin explaining how his or her loved one was lost. VA-35 on *Enterprise* lost six aircraft and twelve aircrew members, although two returned as POWs in 1973. VA-35 lost both their CO and XO.

In 1972–73, I was the special assistant to the CNO for POW/MIA matters and overall Navy coordinator for Operation Homecoming when our POWs returned in 1973. I got to welcome home many of my friends and neighbors from the Virginia Beach area and the POWs from VA-35. What a rewarding job that was.

[Editor's note: CDR Jerrold "Jerry" Zacharias was awarded the Navy Cross for his heroic and brilliantly executed bombing of the port facilities in the heart of Hanoi.]

CDR Jerry Zacharias wearing his Navy Cross
(Courtesy Capt. Jerrold Zacharias, USN)

And I Never Even Volunteered

Fred Adair

I t was early 1957, and there I was, skipper of a seagoing tug in Aleutian Island waters, my third ship since 1952. One day while at sea, the radioman brought me an odd message, odd in that it ordered me to tie up the ship, appoint an acting commanding officer, and fly to Washington, D.C., for an interview with a man affectionately known as the "Kindly Old Gentleman," VADM Hyman G. Rickover, the head of Naval Reactors.

I thought it was a joke until we returned to port and my wife met me with the same message. So off I flew to Washington and reported to Admiral Rickover's headquarters as ordered. In the admiral's office, the interview proceeded. "Where did you go to high school?" he asked.

"Garfield, in Seattle, sir."

"Named for?"

"A president, sir."

"What about him?"

"He was shot, sir."

"Where?"

"I don't know, sir."

"Where do you think?"

"I guess New York City. It's the largest place."

"You're wrong, it was Buffalo."

Rickover would sometimes plant an error in his questions to see if the interviewee would later point out the error. The correct answer was the train station in Washington, D.C., and I have long lamented that I didn't go back to correct him. It would have been interesting to hear his comment. *[Editor's note: Not only interesting, it would have been downright scorching.]*

The conclusion of the interview was interesting. "Did you apply for the program?" he asked me.

"No, sir."

"Then get the hell out of here!"

Three months later, with only six months at my first command, I was in the Idaho desert, beginning nuclear-power training with other surface officers. We were an early group of trainees, and over the next two and a half years, we trained and qualified ourselves while helping with the construction of what eventually became the large ship prototype, the carrier *Enterprise* engine room, a difficult engineering space with things like air compressors (mockups made of wood) and other machinery, so trainees would be at home once on board the ship, which was yet to be finished. We also participated in construction follow and systems testing while developing a training curriculum for the larger groups of trainees to follow.

The prototype was completed in 1958. *Enterprise*, with two reactors supplying one engine, raised questions as to what would happen when the two reactors were brought on line together, supplying the same engine. I was chief reactor operator for the first time this was tried. Not surprisingly, there were a lot of key people in the control room, including Admiral Rickover. Happily, the reactors turned out to be very stable together, and so were those in *Enterprise* for her fifty-one years.

The secretary of defense, Robert McNamara, was not a fan of nuclear-powered surface ships. Two oil-fueled carriers, *America* and *Kennedy*, were built after *Enterprise*. Scheduled by the Navy to have four reactors each, they were reverted to conventional propulsion by McNamara. It was only when Naval Reactors said they could power carriers with just two reactors that McNamara relented.

I left Idaho for Quincy, Massachusetts, in the fall of 1959 to do much the same thing in the nuclear-powered cruiser Long Beach that I had done in Idaho. I was the main propulsion assistant in the precommissioning crew and served on board for a year after she was commissioned in September 1961. Long Beach had two reactors, considerably fewer than *Enterprise*'s eight-reactor arrangement, with each reactor driving a shaft, but they could be cross-connected and run both engines on one reactor. From Long Beach, I went to a destroyer as executive officer.

I do not know why I was called for nuclear-power training, but I know that the majority of the officers with whom I trained had not requested nuclear-power training. It is my understanding, from second- and third-hand sources, that destroyer chief engineers and those with an early command were of particular interest. Possibly another factor was my finishing first in CIC Officers School.

Regardless, there I was, learning all about nuclear power, and I had never even volunteered.

One-Plane Airline

Bill Laux

I n the summer of 1965 I was the navigator of the seaplane tender USS
Currituck (AV-7). We had deployed to Okinawa early in the year, and
we were then ordered to proceed to the Con Son Islands in the South
China Sea, about eighty miles south of Vung Tau, which is near the entrance
to the Saigon River. We established a seadrome from which a squadron of
SP-5 Marlin seaplanes would operate as part of Operation Market Time.
Earlier that year it was discovered that the North Vietnamese were supplying the Vietcong in the south by sea, transporting men and materials in
junks and fishing boats, usually at night. Our seaplanes, along with other
aircraft and surface forces, were to put a stop to these activities.

Commander, Patrol Force Seventh Fleet was in charge of Market
Time. The admiral and his staff were embarked in *Currituck*. This arrangement worked fine in Okinawa, where the staff lived ashore and drove to
work each day, but it meant nearly total isolation in Con Son. The admiral requested the assignment of an amphibious airplane so that official
mail might be transported to and from Saigon. The airplane, an HU-16
Grumman Albatross, was delivered to the ship by a couple of ferry pilots.
Then it was discovered that while there were several aviators on the staff,
none had seaplane experience.

As the navigator of a ship at anchor, I had very little to keep me busy.
Supervising nautical chart corrections, and overseeing the daily wind-
ing and comparing of the ship's chronometers, didn't take a whole lot of
time. When I learned that the staff needed a qualified seaplane pilot, I
offered my services. I had been a designated patrol plane commander in
PBM Mariners and SP-5 (formerly P5M) Marlin aircraft. Earlier, while
an instructor at the Naval Academy, I had been designated a utility plane
commander, in the very same HU-16 aircraft (formerly designated UF) for
which they now needed a pilot. After a qualifying flight in which I demonstrated my competence, I got the job. I was designated a courier, given a
rifle and a pistol, and admonished not to let myself get shot down.

I was in business. Most days I would make the one-hour flight to Ton
Son Nhut Airport, at Saigon. Some days I made two flights. Some nights

I had to lay over in Saigon, and I would head downtown and find a hotel room, usually at the Caravelle Hotel in the center of town. It was a popular place. It housed the Australian and New Zealand embassies and the bureaus of all the U.S. television networks. There was a rooftop bar, and I would sit up there with a cool libation and watch artillery duels in the distance, an eerie experience.

As the summer wore on, the Marlin seaplanes encountered resistance—people on some of the junks started to shoot at them. One bullet went through the cockpit of one airplane. The Marlin at that time carried no weapons, but someone figured out that they could rig recoilless machine guns in the waist hatches with bungee cord. I was tasked to get some machine guns. At Ton Son Nhut Airport, there was a supply yard, or supply dump, of enormous size, with pallets, boxes, crates, and equipment of all types all over the place. I found a supply sergeant, a short stocky type, in sweat-soaked fatigues but hatless, with a big cigar. I told him what I had in mind, and very quickly he delivered a stack of machine guns and ammunition to my airplane. No paperwork, no signatures—I asked and I received. It took several more trips, mostly because of the ammunition. Ammunition is very heavy, and the HU-16 could carry only so much. As to the effectiveness of the machine guns in the seaplanes, I have no information.

Summer wore on, and eventually it was time for us to be relieved as the flagship of ComPat, Seventh Fleet. We turned over the HU-16 Albatross, and my fun was over. I resumed my duties as navigator of the *Currituck*, and after twenty-one days of morning and evening star shots, and local apparent noon sun lines, we were back in San Diego. My UF plane captain and I were each awarded two Air Medals for our efforts.

Hurry Up and Wait

Earl Chinn

It was November 1957, and I was finishing my tour as commanding officer of the minesweeper USS *Bobolink* (AM 20), home ported in Boston. I was expecting orders for shore duty and was shocked to learn I would be going to Korea for a one-year unaccompanied tour as the mine warfare and harbor defense advisor to the Korean navy.

"What kind of duty assignment can I expect following my tour in Korea?" I asked the Bureau of Naval Personnel (BuPers) detailer.

"We'll give you anything you want!"

I couldn't believe I actually heard him say that, but there it was. To say that I was thrilled would be an understatement. Since my relief would be in December, I asked if I might take thirty days' leave en route to spend Christmas at home. It would also allow me to find proper accommodations for my wife and son for the year I would be gone. The answer was no. The need to fill the billet would not permit delay and I would have to report for travel to Korea on 15 December.

We had relatives in Albuquerque, New Mexico, so we decided that would be a suitable place for my wife, five months pregnant, and our two-year-old son to live while I was in Korea. On my twenty-ninth birthday, 14 December, I flew to Travis AFB for transportation to Korea. About thirty hours later, the fully loaded four-engine propeller aircraft began its twelve-hour flight to Honolulu. We were five and a half hours out of Travis when the pilot announced we had lost an engine and were returning to Travis. There we had another layover. Finally, I landed at Kempo Air Base near Seoul, Korea.

When I stepped out of the airplane, it was like stepping back in time. The terminal was liberally decorated with bullet holes in the walls and windows, a testament to the recent fighting there.

After scouting around the terminal for half an hour, looking for anything resembling the U.S. Navy, I met the chief of staff of the Naval Advisory Group, who had just returned from Japan. He gave me a ride to Advisory Group Headquarters at Seoul. He also told me that I would be going to Chinhae, on the southern tip of Korea, the location of the Korean

Naval Headquarters. I left by train that night, heading for Pusan, where I would be provided transportation to Chinhae.

Still in my Navy dress blues, I stepped off the train at Pusan into a sea of Korean travelers. It was about 6:30 a.m. After some searching among the crowd, I spotted a young sailor in dungarees. With a sigh of relief, I approached him and was greeted by "Are you Lieutenant Chinn?" When I said I was, he also sighed with relief, thinking that he would never find a man named Chinn among all those Asian faces, not realizing I was Caucasian. We loaded up his haze gray Navy Jeep and drove to the Eighth Army Base at the other end of Pusan. There he dropped me off at the base post office, where a mail carrier from Chinhae would be arriving at about 10:00 a.m. He, the sailor told me, would get me to Chinhae. Right on time, a three-quarter-ton weapons carrier pulled up and, after loading mail, picked up me and my luggage for the thirty-five-mile drive to Chinhae.

The trip took almost an hour and a half. The parts of the road that were free of bomb craters had some gravel cover, but the road was mostly plain dirt or mud. Upon arrival, I was taken to my room in a Japanese-style house shared with eight other junior officers on the staff. It was Christmas Eve 1957. After a shower and change into a clean uniform, I joined my housemates at a reception given by the commanding officer at his quarters. There I met the other members of the staff as well as our counterparts from the Korean navy.

Then it was my turn to meet my commanding officer. It was an eye-opening shock when he greeted me with open arms and proceeded to tell me I was filling a newly created billet—so new it did not yet have a job description—and since it was the holidays, I should relax and enjoy myself and then come and visit him at his office to discuss my job description, say, on Monday, after the first of the New Year.

Yep, it was a classic case of hurry up and wait.

Suez Canal Reopening

Bob Hill

T
he operating schedule for the Sixth Fleet flagship was always published well in advance of sailings, since commander, Sixth Fleet protocol requirements for official visits required meticulous advance
planning. It was highly unusual, therefore, when USS *Little Rock* (CG 4)
departed her home port of Gaeta, Italy, on Sunday, 1 June 1975, for "operations at sea." Sailing orders became known after departure. The ship was to
sail to Port Said under darken ship and electronic silence to arrive early in
the morning of Wednesday, 5 June, for participation in the reopening cere-
monies of the Suez Canal.

Transit was made without incident, except that late in the evening prior
to arrival in Port Said, target acquisition radar was detected coming from
the east. With thoughts of the 1967 *Liberty* incident, orders were given
to break electronic silence, turn on the lights, and generally advertise our
presence to the world. It would be only a matter of hours before the ship
would be in Port Said anyway. Target acquisition radar soon ceased, and
Little Rock arrived at Port Said on schedule.

At the conclusion of the activities and events of the canal reopening,
the ship was to proceed to Alexandria for a port call. While at sea en route
to Alexandria, I wrote to my family recounting the events of the previous
thirty-six hours. What follows is a verbatim copy of that letter—no editing.
I wrote about what I saw and heard, giving my impressions and expressing
my opinions of the moment. Where appropriate, amplifying information
has now been added, italicized, and set off by brackets:

> These last two days have indeed been something to write home about,
> so while the events are still fresh in my mind, I thought I might as well
> make a family letter out of this to pass on what has been a most unusual
> experience. It would be a blasé person indeed who would not have
> been swept up to some degree in the excitement of where we were and
> what we were doing. For those not affected by the political significance
> of our participation in the Suez Canal reopening, or moved by the
> sense of history surrounding the occasion, then at least they must have
> been impressed by the current aspect of Suez. Each, in turn, deserves

consideration. But lest this turn into a veritable treatise, let me just give you a brief run-down of how this Suez Canal adventure seemed to us.

To begin with, our participation was not certain until the completion of the discussions between the Egyptian and U.S. presidents last Sunday in Salzburg. We left Gaeta with no certain idea that we would be invited to come. So we steamed across the Med in a condition of silenced electronics, avoiding shipping insofar as possible, and hoping the Russians didn't know where we were. As it turned out, we must have been completely successful, for when we steamed into Port Said early Thursday morning we were definitely the surprise guest at the party. We moored to one of the big freighter buoys in what would be the outer parts of the harbor, and Admiral Turner [VADM Frederick C. Turner] went off with his aide to attend the official opening ceremony. He reports that his arrival caused somewhat of a stir among the gathered officials—particularly military officials, but then Admiral Zikri (the Egyptian CNO) called all flag rank foreign military up to the front to await President Sadat's entrance. During the introduction, President Sadat took the opportunity to make a minor speech of thanks to Admiral Turner for the U.S. Navy assistance [mine] in clearance operations, which was given so all could hear. The listeners included the Russian contingent of several admirals (one of whom outranked ours), who were conspicuously at the end of the line. Also, the Russians were seated on the back row of the military, even behind a couple of USN captains. Obviously, President Sadat is playing his politics for high stakes!

Meanwhile, back on the ship, we waited time for the procession to begin—while Russian helicopters circled overhead, silvery MIG-21's streaked high above, and the soldiers began emerging from their barbed-wire, foxhole, tent camp just opposite us on the shore. The bombed out Said Hotel was just behind them, and a half-collapsed office building next door.

The procession got under way about 11:30, with President Sadat in an Egyptian destroyer, 6th of October, in the van (a date I will not soon forget). [Editor's Note: The start of the 1973 Yom Kippur War.] Then came a second Egyptian destroyer, then an old yacht (at least that's what they called it—maybe it was King Farouk's yacht) for VIPs, [The presidential yacht, Hurriah, which was rumored to have participated in the original Suez Canal opening in 1869.] then USS Little Rock, followed by two small liners with the press and lesser VIPs. No other warships or other nationalities represented. The long, narrow harbor (see page 804 of your June National Geographic) was teeming with boats of all sizes, shapes, and descriptions—all of them filled to the gunwales with cheering, applauding people waving flags—and all of them covered with flags and bunting! What a sight. Anyway, as Little Rock hove into sight, it was apparently the first inkling of the people that we were there—and the enthusiasm seemed to know no bounds. Every square inch of waterfront as we approached the old Authority Building where the ceremony had been held was covered with screaming, waving humanity—virtually a mass of flags and arms and faces. At one point a barricade gave way and people poured over onto the narrow strip of rocks below the seawall.

In the midst of all this I became aware of a sound that was almost drowned out in the multitude—and it could be discerned from some of the boats steaming alongside: it was an Arab woman's wail, which we remember from some movie. Perhaps *Lawrence of Arabia*. It sounded like nothing so much as a child's version of the old Indian war dance. But of all things it sounds like a sound from antiquity! I would never have picked it out, if I had not already heard it before. Then, once attuned, I heard it from each crowd's cheers the rest of the day, whenever women were present.

Back to our parade through Port Said, there were already 15 to 20 freighters waiting to transit the canal as soon as it opened. From each of these came the three blast salute of welcome—including the Russian ships. Finally, in response, *Little Rock* let loose with a series of whistle blasts that were deeper, louder, more authoritative than any other noise around. A beautiful gesture, superbly timed, which for once magnificently embodied the presence of the United States, in a manner which we have grown to long for. The United States was, at that moment, the way the United States should always be. The rails were manned; salutes from military ships were received and returned; and silently as each merchantman dipped her ensign in salute that salute was officially and formally returned by dipping ours. I say silently simply to point out the presence of strict international protocol even as the cheering and whistling went on.

With a slight turn to port our bow entered the canal, and one by one the small boats dropped behind and the cheering faded. From there to Ismailia is about 6 hours, and Ismailia is roughly at the mid-point of the Canal. That was to be as far as we were to go in our little ceremonial convoy. The countryside along our passage divided itself into three general types of ground: first, tidal flats and salt pans; second, just plain dirt, flat at first and then growing humpy, but totally unrelieved by green or anything growing; then finally sand. The transitions are gradual, but that's the general effect.

If one thing quickly became apparent from the 50 mile trip we made to Ismailia, it is the fact that Egypt is still at war. Let there be no doubt about it. Bunkers, pillboxes, barbed wire, tanks, anti-aircraft guns, and soldiers, soldiers, and more soldiers. Among the billboards posted along the route of the canal in English, French, and Arabic is one which quotes Anwar Sadat: "We have opened the canal, and it will remain opened." From the fortifications we passed, there can be no doubt that he meant what he said.

Also along our route were the ruins of war: the bomb craters, the burned out tanks, the upside-down hulks of burned trucks, the piles of twisted metal—now unrecognizable, the bare metal spikes jutting from exploded reinforced concrete bunkers, and—most poignant—the completely destroyed and apparently uninhabited town of El Qantara. A few flaming red poinciana trees in full bloom harked back to other days, but now stood in stark contrast to the desolation around them. At first, all these signs of the past wars were novel and were commented on. But then they, too, became commonplace and hardly worthy of note.

But the soldiers along the route were all drawn up in ranks to salute their president as he passed, and remained in formation as we passed. It was something to see! Each littler bunker—each antiaircraft battery— each tank—each little construction group with their bulldozers—all drawn up at attention on the sand. For each one that rendered military honors to *Little Rock*, he received full military honors in return—I add that this applied only to groups in formation and not to individual soldiers. How improbable to see a tank captain, in front of his three crewmen, in turn in front of their Russian T-62 tank, saluting a USN cruiser! But each one received an "Attention—Hand Salute—Carry on" from *Little Rock*. It was a day of paradoxes and improbabilities.

Along that line, one comment that was made around the ship was that as long as there were Russian MiG-21 jets streaking across the sky we had no cause for concern. However, if they had been French Mirages or U.S. Phantoms we might have reason for concern, for they would bear the six pointed star of the neighbors to the east.

As I stood there on the deck watching the sands of the Sinai go by a few yards away, I couldn't help but reflect on the changing patterns of our global politics. We are no longer welcome in Greece. Where is NATO headed? Portugal may be closed next year at this time. Yet, here we were, the flagship of the Sixth Fleet, and the sole foreign participant in an otherwise totally Egyptian procession. And Egypt remains the political giant, if not the financial one, of the Arab world. The bits and pieces of international politics may be small, but collectively they point the way of the future. It's interesting to consider if our Suez trip might not be one of those bits or pieces.

So we spent last night in Lake Timsah. No one went ashore in Ismailia, but we watched the fireworks commemorating the occasion for that beleaguered city. Within a few hours of our anchoring, the first southbound convoy entered Lake Timsah from the north, made the sharp left turn into the next leg, and headed south toward the Red Sea. They were the ships that had saluted us a few hours earlier in Port Said. Led by a ship from Kuwait, followed by Russians, Yugoslavians and Norwegians, the Canal did, in fact, open.

We came back out this morning, *[Editor's Note: June 6]* and still the few stragglers who happened to see us pass greeted us warmly. One lone Arab standing on a sand dune, his djellabah flapping back in the desert wind, stood there and applauded. As we left Port Said harbor, a Communist Chinese ship waiting its turn for the Canal dipped its ensign in salute to *Little Rock*. The salute was not returned.

The subsequent port call in Alexandria was notable in that a significant number of the Russian Mediterranean fleet was present. *Little Rock* tied up across the pier from the Russians. Across the harbor were at least a couple of the newest Soviet submarines, known to have been coated with the latest anechoic material. A number of creative ideas were floated on board *Little Rock* about a way to obtain a sample; however, none proved acceptable. Late in the first evening, the quarterdeck of *Little Rock* received a phone call from the quarterdeck of one of the Soviet ships up the pier. It was requested that someone be sent to retrieve one of our sailors, who was creating a bit of a stir on their quarterdeck and wouldn't leave. The request was quickly filled and no incident report was forthcoming. It remained unclear whether our intrepid sailor was trying to singlehandedly fight the Cold War or solve it.

The Silent Service Speaks

Al Kelln

ollowing my graduation and commissioning, my first tour of duty was in the destroyer USS *Blue* (DD 744), where I qualified as officer of the deck, while awaiting orders for flight school, my intention then being to get my wings and be a carrier pilot. However, when the expected date for my orders to Pensacola passed with no orders, followed by week after week of no orders, I finally went to my skipper and told him of my concern that my expected orders had somehow been lost. He took me aside and told me that he could not recommend me for naval aviation. His two Academy roommates had been killed while flying from carriers during the late war, and while he would gladly recommend me for submarines, he could not do so for aviation. My orders had arrived on time, but he had held them from me.

Much of our duty in the waters off Korea had been as part of the destroyer screen assigned to Task Force 77, and it was not uncommon to see pilots come back from a mission with their aircraft so badly shot up that they ditched the aircraft in the sea, usually near a destroyer, rather than try to land on board the carrier. The frigid temperature of the sea during the winter months while we were there meant that the pilot, if he survived the ditching, had only a few minutes in which to be rescued before the cold water would claim his life. Listening to my skipper, it did not take too much of an argument from him to persuade me to change my mind about being a pilot, and I volunteered for submarines.

Upon completion of submarine school at Groton, Connecticut, I received orders to USS *Ronquil* (SS 396), a Pacific Fleet boat, home ported at San Diego. I arrived in time to participate in *Ronquil's* workup for deployment to the Western Pacific. I had a knack for using the strip plot, a method used by submarines at that time for determining target speed and range, so I was assigned to the battle action team that manned the conning tower at general quarters.

Shortly after reaching Japan, we were assigned the special mission of landing a group of North Korean defectors who had been trained as saboteurs and spies for duties inside North Korea. One person's mission was to become employed in a North Korean explosives factory, blow it up, and then find his way back to safety using a special route formed by resistance supporters, similar to the Underground Railway used by escaping slaves prior to the Civil War.

Landing spies can be exciting, calling for skill and stealth on the part of the submarine. We found a coastal area with deep water near the pre-scribed North Korea drop-off point. The captain carefully maneuvered our sub to within about half a mile (one thousand yards) off the coast, and in the silence of our approach, we could hear voices and cattle in the dis-tance. Silently, with no fanfare, we inflated a rubber raft and loaded the passengers and their tools, along with two strong American sailors, and off they went. From the submarine's bridge, we could see the raft slowly approach the shore and unload the passengers. Soon our sailors were back on board. Whew!

We never learned how successful the saboteurs were. This was war-time, and we quickly focused on our next mission, surveillance of a Russian naval base. Our Navy needed to know what the Soviet navy was doing. A World War II veteran of submarine warfare, the skipper ordered, "Rig for silent running." With course set for northern waters, *Ronquil* was ready and on its way.

Life on board a diesel submarine was an uncomfortable and hard exis-tence. Adding to the discomfort was the need to snorkel, and the constant cycling of the snorkel valve atop the snorkel mast causing rapid changes in the air pressure was never a pleasant experience. The boat had a very lim-ited capacity for making fresh water, so the officers and crew were each rationed a quart of water per week for body cleanliness and shaving. After a few weeks at sea, the odor inside the boat was not very pleasant, the only mitigating factor being our common reeking so that we somehow became accustomed to the smelly atmosphere.

The other factor was the cold. As we proceeded north, the sea water temperature continued to drop, and it was becoming very cold inside the boat. Interior heating was nonexistent, and we all wore layers of clothes, whether asleep or awake. From my bunk, I could touch the steel hull that was covered only with a thin layer of material and paint. It was not long before the inside of the hull was also covered with a thin layer of ice, noticeable when your body happened to touch the hull as you turned in your sleep. Eventually, even the water in the bilges froze into solid ice. We gained some respite by taking turns to go into the engine room when the diesel engines were running and drape our coats, clothes, and underclothes on the hot engines to dry them out and warm our bodies. The engine room odor of fuel oil became as sweet as roses to our frigid senses.

When we reached our patrol area, we found complete inactivity by the Soviet fleet. The Soviet navy was going nowhere. But something else was happening. At first we noticed only small cakes of ice of the 100-pound variety flowing south. We were able to avoid them in the daytime and at night we retreated to ice-free areas by going twenty to thirty miles offshore. We were unaware of a massive frontal storm in the Bering Sea that was breaking up the solid ice canopy and sending massive ice floes south into our area. When solid ice canopies break, they make a loud report, a warning to look out for floes. But we had no such warning and were shocked when massive chunks of ice appeared in our vicinity.

The weather was usually overcast, making it impossible to see a ship at night unless its lights were on. Being so close to land we snorkeled at night to charge the batteries instead of running on the surface. During daylight hours, we were submerged, running on the batteries. In both situations, the OOD manned the periscope. One night, without warning, the periscope was struck by a massive multiton slab of ice that bent the scope at a ninety-degree angle. We now had only the second periscope. After a long interval, the captain raised number 2 periscope for a look around and to evaluate our situation. Bang! The number 2 scope had struck a large, thick cake of ice and was also bent over. We could hear the scope filling with sea water. We were blind.

We headed south and away from land, running on the electric motors powered by the batteries. Now the concern was whether the batteries would last until we were clear of the ice floe. We rigged for reduced power and said many silent prayers. I could sense the determination and resolve of the crew, but first we had to clear the ice floe that was testing the fabric and mettle of the crew.

We ran south at a speed that allowed the optimum balance between making distance while conserving battery life. We calculated we could run thus for about forty-eight hours before we would have to charge the batteries. At reduced power, everything using electricity except the electric propulsion motors was turned off, including the galley range. We even used flashlights rather than the normal overhead lights. In the dank cold and darkness, life was not very pleasant. We put on more clothes and waited.

Suddenly, the forward watch reported that the ice on the inside of the hull was starting to melt. A check of the seawater temperature showed it had warmed to thirty-four degrees Fahrenheit. We continued south another twelve hours, and just at sunset, the captain stopped the boat and we went into a silent hover. With the last of our precious battery power, we started slowly pumping water ballast and gingerly rose toward the surface. As we passed the depth of one hundred feet, we activated the passive sonar and determined that there were no ships in the vicinity. Several minutes later, we surfaced, opened the bridge hatch, and the captain and I went to the bridge. We were clear of the ice floe.

Our two periscopes, bent over at ninety degrees, towered over-head. With no contacts detected either on sonar or on radar, we put two engines on propulsion and one on maximum battery charge and headed for Yokosuka, Japan. Fortunately, a warehouse at Yokosuka, filled with material from the war, yielded two good periscopes, and we were back in business. I qualified in submarines shortly thereafter.

Fast forward to 1957. Having successfully completed nuclear-power training, I was now assigned to the commissioning crew of USS *Skate* (SS 578), under construction at Electric Boat in Groton, Connecticut. *Skate* was the lead boat in a series of four submarines designated swift attack submarines. The Cold War was heating up a bit and the Soviet Union was trying to extend its dominance over much of the world. The Soviet navy was constructing a large nuclear-powered submarine fleet, and the numbers alone were intimidating. To counter this would require much personal sacrifice from our Navy, including long periods of time away from our families. It was our time to step up and do what had to be done. Our submarine fleet did so in ways that even today cannot be described in any detail. None of us in *Skate* knew what lay ahead. We only knew that we were trained and ready to make whatever sacrifices our duty called for.

The summer of 1958 was busy, with long days spent getting *Skate* and the crew ready for our next deployment. But this time we were not heading west, we were heading north. The officers were reading every book they could find that involved the history of Arctic explorations.

One piece of required information could not be found in the books, and that was the density of the openings that naturally occur at random in the Arctic ice cap. Called polynyas, these openings would be useful for surfacing in the ice cap. Getting that information would require going to the Arctic and counting any polynyas found. The group selected to go comprised the squadron commander, CAPT Dennis Wilkinson, the executive officer of *Skate*, LCDR Nick Nicholson, LCDR Jeff Metzel, and me. A P2V patrol aircraft was selected to fly us there, since its clear plastic nose provided an excellent spot from which to photograph the ice and polynyas. Nicholson and Metzel were the navigators, Captain Wilkinson was there to double-check the scope of preparations and modifications being designed and installed by Electric Boat, and I was the photographer.

The flight to Thule, Greenland, was uneventful, and we spent the night there. The next morning, as we flew over Baffin Bay, we could see hundreds of whales migrating south to the Atlantic Ocean, a once-in-a-lifetime sight. Flying north over the last point of land, called Alert, we saw for the first time the majestic beauty of the Arctic ice cap. Nevertheless, it was a forbidding sight as well, since any aircraft forced to go down onto the cap would find the rough surface of the ice far from friendly for a safe landing. Our group became a bit sober when we discovered that the port engine had been shut down and the plane was slowly losing altitude. We had been flying at thirty-five hundred feet, so we did not have much of a cushion to work with. The plane was equipped with a JATO (jet-assisted takeoff) bottle under each engine, so the pilot fired up the JATOs now and then to regain altitude as needed. When Thule's runways appeared, we relaxed and I silently thanked God. With the engine repaired, we once again headed north in our P2V. I took hundreds of photographs, counted the density of the polynyas, and filled my log book with data.

There were a number of special pieces of equipment being installed for the journey, including newly designed underwater TV cameras, upward-beamed high-frequency ranging sonars, and mine-detection sonar installed on the sub's deck to locate polynyas. Most fascinating to me was the inertial navigation system. Above 85 degrees of latitude, magnetic and gyro-compass systems are useless, so the use of inertial systems was the answer. We needed a system that could be run for days, unlike the inertial systems already in use on aircraft. Luckily, the U.S. Army had just developed such a system for their new Navajo missile. To make room for the nose cone from one of their missiles, we removed three sleeping bunks and installed the nose cone upside down in the crew's quarters. A hand-cranked Swedish computer was used to transform the inertial system's digital output to numerical latitude and longitude degrees.

Skate's Arctic mission was vital. In order to have a credible deterrent force, survivability of the nuclear-warhead launching platforms was critical, be they aircraft, land-launched missiles, or sea-launched missiles. If we could station a few of our fleet ballistic missile submarines under the Arctic ice cap, the entire northern coast of the Soviet Union would be at risk. We were tasked to gather the data that would make it feasible to do so.

Skate and her crew were ready. As we sailed, I said the mariner's prayer: "O God, Thy sea is so great and my boat is so small." On Sunday, 9 August 1958, *Skate* reached the Arctic ice pack. The ninety-seven members of the crew and the nine civilian experts were about to do what no man had ever done; we were going to operate under, and surface in, the Arctic ice cap, a feat that would ease man's fear of this massive unknown area of the world.

Proceeding north, we found that the ice cap averaged about ten to twelve feet in thickness, with upended ice called "hummocks" protruding down about thirty to forty-five feet in spots. The ice cap is affected by both current and wind. The effects of the wind on the ice can occur at great distances from the actual location where the wind is acting, causing a polynya, for example, to suddenly start closing without any warning. A submarine or ship in a polynya in that situation could be crushed by the closing ice, and indeed the wooden ships of early explorers experienced just that.

Commander Calvert, our skipper, decided to test our procedures for surfacing amid the ice cap. At the next large opening, our surfacing team went into action. We maneuvered the boat under the opening, and then, allowing for current and ice movement, we carefully pumped out ballast to slowly bring *Skate* up to the surface. Other than a few polar bears whose nap we had interrupted, there was nothing but the vast expanse of ice. In just a few minutes, we had accomplished what we had spent months training to do.

The scientists gathered some data, and then we again submerged to continue north to the Pole. It was Sunday, and during the afternoon worship service, we read Psalm 139, which reads in part that God is there in the uttermost parts of the sea and his hand is leading us. We were entering an unknown world and all knew that the sea was the jealous possessor of the domain into which we had intruded, and was not forgiving if we made any mistakes.

We traveled north under the ice cap at a depth of 230 feet at sixteen knots. When we were a mile from the Pole, we slowed to five knots and adjusted course. At 1:47 a.m. Greenwich Mean Time, on 12 August 1958, we passed directly over the North Pole. The ice canopy was solid at the

Pole, and the deep ice hummocks made it unsafe to try to force our way through the ice canopy, so we circled the Pole at a few yards distance and, in less than a few minutes, had gone around the world. Now it was time to report our accomplishment to our superiors. While searching for a polynya, we stopped and hovered at 120 feet. Suddenly, the stillness in the control room was broken by noise from the radio room. Morse code signals were being received as clearly as if we were on the surface. In the run to the Pole, I had forgotten the floating wire antenna.

In the past summer, a friend from the Naval Submarine Sound Laboratory had informed me that an employee there had developed a concept in which a wire that could float on the surface might be able to receive radio signals while the submarine to which it was attached was deeply submerged. This involved encasing a flexible wire in a newly developed buoyant material. While test results had been mixed, with the help of several five-pound cans of coffee, I had persuaded the lab to fabricate one for me.

The duty radioman, while checking the antenna switching panel, had remembered my floating wire antenna and turned on its switch to the radio speakers. I rotated the deck-mounted TV upward to the ice, and there it was; the wire was neatly coiled at the underside of the ice canopy, and without any degradation of signal, it was receiving the normal submarine broadcast from the United States. We had proved that my floating wire antenna was a way for our ballistic missile submarines, then under construction, to be in constant reception of the submarine broadcast, ensuring that the president could contact us without the necessity of surfacing. The communication link had been the single big problem that had to be solved so that our fleet ballistic missile submarines could be ordered to release their missiles if the United States came under attack.

The skipper said, "Nice job, Kelln" and ordered me to get on with locating a polynya. We needed to notify our superiors as to where we were, what we had done, and that we were safe. They tend to get excited and lose sleep if they think one of our subs is in trouble. Word also had to be sent to the president; much was at stake in the Cold War, and he needed to know that the missile-carrying submarines could be relied upon in the event of an attack.

We surfaced about forty miles from the Pole and sent our progress report. It was heard by a Navy radioman in the Philippines who took some persuading before being convinced to relay our message, we being an

Atlantic Fleet unit. For the first time ever, a submarine had surfaced in the Arctic ice pack, not once but twice, and had reached the North Pole.

It was 1958, and the Cold War was intensifying. The Soviet Union was increasing the size of its armed forces, including the Soviet navy. Although the possibility of a nuclear war was low, it was a possibility that could not be ignored, as Russia never let up in its effort to attain global communism. It thus became vital for our submarine force to patrol hot spots, to collect intelligence, and to be ready to strike the foe whenever our commanders so ordered. However, we had only three nuclear submarines with which to tame the bear, if called upon, so all three were heavily employed in peacetime special operations. The training for these was intense. We sharpened our tracking and torpedo approaches over and over again. Our intelligence collecting team was likewise busy. With one last check from the squadron commander, we were off to the front lines of the Cold War. It is often said that a submarine is one of the few defense systems where we actually interact with a potential adversary during peacetime.

Here I must state that most of our missions remain highly classified, even over half a century after their occurrence. This protects both the information gained and those submariners who are on station today. Today's submarines not only engage in special operations but also carry long-range cruise and ballistic missiles that can neutralize any enemy's communications and defensive infrastructure within hours of the commencement of hostilities.

Skate and her sister submarines successfully completed their special missions such that it was evident to all, from the president on down, that the nature of naval warfare had dramatically changed with the advent of nuclear propulsion in ships and submarines. Admiral Rickover, now recognized as the Father of Nuclear Power, had introduced a new and significant factor in the equation of world affairs.

[Editor's note: During a subsequent deployment to the winter Arctic Ocean, Skate surfaced at the exact geographical North Pole, a historic first. Thus RADM Al Kelln became the first person ever to fly over, pass under submerged, and stand atop the ice at the North Pole, a truly distinct achievement. However, he prefers to be seen as a dedicated submariner rather than an Arctic pioneer.]

Looking Back at a Near Miss

Jim Nunneley

In early 1958, I was serving in USS *Northampton* (CLC-1) as chief engineer. The commanding officer was CAPT Hal Bowen (later to become vice admiral). The ship was flagship of commander, Second Fleet, who at the time was leading a group of about fifteen U.S. Navy ships down the St. Lawrence Seaway for a Montreal port visit. The ships were steaming in a single-file configuration as the channel was fairly narrow during parts of the passage.

There were some seven or eight ships ahead of *Northampton* steaming in single file. USS *Norfolk* (DL-1) was immediately ahead of *Northampton*. *Norfolk* had quite a reputation in the Atlantic Fleet for engineering unreliability, stemming from the problems associated with being the first ship with a 1,200-psi steam plant to join the fleet. At that time, all Navy ship steam plants used 600-psi steam.

Captain Bowen had turned in, leaving me in charge as officer of the deck during the midwatch. I cautioned all of my watch standers on the bridge to keep a sharp eye on *Norfolk* because her engineering reliability was questionable. About thirty minutes into the midwatch, all lights, and I mean even the navigation lights, went out simultaneously on *Norfolk*. I quickly ordered right standard rudder followed soon thereafter by left standard rudder while backing the engines for a short time to slow our speed. We pulled up alongside *Norfolk*, which still showed no illumination. Ships astern of *Northampton* followed our lead, steering clear of *Norfolk* to the extent possible, constrained somewhat by the narrow channel.

Captain Bowen came out to the bridge, having been awakened by my messenger and wanting to know what all the excitement was about. Fortunately, *Norfolk* was able to restore power after a brief interlude and no damage was done to any ship in the task force. CAPT Denny Downey, CO of *Norfolk*, a good friend and neighbor in Newport at the time, had some explaining to do, but everyone knew of *Norfolk*'s continuing engineering problems and tended not to make the CO the fall guy. As proof, Denny went on to wear the three stars of a vice admiral before retiring.

To top it off, the port visit to Montreal was a huge success. So what could have been a major setback for the Navy was a success, and what could have been a major embarrassment to the Navy turned out to be just another near miss!

Sound Surveillance System

Robert E. Jacob

S tarting my naval career as a naval aviator in patrol seaplanes (VP-50) with two lengthy deployments and a year instructing all-weather flight, my orders to Naval Postgraduate School (NPS) presented an interesting change of direction. Shortly after starting the electrical engineering course, several of us were asked if we were interested in also studying underwater sound as a minor course: five said yes and four were interested in the relatively short range of sounds as they affected shipboard sonar systems. I was offered a chance to study very low frequency, long-range acoustics with two provisos: a top secret clearance was required, as was a so-called payback tour with the Bureau of Ships (BuShips), which would be funding the course. The deal was made, the top secret clearance was approved about three months later, and after a short but classified thorough briefing and a tour of a nearby operational facility by the BuShips Project Caesar officer (who also explained what was ahead of me), that very different career path started. I was now an early participant in the Navy's venture into a long-range undersea acoustic detection and tracking system, originally under the cover story of oceanographic research and now publicly acknowledged as the Sound Surveillance System (SOSUS). The system was developed and implemented under the title Project Caesar with a "brickbat three" priority assigned for rapid funding and procurement authority.

My immediate tours following NPS were a "skinny" teaching course at the Naval Academy, followed by Naval Air Station Lakehurst in New Jersey with ZP-3 as a student blimp pilot. The blimps were decommissioned on the day I was awarded my LTA wings, and we were off to Naval Air Station Bermuda and VP-49, again doing ASW patrols, flying the P5M-2 seaplanes, but I was also spending part of the time learning more about the operational SOSUS, both with the squadron and with the U.S. Naval Facility (NavFac) Bermuda, the classified facility located just outside the NAS. The commanding officer, NavFac Bermuda was a 1952 classmate, Bob Craven, who was extremely helpful to my learning and encouraged me to participate in the daily activities. During the Cuban Missile Crisis of October

1962, VP-49 carried out extensive ocean surveillance patrols, many with SOSUS inputs, and deployed six aircraft to Guantanamo for seven months with me as the detachment OinC (officer in charge), providing surface surveillance for the Cuban area.

With the transition of VP-49 from P5M-2 seaplanes to the new P-3B landplanes, I was given command of the earliest commissioned SOSUS facility, U.S. NavFac Ramey in Puerto Rico, co-located on Ramey Air Force Base. My career path change was taking hold at last. At that time, SOSUS operators were an odd mixture of electronics technicians, sonar men, cooks, yeomen, and boatswains—whatever and whoever could qualify at reading the "grams" depicting underwater sounds. There was no Navy enlisted rating path; instead we found people who could be trained to look at the grams and decide what the targets were. With more than a little bit of complaining about this lack of personnel development, I was ordered to Norfolk for temporary additional duty to head a committee to evaluate the question and make recommendations.

In a ten-day period, we consulted the various SOSUS stations in both oceans, reached a consensus, and presented a formal program proposal to the Bureau of Naval Personnel: (1) create a dedicated operator rating (I proposed the name Oceanographic Technician or OT) that would maintain the still-classified security of the program; (2) establish a school training program; and (3) develop a rating badge. After some haggling with BuPers, I drew my pencil version of the badge. All of our proposals were finally accepted when the rating was authorized nearly seven years later.

On an earlier trip to NavFac Shelburne, the Canadian SOSUS station, I noted that not only did the station consistently win the Atlantic System "E" for Operations, but its operators were all women. With the continual influx of Soviet submarines into the Atlantic, Ramey and the other East Coast facilities detected and reported many targets of opportunity, both surface and subsurface, including the very long-range detection of the first Soviet nuclear submarine Atlantic deployment. As my CO tour reached an end, my initial orders were to commander oceanographic systems, Atlantic as operations officer, but my NavFac Ramey change of command ceremony was literally interrupted by a telephone call from VADM Charles Martell, the CNO's antisubmarine warfare czar (Op-095), and I was simply told to forget my written orders, get off the plane at Washington, and report for duty as the head of fixed surveillance systems for the CNO.

Office of the Chief of Naval Operations (OPNAV) for a lieutenant commander was exciting and at first a bit deflating; as a NavFac CO, I'd had a small, beautiful, and remote duty station right on the Atlantic shoreline, an assigned car, wonderful Air Force quarters, a nice office, and some 110 officers and men to carry out our assignments. In the Pentagon I had about a four-by-four-foot space with a desk and chair, a part-time yeoman, and a setback to my personal esteem—that is, until I went to one of the Pentagon midget cafeterias for lunch and found myself in line behind two vice admirals (so much for my hurt pride). But the job was more than justified. I basically worked directly for Vice Admiral Martell, and what program proposals I suggested, he approved, and they rapidly became fact. Recalling my visit to Shelburne, one of my early thoughts was the use of female operators. I found a sympathetic ear with a female captain on the SecNav staff, and with considerable speed, she and Admiral Martell assembled our first group of female volunteers, who were eager to prove their ability by asking for the most remote of the Atlantic stations, that is, NavFac Eleuthera in the Bahamas. Their performance quickly proved successful, and soon, female officers and enlisted were authorized for all stations.

During one of Admiral Martell's early evening meetings on what to do about the submarine threat, the decision was made to build a NavFac in Iceland. I was given a torn half of an envelope reading, "NavFac Keflavik approved" as my authority to proceed. A Friday call to the office of Senator Margaret Chase Smith resulted in her primary assistant giving approval in her name, and on Saturday the Project Caesar officer had a local contractor building the facility at Keflavik (how government to government approvals were so rapidly arranged I never heard; formal DOD approval was actually provided nearly a year later, one month *after* the facility was fully operational). I kept that half-envelope in my wallet the entire time, in fear of a court-martial for taking an unauthorized action.

With those successes, a major improvement effort was suggested for the underwater hydrophone and cabling systems as well as for the entire shore processing equipment. Digital technology would solve many of the current restraints. It would obviate the need for the selecting stations being right on the shoreline (cable transmission capability being limited by technology—it was simply copper wire with some protective wrappings) and well away from electric impulses that would distort the signals in the cable (another technology issue), and by shifting to digital processing and displays within the shore station, changes could be quickly implemented with modular systems design. My proposal included establishing a large station on the eastern side of the Atlantic to provide coverage in that area and, using the new technology, terminate several underwater sensors at a single shore station, thus reducing the manpower requirements caused by several widely separated small stations. With help from the Bell Labs unit that supported the system and with that of the Project Caesar office, the proposal was prepared in five days and submitted and approved by Admiral Martell, who applied a top secret very limited distribution. Then he and I hand carried it to the secretary of the navy, who concurred. We then hand carried it directly to Secretary of Defense McNamara, who immediately approved both the proposal and the funding. In fewer than ten days, a significant change was made to one of the Navy's major programs, vastly enlarging and improving the detection and tracking system across most ocean areas, a system that would eventually result in an annual budget of over $900 million dollars.

The next change to surveillance capability was the result of a direct telephone call to me from the SecNav: "Can you make your system work on board a ship?" Once I realized the caller was the SecNav himself, I dashed down the hallways to his office with a quick sketch on a notepad showing one of the project's survey arrays being towed. Following a short discussion with the secretary and RADM William Groverman (OP-32 and my immediate supervisor), the secretary directed another fast track effort and the Surface Towed Array System was initiated. During this time period the conflict in Vietnam was under way and a question came up about using sonobuoys to detect enemy truck and troop movements. My short answer was basically to change the battery from seawater initiated to a normal stored charge battery and change the hydrophone to a microphone with a weighted wedge to place it along the suspected enemy trails. This was done by another OPNAV office and by contractors, who even disguised the units to look like the typical bushes found in the area. Navy patrol aircraft flew missions along the line of buoys to pick up the sounds; trucks and even troops walking were clearly heard.

At one point I became aware of the efforts of Air Force Technical Applications Center (AFTAC) and its concerns for nuclear detonations and the resultant earth-borne, very low frequency sounds or vibrations (much like those of an earthquake). With AFTAC's need for sensor locations and its recording equipment being similar to SOSUS, it seemed logical to be cooperative. An arrangement was made and approved by authorities for AFTAC to jointly share facilities where needed. That arrangement proved invaluable in April 1963, when USS *Thresher* (SSN 589) failed to return from deployment. Quick telephone calls to the fleet SOSUS Headquarters, to the ONR field units studying underwater sound, and to AFTAC Headquarters were made, with a request to save all recorded data for the days before and subsequent to *Thresher's* apparent loss. I then formed a small *Thresher* acoustic analysis committee for the CNO; the resulting analysis of the acoustic data was significant in locating the sunken submarine. To this day, analysis of that data, and considerable conjecture, are still a matter of controversy as to the reason for the loss. Over the years that group of analysts was called upon to review SOSUS data and that of other sources (earthquake recordings) and were instrumental in locating several other submarine disasters involving foreign navies.

With a three-year OPNAV tour ending, I received orders to the new Naval Electronics Systems Command (NavElex) as the deputy and then later the Project Caesar officer; the earlier proviso of a repay tour for NPS was to be collected. As deputy and later project officer, my primary effort was the development of the new system as well as continued support and improvements to the existing systems. With the same small project staff we were able to find ways to improve the hardware, install further installations in the Pacific and other areas, and participate in several agreements with foreign nations for joint facilities, including what became U.S. NavFac Brawdy in Wales, the selected location for the eastern Atlantic system. It was in 1973 that Vice Admiral Shear called me and asked, "All right you wise-ass engineer, are you ready to put your foot where your mouth has been and make Brawdy operational?" He then went on to congratulate me on my captaincy promotion and tell me I was being ordered as the commissioning CO of NavFac Brawdy. Actually, it was a dream come true. All those years of work at the Pentagon and NavElex meant my earlier system improvement program vision was coming true. In February 1974, I arrived at Brawdy, eager to prove the new design was working and was an improvement in operational performance and simpler in maintenance.

U.S. NavFac Brawdy was co-located with RAF Airfield Brawdy, about ten miles north of Haverfordwest, Wales. The RAF reopened and updated the World War II airfield and relocated a major RAF flight training unit, providing the U.S. Navy with needed housing and other support, and the local community a much needed economic lift. Haverfordwest was the location of much of the personnel housing. The NavFac building was designed and prewired such that when the terminal, or shore, equipment arrived, the cabinets would be simply placed in their assigned positions on the floor and plugged in, no additional specific wiring required. And that idea worked! The project office in the Naval Electronic Systems Command (NavElex) had arranged for the equipment to be picked up and packed into six standard moving vans and then carried to Mildenhall, England, on a single USAF C-5, where local tractors made the haul to Brawdy. In only four hours after the trucks arrived, NavFac Brawdy detected and reported its first Soviet submarine target; digital modular systems were proven.

Formal dedication and commissioning was delayed several weeks until sufficient personnel were on hand and given basic familiarization with the new system; these included an RAF and a Royal Navy officer. At the commissioning, Shear, now commander in chief, United States Naval Forces Europe (CINCUSNAVEUR), was present with a number of Royal Navy and Royal Air Force senior officers, and we were fortunate in being able to show these gentlemen Soviet submarines being detected and tracked in real time. One of the digital design features we wanted at the project office was ease of maintenance; this was actually demonstrated when a visiting secretary from the Western Electric–Bell Labs support group was asked to detect a reported unit fault and make a repair. The maintenance computer located the cabinet and slot of the faulty unit, the secretary selected the part as noted by the computer program, removed the faulty unit, and installed the replacement, as we watched the system return to full capability—another digital modular systems demonstration.

The tour at Brawdy, with my wife, Nancy, proved a wonderful experience and introduction to the local Welsh people and culture. The pub singing sessions there were memorable. Welsh hospitality was beyond reproach, and we made many friends in the local and RAF communities. We were constantly reminded of the wonderful work done by the Navy SeaBees during World War II. Although not cleared security wise, they proved to be totally security conscious and kept me and the British CID/MI5 people aware of any unusual activity by the press or outsiders visiting the area and getting too curious about this "new U.S. base."

Admiral Shear came to visit Brawdy and informed me that for my next assignment, I was returning to the Pentagon as the head of Undersea Surveillance Systems in OP-095. Once again I was in position to use my experience and influence the system and its capabilities; this time my concentration was on furthering the surveillance towed array sensor system (SURTASS) development, including a catamaran tow ship with greater sea-keeping capability than the original standard hull ships, and to start a deployable capability that could be rapidly inserted where needed. With the suggestion of the project office, we also directed an expanded reporting system to demonstrate the system capability and performance. A major effort was negotiations with foreign governments to establish their own SOSUS capability and to operate in coordination with the U.S. system. These involved numerous overseas trips and technical discussions with foreign nationals, with resulting new capabilities in the ASW effort and many new friends.

Following active duty, I joined Planning Systems, Inc. as principal scientist for undersea systems, and Vice Admiral Waller requested that I report back to my old office for assistance and training of the staff. For ten years Planning Systems provided the detailed analysis of the reporting SOSUS target detection data from all operating stations, assisting both OPNAV and the Project Caesar office in their decisions for further improvements and change.

All told, I spent nearly thirty years in one manner or another in that different career path taken, and I enjoyed every minute of it. My family and I lived in areas most people pay a small fortune just to vacation in but never really see—or learn just how beautiful and wonderful are the areas and people. The children went to schools much different from those in the American system and learned a lot about the upbringing process in foreign countries.

I am forever humbled by the various citations received for my performance in that each was supported by and largely due to the outstanding support of my superiors, my staffs, and my crews and contractors, and I am forever grateful for the loving support of my Nancy and our daughter Christine. They have proven themselves loving supporters of my career choice and instantly available when needed. Life has been good. Very good.

Service Memories

Richard J. Laulor

O n 10 March 1945 I enlisted in the Navy and reported to the U.S. Naval Training Center at Sampson, New York, for ten weeks of boot camp. In late June, I boarded USS *Carlisle* (APA 69) in San Diego, and on 14 August, I arrived at Samar, Philippine Islands. It was V-J day, the end of World War II. Six weeks later, I traveled to New Guinea on the SS *Extavia* (IX134), becoming a Shellback while en route.

I reported for duty on board USS *Arayat*, a tanker for destroyers. We departed New Guinea in October 1945, stopping at Pearl Harbor, then headed east for the United States. On Christmas Eve, seven hundred miles off the coast of Mexico, the fuel oil became contaminated with salt water, causing the main engines to stop and leaving us dead in the water. A fleet tug responded to our SOS and towed us to Panama City, Panama.

After clearing our fuel, we transited the Panama Canal on 3 January 1946, and arrived at Mobile, Alabama, on 14 January. The good ship *Arayat* was decommissioned on 15 February, and I was transferred to USS *Mellette* (APA 156), one of four APAs being readied for the mothball fleet in the York River near Yorktown, Virginia. I was one of ten seamen who made up the decommissioning crew, led by a chief petty officer.

Seaman First Class Laulor was honorably discharged from the Navy on 29 July 1946. However, Navy blue called once more, and on 30 June 1948, I was sworn in at the Naval Academy, joining the Class of 1952. In June 1952, now a new ensign, I reported aboard USS *Witek* (DDE 848), where I served for a year before reporting to submarine school at New London, Connecticut, from which I graduated in December 1953.

My next duty station was USS *Halfbeak* (SS 352), in which I served until July 1956, during which time I qualified in submarines. The executive officer of *Halfbeak* was LCDR Jon L. Boyes, who later went to command of USS *Albacore* (AGSS 569). *Albacore* was the first U.S. submarine to have a hull designed for optimum underwater performance, surface sea keeping being a secondary consideration. An experimental boat, *Albacore* set a world record for that time for underwater speed. One of Lieutenant Commander Boyes' proudest moments was when his crew showed ADM

Arleigh Burke, accompanied by Lord Mountbatten, that *Albacore* really could "fly" underwater.

In July 1954, during a weekend trip to Portsmouth, New Hampshire, I visited Boyes. He told me that Admiral Rickover was going to ride *Albacore* on Monday as the final step in the decision to use nuclear power in submarines. I accepted his invitation to be on board for the demonstration. Rickover demanded numerous deep dives, sharp up-angle changes in depth, tight turns, one after the other, and all at high speed. *Albacore* had "subway straps" attached to the overhead throughout the boat. Without them, bodies would have been strewn all over the deck.

The first nuclear submarine, USS *Nautilus* (SSN 571), and the subsequent *Skate* class of nuclear attack boats were designed with the fleet boat hull configuration. It was not until the 637-class ships were built that the *Albacore* hull form was incorporated into the submarines' design.

After a fourteen-month stint on the Submarine Squadron 8 staff as division engineer for Submarine Division 81, I accepted a commission in the Naval Reserve, in which my final tour was commanding officer of the newly established Naval Reserve unit in the Naval Material Command Headquarters in Crystal City, Virginia. I retired in the rank of captain, USNR.

My years in the active Navy and in the Naval Reserve were good years.

A Boy from Brooklyn

Don Masse

A product of parochial schools in Flatbush, a section of Brooklyn, New York, I entered the Navy in 1947 at the age of seventeen and enlisted in the Naval Reserve, from which I was appointed a midshipman by Secretary of the Navy John L. Sullivan, entering the Academy in the summer of 1948 with the Class of 1952. In retrospect, a year at the Naval Academy Preparatory School would have helped me a great deal in plebe year, indoctrination taking more of my time than studies.

Upon graduating, I entered flight training at Pensacola, Florida. My first solo flight was both memorable and short. I taxied my aircraft out to the runway, and when cleared for takeoff, I added full power, but just as I lifted off the runway, my engine began losing power (and making sounds like firecrackers popping). I reached about three hundred feet, and with my landing gear still down, turned downwind. The tower hit the crash alarm, and I was given clearance to land on any runway clear of other aircraft. With the help of my guardian angel, I made it all the way around and landed. I was given another plane, and when airborne, as I climbed through the clouds, it was like starting a new life. My flights in N3Ns at the Academy while a midshipman had hooked me on flying, and I was now on my way to becoming a naval aviator.

I won my wings in early 1953 and was assigned to the Naval Air Ordnance Test Center at Naval Air Station Patuxent in southern Maryland. I was in charge of a twelve-man unit, testing the Sidewinder, Sparrow, and other self-guided missiles, some of which are still in use. We also tested BAT, a 500-pound guided glide bomb, the accuracy of which was dependent on the ability of the controller in the delivering aircraft. Because of its size, it was carried by the PB4Y-2, the Navy derivative of the B-24 Liberator bomber. We also tested a new missile called "Petrel," a 2,000-pound flying missile equipped with wings, a jet engine, radar, and a World War II torpedo and intended for delivery by the new P2V patrol aircraft. The plane had to dive in order to gain enough speed to launch Petrel, and once launched, its flight was monitored from the delivering plane throughout its flight to the target.

We were required to go through escape and evasion training. Without warning, a vehicle would meet a returning aircraft and the crew would be taken to a wild area with only their flight suits to wear. They were dropped off two at a time and given fifteen minutes to escape before the arrival of Korean War veteran soldiers. For two weeks, I hid alongside snakes and alligators, drank swamp water mixed with iodine tabs, and lived off of whatever edibles I could find, whether animal or vegetable. I was the only one who escaped capture, and when I turned in at the end of the exercise period, I learned that three of our crew needed medical attention after being interrogated following their capture. One had fainted, and the interrogators, thinking he was faking, bound him and put him in a wire cage. They said it was an accident that the cage was on top of an anthill.

My squadron, VP-24, was sent to Malta, which was much closer to our assigned targets in the Black Sea. The airfield at Helfar, Malta, had no runway lights and only one runway suitable for our P2Vs. At one end of the runway was a three-hundred-foot cliff overlooking the main part of the town. There usually was a stiff crosswind, so we took off toward the cliff and landed over the cliff. Although the British placed flare pots along the runway, landing at night on that black runway, between the flare pots, over the three-hundred-foot cliff, and with a stiff crosswind, took some getting used to.

I left VP-24 with orders for flight instructor duty at the Flight Training Command at Hutchinson, Kansas. I had to train a new radio operator and a navigator. As we taxied out one night for night training, we received a fog warning. However, our ops officer told me the flight was needed, so off we went. Two hours out, the navigation equipment became inoperable. We were over the Atlantic somewhere, with only an approximate position, so I decided to contact the East Control Center. I was told the East Coast was completely fogged in and my nearest alternate was Pittsburgh. We had enough fuel, so I decided to try a ground-controlled approach (GCA) to Chinco. Responding to our call, the GCA crew took us in, but when we were over the field, we saw we were too far left of center. I pointed this out to them, and they promised to try harder if we really wanted to try again (as if we had a choice!). The second time, they brought us right down the centerline and we landed, the only plane to do so that night.

Weather continued to give me problems. Since I was a "green card" pilot, I was often given the first flight, the weather-check flight. The weather in Kansas that winter varied from bad to terrible, but even if the ceiling was almost zero and the temperature below zero, they wanted to know if we could get some work done above the weather. One morning I took off in a freezing drizzle with a student at the controls. I told him to make a slow, climbing turn to the left. Nothing happened. I told him again, and still nothing happened. The look he gave me encouraged me to take the controls, and when I did, I discovered that they were literally frozen and could not be moved. Luck was with us, and we popped out of the clouds. Flying with the trim tabs, I called the field and declared an emergency. GCA brought us back down, where we found that the slush on the runway had splashed up into the wheel wells, freezing the control cables. As a result, the aircraft were modified and the runway condition was made a factor to be checked before flying. We had some close calls during my tour, but we never lost an aircraft or a student.

One of the most difficult assignments I had was catapult/arresting officer on USS *Forrestal* (CVA 59). The ship wanted me to report ASAP, but it was in the Med and its exact location was not known, so I flew to Naples, Italy, and checked in with the Naval Command. They sent me out to the ship in a COD (carrier-onboard-delivery) aircraft. Once on board, I was quickly put to work. Daytime operations were not too difficult, but night operations were terrifying, at least at first.

At that time, there were no flight-deck lights, and *Forrestal* had a mix of jets and propeller aircraft. We had to check in with flight-deck control before going out on the flight deck. They had a spot diagram showing where the aircraft were supposed to be. The first time I went out on the flight deck at night, I was with Jack Verser, the officer I was relieving. Twenty-two aircraft were scheduled to be launched, some jets and some props. The "spot" was in progress, and we had to get out there to get set up for the launch. I took hold of the back of his belt and followed him out onto the flight deck. It was a moonless, pitch-black night; I couldn't see anything. There were propellers spinning and jet engines roaring all around us. I held on to his belt, and as we made our way out to the center of the deck, I felt the wind from the propellers and the burning heat from the jet exhausts. Jack got us out to the center of the deck without incident, however, and we began work. Two jet planes were being maneuvered onto the forward catapults, while two more were being connected to the other catapults by the assistant cat officer and his crew. We leaned into the prop wash and turned our backs to the burning jet exhausts; the noise was deafening.

Jack checked the type and weights of the first two to go, and using his red flashlight, he checked the steam pressures required for launch.

During day ops, he would signal the pressure to the deck-edge crewman, but at night, he had to go over in front of the aircraft and shout the pressure to the crewman. We did this for the two aircraft on the cats, then went back to the center of the flight deck and signaled the aircraft to go to 100 percent power. We made one more check of the aircraft, checked forward to ensure the deck was clear, and then waited for the pilot to signal that he was ready. The pilot turned on his aircraft lights—the ready signal—and Jack gave the signal to the deck edge for launch. The crewman once again checked the steam pressure and then pressed the launch button. Down the track went the aircraft. We immediately turned to check the second aircraft—lights came on, signal to deck edge, and launch, all in less than one minute.

While the next two aircraft were being positioned for launch, the waist catapults launched their two aircraft. We stared toward the bow for a signal from the crewman stationed there that the bridles had been recovered and were back on the deck edge. He showed a steady red light until the bridles were back in place for the next launch, at which time he showed a green light. Until the green light appeared, the cat officer would not let the aircraft launch, even with the two waiting aircraft at 100 percent power and the air boss screaming for the launch to go. It could be pretty hectic, but if we did not get that green light, we would stand in front of the aircraft until the situation was okay. This was a very tense time for all concerned. At times, it was necessary to signal the aircraft to reduce power, something the pilots did not want to do while sitting on the catapult. The reason for this strict practice was to ensure the safety of the crewmen who had the task of retrieving the bridle.

A picture of an aircraft carrier in the 1950s would show two projections on the front of the flight deck called "horns." Two men were assigned to each horn on the *Forrestal*, and immediately after a launched aircraft roared by at 130 mph, they would jump out onto the track, and one of them had to run down the horn (three hundred feet above the ocean), grab a bungee cord to which was attached a forty-pound metal strap, haul the bridle back to the flight deck, and stow it into the deck edge just before the next aircraft came roaring down the track. The man on the horn had to buck a thirty-plus knot wind and run through hot steam and water on the horn, all the while the deck was pitching up and down. This was done every time an aircraft was launched, rain or shine, day or night. It was a challenge to walk down that horn on a calm, sunny day in port, yet those sailors did it routinely under any and all conditions. I doubt that a Hollywood stunt man could be paid enough to do what my crew did as a matter of routine. During my tour, flight-deck lighting was installed, a catapult officer control pit was added to the center of the flight deck, an automatic retrieval system for the bridles was installed, and the horns were being gradually removed from carriers. These changes were long overdue, and by the time they arrived, my hair had turned gray and the air boss had an ulcer.

I was also responsible for retrieving the aircraft with the arresting gear and cables on the rear of the flight deck. This operation had its own set of problems and dangers, too numerous to mention here. As an example, during a retrieval, the cable broke when it was caught by an A3D, the heaviest and largest aircraft we were operating. The severed cable end whiplashed forward, killing three crewmen and slicing the shins of the assistant cat officer.

Flight quarters was usually sounded at 4:00 a.m. and ended with the recovery of the last aircraft, sometime around midnight. During this time, my crew and I were continually on the flight deck, launching and recovering aircraft. We had sandwiches brought to us at mealtime. Since we were operating continuously while at sea, any maintenance of our gear had to be done while in port, resulting in little liberty for my crew.

The American public has little knowledge or appreciation of what our sailors did then and do now to earn their bed and board. My crew did a magnificent job, at the risk of their lives every day.

After my retirement from active duty, I continued my service with the Navy, establishing a Junior Reserve Officer Training Program at a high school in Texas, where I taught naval science, chemistry, and history.

Looking back on my years in uniform, I can say that I served my Navy and my country to the best of my ability, and I am proud of my years of service. I am also grateful to my beloved Kay and my children, who have stood by me in all the ups and downs of life. And lastly, I have tried to "walk humbly with my God."

Vignettes from the Surface Navy

John Derr

Life after Annapolis graduation starts with many exciting events for the young officer: first duty station, marriage, freedom from Academy's tight routines—all part of the "real world." My arrival on a destroyer operating off Korea was a pressure tank for learning. Operating in a screening destroyer, one of some twenty circling the carrier task force, was a good learning experience for a young officer. I was the first division officer and junior officer of the deck (JOOD) for bridge watches, and shortly after my arrival, the ship was assigned shore bombardment duties that continued for nearly six weeks.

As the landing force officer, I was responsible for riding our twenty-six-foot motor whale boat with the three-man crew into shore at the bomb line to pick up two Army spotters. This was at or near the then-current combat zone, and there was much concern about having selected the proper landing place. It was the right one, however, and the spotters came on board, enjoyed some ice cream, briefed our Weapons Department, and then went back ashore. Just as we began receiving their portable radar signals for offset firing, they were knocked out by enemy fire. When near shore, we could often view enemy personnel moving about and at night see the tracers from engaged fire parties. That made the destroyer seem a much safer and more comfortable place, yet destroyers' expected life during sea battles could be very short.

Naval officers are expected to be good ship handlers, but that is a skill that one is not born with. My learning started on a destroyer docking one night in Norfolk. While making a port-side-to landing alongside another destroyer, I inadvertently left the starboard engine at ahead one-third. The resulting crash severed a fire main riser, resulting in water shooting some ten feet high and the "attacked" destroyer sounding general quarters. My eternal gratitude goes to the ship's ship fitters, who rapidly welded and made things whole. My courtesy visit to the alongside destroyer found their commanding officer sitting in their wardroom, holding his head and thinking it was his career that was ruined.

One of my shore duties was with the Key West Sonar Test and Evaluation Detachment. Whitey Platt and Tex Proctor were in the area then, and many of our class know both men. One project I had was called SCAT, for the submarine classification device. This was a device with a hammer attached that was fired from the "hedgehog" weapon launcher at suspected sonar targets. The device, when successful, magnetically attached to the submarine's hull, at which time the hammer deployed, lined up with water flow, and beat away on the hull. The beating enabled surface units to use passive sonar for tracking the contact with great detail. The idea seemed like a good Cold War plan, but later I heard differently. The fleet never used this submarine tracking system due to fears about the reaction from the submarine being tracked. Real fears from the Cold War era.

Hurricanes have featured heavily in my life, both in uniform and while working for ten years as director of Charlotte County Emergency Management (in Florida) immediately after Navy retirement. It was about 1958, and I was assigned to a destroyer home ported in Charleston, South Carolina, when we were ordered to sea as a hurricane neared Charleston. Mine craft scattered in the mud flats for safety but combatant ships went to sea since damage to both piers and ships can result if docked. Hurricanes follow their own paths, and we had estimated wrong, ending up directly in the storm's path. We suffered high waves, many at least as high as the bridge at thirty-five feet, some higher. The ship rolled to dangerous degrees. One of our two main shaft sleeve bearings wiped, demanding that the shaft be locked and the bearings be replaced. The babbit-bearing surfaces must be polished to a fine tolerance, and each half weighs about 150 pounds. Our "black gang" performed this heroic feat while sick, scared, and working in cramped space. Had the other shaft failed then, our ship would have fallen victim to the storm, wallowed in the trough, and been lost. The American sailors performed duties that night equal to any combat challenge and saved this U.S. Navy destroyer. No medals given, no hazardous pay, and no special uniforms, just good, solid, loyal, and professional performance.

While I was executive officer on USS *Abbot* (DD 629) in the mid-1960s, operating as Destroyer School training ship and later Naval Reserve training ship, short cruises were the norm. On one trip to Halifax in company with a sister ship, *The Sullivans* (DD 537), a speed run was conducted. On arrival in Halifax, the ships were nested together. Sometime during darkness, some person or persons unknown, repainted the stern where the ship's name is shown, with "Costello" over *The Sullivans*. There one could see two USN ships, "Abbot and Costello." (For those too young to remember, Abbot and Costello were a famous comedy team in the mid-twentieth century.)

Our Navy's fleet operations in the Mediterranean during the Cold War might be compared to Homer's Ulysses in the Odyssey saga, as ports from the Pillars of Hercules to Turkey were all visited. It was about 1954 and I was serving in USS *Salem* (CA 139) when a serious earthquake hit Greece and *Salem* was the first ship to arrive and start to render aid. The citizens of Cephalonia, Greece, who survived were seen at the edge of the little port town—fear kept them away from buildings. Several teams of half a dozen men, me included, searched for survivors. None were found alive, but we saw many dead, including some under vehicles that apparently had bounced on them. One man was completely covered with debris, dead, and when I felt something soft under foot and scraped away the dirt, it was the face of another victim. *Salem's* helicopter flew over the area, and some natives threw stones at it. Food and medical supplies were of real value for this mission.

After my four years of obligated service, I resigned, attended Westinghouse's Graduate Student Program, and spent two years as a sales engineer with their automated small motor factory near Lima, Ohio. One day in 1958, a phone call from the Detail Desk at BuPers offered me operations officer on a fleet operating destroyer and regular commission in about six months. I accepted. This ship then became a critical part in Weapons Systems Evaluation Group (WSEG), much like a repeat of the Billy Mitchell fight over a bomber's ability to sink us all. My ship had the AN/SPS-31 radar capable of picking up a target about one meter square at some 250 miles. The budget process in Washington was apparently in full swing with this bomber challenge on the table. We were able to not only detect their RB-66 bombers but also photograph their side numbers using fighter aircraft flying out of Oceana Naval Air Station to our location far out in the Atlantic.

Memories

Wayne P. Hughes Jr.

When I was a boy in Chicago, I read Fletcher Pratt's *Our Navy: A History*. My romantic spirit wanted to be another Isaac Hull, Farragut, or Spruance and win exciting sea battles. I was dumb lucky enough to get an appointment to the Naval Academy, but my naval service never matched those dreams of heroism. However, three landmarks came in December 1955. In short order I was selected for lieutenant, married the best Navy wife a sailor could ask for, and got orders to command the mighty USS *Hummingbird*, a bird-sized minesweeper.

After that command, I was a flawless ship handler and navigator—there is hardly any greater satisfaction short of sinking an enemy submarine than ship handling—and I did not want to leave the Navy until I commanded my own destroyer. I made three deployments to Korea and Vietnam and two around-the-world cruises. I was only shot at once, off North Korea, when my first ship, USS *Cushing* (DD 797), was firing at a coastal railroad. But in 1968 I was foolhardy enough to take the destroyer USS *Morton's* 5-inch 54-caliber guns five miles up the Saigon River to do air-spotted call-for-fire into the jungle. It is well that we did not annoy the Vietcong enough to shoot back, because we had to head up river to stem the current, and twisting ship to flee the scene would have been awkward and slow.

Amid these operational tours I got a master's degree in operations research in 1964, after which I was either at sea or in an OR billet in the Pentagon, working for inspirational leaders such as ADM Bud Zumwalt, ADM Harry Train, VADM Staser Holcomb, VADM Jim Wilson, ADM Al Whittle, and ADM Ike Kidd. Yes, Kidd was an inspiring leader too, if you didn't let him bully you and all your answers, including "I'll find out, sir," were unfailingly correct. After serving as aide to Under Secretary of the Navy Jim Woolsey, I finished my active duty at the Naval Postgraduate School.

My best contributions to the Class of 1952, since I didn't leave my shoes on Worden Field, were as biographies and sports editor of our *Lucky Bag* for editor Bob Maich, and fifty years later, writing the class retrospective in our *Golden Lucky Bag* for Howard McCallum: "Longest Conflict, Greatest Victory: A Celebration of the Class of 1952 in the Cold War."

I think it was family roots that steered me to serve a second career at NPS. There are more teachers among my parents, uncles, aunts, and cousins than relatives who served in the armed forces, so teaching and writing came naturally. While on the faculty of NPS, Joan and I took time off for six months to Singapore, where I helped organize the new Operations Research establishment. I taught many young officers and civilians who are still friends and have now risen to be top managers and leaders in the Singapore armed forces. Even more fun for Joan, we went to England, where I advised CINCUSNAVEUR London on a tricky analysis problem. We had time left over to see the sights, including some in Normandy, France.

Even now I am still teaching, because the young officers who attend the Naval Postgraduate School are the best students in any university, anywhere. They are motivated, experienced adults who know it is a luxury to attend graduate school while drawing a lieutenant's pay. Once I was asked to give the graduation address. It was a popular talk, doubtless because it was over in twelve minutes and shorter than a Presbyterian sermon. It was also well received because I only gave the graduates one piece of advice. Quoting Abraham Lincoln, I said, "Whatever you are, be a good one." I pointed out that lawyer Lincoln always chose his words carefully and he did *not* say, "Be the *best* one," because best implies hubris, single-mindedness, and self-centeredness, whereas being "a good one" implies teamwork. I said whether you serve in a ship when everyone sails in harm's way together or on a study team, where the participants bring different backgrounds and skills to solve "wicked" problems, the result will be good to the extent that all the contributors are good at teamwork.

That is our Class of 1952: some have been the best, like our astronauts and our many flag officers, but whatever we were, almost all of us were good ones.

Master Spy

Jim D'Orso

The name is D'Orso, James D'Orso. Before I have a martini, there are some tales to be told. You see, during a shore tour associated with naval intelligence in Europe, I had a few experiences that might be of interest. My assignment was with the CINCUSNAVEUR representative, Germany, stationed in Frankfurt from 1960 to 1962. It was tough duty, but someone had to do it. Our small unit consisted of four or five naval officers and a few yeomen, together with a Navy scientific and technical team of a few naval officers and civilian scientists.

My job was in intelligence collection, which devolved into seeking assistance from various American and allied sources. The U.S. Army and Germany's BND (Bundes Nachtrichten Dienst) were exceptionally helpful. A large part of my time was spent in traveling in northern Germany visiting various outposts and sources. (Until I had a ten-day leave in 1962, I never got farther south than Nuremburg, thereby missing most of Germany's scenic beauty. Like I said, it was tough duty.)

Our Army had an intelligence headquarters in a small town near Frankfurt that I'd visit about weekly, keeping up with events. One senior NCO there was Master Sergeant Svoboda, who acted as the custodian of classified material. He was a very interesting character, having been recruited from Soviet forces in Germany in 1945, opening the path to U.S. citizenship under the Lodge Act. We often exchanged friendly greetings. Early in 1961, before the Berlin Wall was built, my pal Svoboda went to Berlin on a weekend pass, easily crossed over into East Berlin, and rejoined his old outfit (probably as a colonel in the Soviet army).

Apart from the explosive effect the Svoboda affair had on our Army's intelligence organization and those of our allies, there was an added humorous item. Later on, I was informed that in his debriefing, Svoboda had named me, D'Orso, James D'Orso, as the U.S. Navy's director of covert intelligence activities in Europe. I most assuredly was not, but I was cautioned by senior authority to never, ever travel to Russia or any other part of the Soviet Union. "James D'Orso, master spy." Hmm, has a nice ring to it.

As the closest submariner at hand, I was enlisted by our science and technology team as their underseas expert. One day, the BND office in Hamburg informed them that a Baltic fisherman had brought in a mysterious device found floating in that sea. They requested help analyzing it. I was headed for Hamburg anyway, so I agreed to stop by there and check out what we assumed to be a sonobuoy. Sure enough, there on the table in the BND office, surrounded by half a dozen officials, was a typical older model of such a device. It had a classically primitive mechanical timer, which was intended to open a flood port, causing the buoy to sink. The timer was stuck. Instinctively, I turned it to restart it, and the timer commenced ticking. Have you ever seen six fully grown men trying to get through one doorway at the same time??

The last item I have to report happened while I was CO of USS *Bream* (AGSS 243) in the western Pacific in 1967. I received an odd request in a letter from our class president (or maybe secretary). It seems that back in 1961, one of our classmates, "Jake" Kermes, was in Germany as a civilian, having been medically surveyed from naval aviation with a serious heart condition. He passed away there, peacefully. At about the same time, one of our cohorts from our Berlin office was injured in a near-fatal car crash in the East Zone. Somehow these events evolved into a story that Jim D'Orso had been killed while on a spy mission in East Germany. Our class had a fund for memorial plaques in the stadium, and one was placed there in my honor.

Thanks, guys, but nobody told me or my wife about that. The letter I received asked whether it would be okay if the stadium plaque were changed to honor a classmate lost in Vietnam. I agreed, but I neglected to ask for the old plaque, which would have made a grand souvenir.

Now I'll have that martini. Shaken, not stirred.

First Command at Sea, USS *Takelma*

Tom Dyer

I received orders to take command of USS *Takelma* (ATF 113) when her commanding officer experienced a serious health problem that required his immediate hospitalization. I reported aboard *Takelma,* contacted my immediate administrative superior in command (COM SERVPAC), and advised him I had taken command and would be sending a message report of my findings after meeting with the executive officer and the department heads. I told the executive officer to break out the instruction on admin inspection and see to the preparation of all departments for an admin-type inspection to be held by me in the next seventy-two hours. This somewhat startled the XO, an ensign who had been in the position about a year and had never been through an admin inspection (I had been through several). So I had to lead them through it.

Additionally, I scheduled the ship for a one-day operational, underway familiarization cruise for my benefit. This being my first single-screw ship, it was somewhat of a challenge, particularly when backing out of the innermost berth with ships moored aft. I was pleasantly surprised to find that the XO and the first lieutenant (boatswain) were capable ship handlers—the other two officers not so much. We went through a series of emergency drills, most of which needed some brushing up, and returned to the berth. As I was conning the ship into the berth, I noticed that the ship was making a perfect approach, but the helmsman was not specifically following my commands. Later I discussed this with the XO. He told me that the helmsman, Signalman Second Class Whitney, a native Hawaiian, had been the ship's helmsman for some six years and was so good that he could actually bring the ship alongside himself. This was all well and good, but it did nothing to train the officers in ship handling. So I talked to Whitney, congratulated him for his excellence as a helmsman, and told him that I needed his help in training the junior officers. He said he understood and would cooperate in this effort.

As for the assigned officers, fortunately the XO, though just an ensign, turned out to be one of the finest officers I encountered throughout my entire career, which included two more ship commands. However, other than the boatswain, the other officers were pretty green. The chief engineer was a noncommissioned warrant machinist, having been advanced from chief engineman. He seemed to be competent at first, but later I found many discrepancies in his department for which there were no excuses. The most glaring one was his failure to ensure that all fuel was run through the centrifugal fuel-oil purifiers before running to the day fuel-oil tanks. Additionally, the lube oil was not being continually purified, which is like giving poison to diesel engines.

One of the first assignments after my assumption of command was to tow a large deck barge loaded with U.S. Army wheeled and tracked vehicles from Oahu to the big island of Hawaii. This was an overnight trip along a line running south of the Hawaiian island chain. This is the most direct route, but it exposes the ship and its tow to the conditions caused by the wind and seas funneling through the channels separating the islands. At about 10:00 p.m., as the ship was proceeding across the Kaiwai channel between Oahu and Molokai, we encountered a three-foot swell. I ordered the OOD to adjust the scope of the tow wire so that the tug and the tow were in sync (meeting the crests and troughs at the same time). That, together with the action of the automatic towing machine, which pays out the wire at a set tension and then retrieves an equal length, smoothed out the jerking of the hawser to a degree that I was comfortable with.

At about 11:00 p.m., I wrote the night orders for the OOD and retired to my cabin on the next level below the pilot house. I turned in at about 11:30 and was lulled to sleep by the hum of the main engines, the whine of the ventilation blowers, and the gentle rise and fall of the tug in the seaway. At about 1:00 a.m. I awoke out of a sound sleep to complete silence (a bad sign). I immediately rushed up the ladder to the bridge just as the OOD was shouting down the voice tube for me to come to the pilot house. The ship had lost propulsion and steering. The tug still had way on. The chief engineer (CHENG) called me from the engine room to report that the 500-kW ship's service generator had "thrown a rod." These are words that strike terror in the heart of the chief engineer and ultimately the captain. No one wants to hear those words. The fun was just beginning.

As the tug lost way, the barge surged ahead. Fortunately, it had yawed somewhat, so it didn't collide with the stern of the tug. However, other big problems were developing as the tug continued to lose way but the barge surged ahead up the port side. I could just visualize all the possibilities. The barge could, if it kept going, start pulling the stern of the tug around and/or the towing hawser could snag on the bottom due to the increasing catenary. With no steering and no propulsion, the tug was helpless. I had read stories where a tow had done something similar and it actually capsized the tug.

While thinking all these unpleasant thoughts, I called the engine room and asked when we could expect power from the two standby generators. At that moment we got back steering and propulsion. I steered the tug away from the barge, which by now was up on the beam, ordered the towing watch to shorten up the tow wire to reduce the catenary, and we slowly got control of the situation. I reported the casualty and we proceeded on our assignment. The fun was not over yet. My investigation revealed that sufficient attention was not being paid by the engineers to ensure that the lube oil filters were regularly cleaned, causing lube oil starvation to the generator. Naturally I was not happy with this result, nor was COMSERVPAC. I took the required disciplinary action and held school on the CHENG and his chief engineman.

As it turned out this was only the first of several engineering casualties that kept recurring. On another trip, the CHENG reported to me that he had found bearing material in the crankcase of the number 3 main engine. On opening up the engine, they found that several of the rod bearings were wiped, as were several main bearings. I filed the casualty report, that engine was secured, and we proceeded back to Pearl. While the crew was removing the pistons, checking all bearings and inspecting the crankshaft for damage, I started my investigation. From my experience as XO on an LST, I knew that one cause for wiped bearings was an insufficient flow of clean lube oil thru the bearings. So the first thing I did was to ask for the log showing operation of the lube oil purifier. I found out it had not been in use for quite some time because of a broken spindle. In fact, both purifiers, either of which could be used for purification of fuel and lube oil, were out of commission.

I had to take some more disciplinary action and hold school again—this time with the whole engineering department. I told the CHENG in private that if he was incapable of performing as CHENG in a positive and professional manner, I would do so and get a replacement for him. That was a turning point. The CHENG got with it and started spending more time with his crew in the engine room and less time in the wardroom.

I requested the staff to come down to Pearl Harbor and do a surprise admin inspection of *Takelma*'s engineering department on the last day of our upkeep period. I then held a meeting with the department. I gave them a couple copies of the administrative inspection check-off list and told them to start churning and burning—and give me a daily report before liberty commenced. I emphasized to them that *Takelma's* engineering department had a black eye and this was a chance to redeem themselves. I was pleased to see the response. The inspection revealed a few deficiencies, but the grade given was "good," far better than I expected going into it. I congratulated them and gave the department early liberty to make up for the extra hours spent getting the department up to snuff. From then on I had nothing but excellent performance from the *Takelma* engineers. This was just one of the learning experiences I had in my first command.

We also experienced some high spots, one of which I'll mention. The first lieutenant also served as gunnery officer. The armament consisted of a single 3-inch 50-caliber slow-fire open gun mount with an associated manual aiming device. I noticed that the gun had an "E" with three hashmarks (equivalent to four Es). On our first air shoot the first lieutenant's goal was to put a gold "E" on the gun mount, and we did just that during my first year as CO. As far as I know, *Takelma* was the only ATF in either the Atlantic or Pacific Fleet to have a gold "E." It was written up in *Stars and Stripes* and was a source of great pride to the crew and to me.

Another noteworthy accomplishment was *Takelma's* successful completion of an inter-ocean tow of a decommissioned submarine from San Francisco to Norfolk, Virginia, without incident.

All in all, I have fond memories of my first command. The learning curve was steep, but the experience served me well throughout the rest of my rewarding career. Most of the time I got through by forehandedness and taking nothing for granted. On a few occasions, I was just plain lucky. I don't know of a single warship commanding officer who wouldn't agree that luck sometimes plays an important role in the successful completion of a command at sea.

A Many-Sided Life

Chuck Pollak

A fter graduation, I was assigned to the USS *Holder* (DDE 819), an ASW destroyer home ported in Norfolk. Since many experienced officers had been transferred to the Pacific because of the Korean War, I qualified as officer of the deck under way six weeks after reporting aboard. Shortly thereafter, during night operations with a carrier, an adjacent destroyer made a wrong turn toward me instead of away, as was required by the Allied Tactical Publication 1, put in operation a year earlier. I immediately went to "back emergency," and we missed colliding by a hundred yards or less. The skipper, who was on the bridge at the time, echoed my thoughts when he stated for all on the bridge to hear, "Thank God for the Naval Academy."

The skipper was George Street, one of four submariners awarded the Medal of Honor who lived to tell about it. Six months later, Commander Street was reassigned as commander of a submarine division in Norfolk and invited any of us who were interested to take a one-week trip on one of his fleet type "boats." I took the opportunity and was tremendously impressed. Immediately I submitted my application for Naval Submarine School and was one of those selected for the July 1953 class, the first for which we in the Class of 1952 were eligible.

After graduation from Sub School in December 1953, I was assigned to *Sablefish* (SS 303) and then to *Trout* (SS 566), a post–World War II sub. I was one of the first three classmates interviewed for the new nuclear-power program but was turned down by Vice Admiral Rickover (George Vahsen in that group was selected). I was then assigned as division engineer of SUBDIV 101, where the division commander was CDR Pat Gray, a remarkable man who many years later was appointed by President Nixon to become acting director of the FBI after the death of J. Edgar Hoover.

After Naval Postgraduate School, I was assigned to the precommissioning crew of USS *John Marshall* (SSBN 611) as the weapons and missile officer. The ship was being built in Newport News, Virginia, and it was the early days of the space and missile programs. As a result, I had many opportunities to travel to the Kennedy Space Center in Cape Canaveral,

Florida, in 1961–62 to witness missile tests, and I met all of the first seven astronauts and most of the second group of six, which included our Tom Stafford, a friend from Academy days.

After my first patrol on *Marshall*, which ended in March 1963, I was again interviewed by Admiral Rickover, accepted into his program, and given two days (!) to report to Bainbridge, Maryland, to begin the next class. A year later, upon completing the school, I reported as XO to USS *Sam Houston* (SSBN 609), made three patrols on her, and then was assigned as CO to USS *Lafayette* (SSBN 616). Then a lieutenant commander, I relieved a captain, James Strong, and believe I was the first in our Naval Academy class to command a ballistic missile nuclear submarine, although others had earlier been in command of fast attack nuclear submarines.

I spent four years on *Lafayette*, including taking her through her first overhaul and being the first sub to receive the then-new long-life reactor, S3G Core 3. Additionally, I made five Mediterranean patrols in command of her. These were challenging patrols, to say the least. The Med is shallow, there were ASW vessels from many countries out prowling the waters, looking for any subs they might find, and there were countless fishing trawlers and merchant ships that were hazards to our operations.

The closest I came to disaster under way occurred one day when we were operating off the coast of Libya, near the Gulf of Sirte. In those days, we were required to come to periscope depth once a day as a check on our inertial navigation system. We turned the ship 360 degrees, listening for any contacts in the area. Hearing none, I went to periscope depth and through the periscope saw a huge supertanker at close range heading straight for us. Her massive hull had blocked the noises from her propellers from reaching us. I ordered a crash dive and had reached about 150 feet when the tanker roared over us. We later identified the tanker; she was over 200,000 tons fully laden and drew ninety feet. *Lafayette* was 8,500 tons. As the ship roared over us, her flat bottom sucked us up to the surface like a cork, and we literally surfaced just 150 yards behind her. Since we were 420 feet long, we were extraordinarily lucky that we lived to tell about it.

I was relieved as commanding officer of *Lafayette* a year later and reported as deputy program manager and chief engineer of the Mk 48-1 torpedo, then under development and in competition with the Mk-48-0/2 torpedo being developed by another contractor. This was a unique situation: two separate contractors and two separate program offices engaged in a winner-take-all competition. The Mk-48-0 had been under development for five to six years and had run into difficulties, so the competitive program was approved. We in the Mk-48-1 program were well behind when I joined the group, but we soon overtook our competition. I was fortunate to be able to play a major role in the 48-1 and successfully led the first two war-shot firings of the new torpedo off Bangor, Washington, both of which sank decommissioned cargo ships of 11,500 tons with dramatic effect. Two weeks later a special flag officers board selected the Mk-48-1 as the Navy's new torpedo, and it shortly thereafter was approved for production. Modified many times since, that torpedo is still the submarine force's primary torpedo weapon, fifty years later. I received the first of three Legions of Merit when I left the program for my next assignment.

That next job was one of the most interesting in my entire naval career. I was appointed a member of the International Negotiation Division, J-5, of the Joint Chiefs of Staff and six months later became the chief of the division. In the division I had officers of all the military services and worked with many different organizations to formulate sound military positions for the president of the United States and the National Security Council to evaluate. The United States was engaged at that time in the SALT II negotiations with the Soviet Union. Salt II was intended to serve as the means through which a permanent treaty could be reached with the USSR that would limit the number of strategic nuclear systems each side could possess. In that capacity, I was privileged to work directly with the members of the Joint Chiefs of Staff, senior White House Security Staff members (including Gen Al Haig and Hal Sonnenfeldt), CIA and State Department officials, and members of the Senate Foreign Relations Committee, especially Senator Henry "Scoop" Jackson (D-WA), the chairman of the committee. I also was assigned to the delegation under Ambassador U. Alexis Johnson and negotiated with the Soviet representatives in Geneva, Switzerland. The SALT talks were considered to have been the most important negotiations by the United States during the 1970s, and I attended nearly weekly meetings in the White House. In the middle of my tenure, Nixon was forced to resign the presidency and Vice President Ford became president. This caused a disruption in the negotiations, but Ford retained Henry Kissinger as his secretary of state and as national security advisor, and the negotiations did not suffer as much as we had feared.

As a result of the transfer of power to Ford, a rather incredible event took place shortly after Ford became president. Under great secrecy, President Ford and Secretary Kissinger made an unannounced visit to

Vladivostok, where they met with the general secretary of the USSR and his foreign minister. There, in secret, they hammered out and initialed a tentative agreement on nuclear weapons. When Ford and Kissinger returned to Washington, they called a special meeting in the White House to report on what they had achieved. Most of us involved in the SALT II negotiations were amazed at what they had accomplished and were ecstatic. The agreement represented by far most of what the United States had hoped to include in a permanent treaty. However, the Air Force chief of staff, Gen George Brown (later the chairman of the JCS), would not give his approval because of one particular provision. Under the tentative agreement, all air-launched cruise missiles of 600-kilometer range or greater had to be counted as strategic weapons. Brown and the Air Force had long argued that those cruise missiles were not nuclear weapons and were necessary to allow the rather slow, subsonic B-52s to penetrate the Soviet missile defenses. Brown called me to his office to discuss this matter privately. I suggested that he accept the provision, and that it would help him sell to the Congress the need to go ahead with the controversial B-1 supersonic bomber intended to replace the B-52s. He listened but would not agree. The tentative agreement fell apart over this one issue, and the B-1 bomber program was stalled for several years.

When I was reassigned to what would be my final position on active duty, I was awarded my second Legion of Merit. Those citations are often overblown, as we all know, but I was truly pleased to have the citation read in part, "SALT . . . the most important international negotiations participated in by the United States during the last decade. . . . Captain Pollak earned an unchallenged reputation as the leading military expert on SALT, both in the military and in other government agencies operating with the National Security organization."

In 1975 I reported to commander, Naval Electronics System Command. I was assigned initially as the deputy program manager for special communications but six months later became the program manager. This was a designated "Major Program" office, with responsibility for the development, production, and support of all submarine communication systems and all special communication systems for all services involved in nuclear weapons readiness and release. I had seventeen separate programs, but two were of particular interest.

The first was Seafarer, an extremely low frequency system that would have allowed submarines to remain deep while receiving messages. Because of the extremely large antenna system that would have been required, the system became an environmental issue and I was featured on the TV program *60 Minutes,* then at the height of its popularity. Interviewed by Dan Rather, I was pitted against a controversial Veterans Administration hospital doctor in a rather unflattering manner. *60 Minutes* failed to indicate that the National Academy of Sciences had unanimously agreed that the system offered no significant threat to the environment. The program was canceled shortly before I retired.

The second program of interest was the design and development of a new, integrated, computer-controlled radio room (IRR) for the Trident submarine, which was then under development. The IRR represented a quantum leap in submarine communication capabilities and became a major feature of the Trident submarine force.

I retired from the Navy in January 1979 after twenty-six and a half years of commissioned service, after having accepted a position as vice president of Research and Engineering for a large division of Gould, Inc., a company that at the time had eighteen thousand employees (it was later sold to a French company, split into several sections, and sold piecemeal). I then worked for Honeywell in Minneapolis in their Defense and Marine Systems Group and, finally, as senior vice president of DRS, Inc., a military electronics corporation.

In 1987 I retired a second time, and my wife, Anne ("Annie"), and I moved on board our fifty-one-foot staysail ketch, the *Reverie.* We lived on board for fourteen years, ten of those outside the country, and visited dozens of foreign countries. Our favorite was Brazil, where we spent three and a half years, sailing as far south as Florianopolis, just a few hundred miles north of Uruguay. Altogether we logged over 36,000 miles on *Reverie* before I ran into some health problems and we needed to "swallow the anchor" and move ashore.

We settled in a small town, Walterboro, South Carolina, in 2002. About that time, I became a very dedicated Kairos Prison Ministry volunteer. This led to ordination as an Episcopal priest (now an Anglican priest) and appointment as a prison chaplain in the South Carolina Department of Corrections. I have volunteered in several prisons in the United States and in Uruguay, worked extensively on South Carolina's death row, and been employed for the past six years at a medium-security prison of about twelve hundred inmates. In Kairos, an international organization of 35,000 U.S.

volunteers alone, I served for six years on their board of directors, including a term as vice chair.

Of some interest, perhaps, I was ordained a priest at the age of seventy-nine and a half, the oldest man ever so ordained in the Diocese of South Carolina. Now, approaching age eighty-four, I am by far the oldest employee at my prison, the Ridgeland Correctional Institution, and am still serving two churches. As the Germans say, "We get old too soon and smart too late."

I am often asked when I intend to finally quit for good. That is solely in the hands of the Good Lord. I will know when it happens. In the meanwhile, I am greatly enjoying my life and savoring each and every day.

Diesel Boats Forever

Red Stein

For those submariners who never made the transfer from diesel to nuclear boats, "Diesel Boats Forever" (DBF) became the phrase that marked a particular and unique segment of seagoing sailors of every rank. That uniqueness was consistently characterized by a novel sense of humor. The first thought that comes to my mind when I hear diesel is the fact that our identity ashore was never in doubt. As the Japanese young ladies ashore would say upon meeting, "Ah, sensokan sailor!" The diesel smell was always there. Stories galore.

Who needed a shower every day? One every five days is good enough. Hemorrhoids be dammed. Pity our stewards, who usually occupied the "bridal suite" under the torpedo loading hatch in the forward torpedo room. But they were food handlers who had to shower daily.

What do we remember about Naval Submarine School? Perhaps escape training made a major impact. How could so many squeeze into such a small space and then share it with water lapping at our chins, trying to cope with the temperature and pressure? And how do you keep blowing air out as you ascend in that tower of water when you feel there is none left in you? Experience helps. I recall that when taking command of *Sea Fox* (SS 402) in Pearl Harbor and leaving the next day for WESTPAC, the crew was undergoing escape training. At the end of the routine effort, some six sailors had failed the test and were given another opportunity to excel. I decided to join them and help them to relax. They did, and on it was to Yokosuka the next day.

Most people question our ability to handle claustrophobia. Did you ever feel claustrophobic? they ask. My response? Once as a junior officer while in overhaul, with the responsibility of inspecting bilges, tanks, and other remote beams and plates for proper preparation for painting, I got wedged in number 2 sanitary tank. I couldn't move. For about ten seconds I felt trapped. Gaining control of my emotions, I forced myself to relax and maneuvered to free myself. A lesson learned.

On board my first boat, USS *Quillback* (SS 424), home ported in Key West, I experienced several firsts. The most important was a storm encountered traveling south from the Iceland-UK gap, after patrolling north of Sweden and Norway. The intensity of the storm was severe. We rolled fifteen degrees while submerged at a depth of 150 feet. It was impossible to snorkel at normal depth. We were forced to snorkel on the surface with the head valve cycling periodically. While on the bridge as officer of the deck, the lookout and I were strapped in with telephone lineman belts and had to hold our breath for ten to fifteen seconds when underwater. I finally convinced the skipper that we would be more efficient on the periscope in the conning tower. We had to make an emergency stop at New London. We had lost all of our antennae, the number 2 periscope, radar mast, forward messenger buoy, forward torpedo loading hatch, and the door leading from the main deck to the bridge. We communicated through copper tubing strung from a stub of a whip antenna to number four cleat.

The only benefit from the storm and stop in New London was that it permitted the crew to buy Christmas gifts for their children. Since I had grown a beard during the patrol, I was designated Santa Claus. I stood atop the bridge as we entered Key West, waving to the children. It was humorous to see the children as they came on board trying to make up their minds who to greet first, Dad or Santa Claus.

Being in Key West was an experience in itself. First there was the Truman White House. This meant a multitude of correspondents during his visits. Where were they quartered? The same sparse Bachelor Officers' Quarters where we were quartered, of course. So returning from weekly operations in the area, we found our belongings stacked in the corridors. Can you imagine that happening today? And then there was Judge Esquinaldo and his brother, Lawyer Esquinaldo. And there was Lieutenant (j.g.) Stein and his sailor charged with DUI. So we paid Lawyer Esquinaldo three hundred dollars, appeared before Judge Esquinaldo, and my sailor kept his license. I was not unhappy leaving Key West for a tour in New London as an instructor at the Sub School.

During my tour as executive officer of USS *Blackfin* (SS 322), we were assigned a patrol in the Bering Sea to determine what our Soviet friends were up to. Early in this effort our formal patrol was terminated and we were directed to visit various islands in the Aleutians to determine what port could be used by a nuclear boat to put a sailor ashore in response to an emergency. We visited Shemya, Adak, and Kodiak. We had to take a helicopter from Adak to get to Shemya. When we landed, red foxes greeted us on the runway. Shemya was impossible for mooring or anchoring. The commercial runway is the point of no return for flights between the United States and Japan. Of course, Adak and Kodiak were perfect for emergencies, and the torpedo facility at Kodiak was in mint condition, but there were no torpedoes in sight.

Contrary to normal operations in 1962, *Blackfin* was assigned to the Eastern Pacific. While we serviced reserve submariners out of Port Angeles for several weeks, we were also assigned the difficult duties of participating in the Seattle World's Fair, the Portland Rose Festival, a patriotic festival in Newport, Oregon, where a Coast Guard chief acting as our pilot swam to our side in a wet suit and came on board to guide us to our pier. However, the major event was in Long Beach, where we helped Doris Day make a movie, *Move Over, Darling*. Tough duty! A brief visit to Victoria had the added pleasure of a reunion with several of my Canadian Sub School students. Yes, we shared food on board *Blackfin* and cocktails on board the Canadian submarine.

During my tour as skipper of *Seafox*, 1965–67, I had two noteworthy assignments that were totally different in nature and results. The first was a search-and-rescue mission of some thirty days in the Gulf of Tonkin. The maximum depth of water in our assigned area was 150 feet. The nights were pitch black, and dozens of local junks surrounded us. We couldn't see the junks, but fortunately they knew where we were, charging our batteries. It was a foolish mission, but when classmate Bill Hipple and I expressed our concern and evaluation of the operation, the sub group commander in Yokosuka reminded us that we were no longer at the Pentagon. Shut up and do what you are told. However, the mission was canceled shortly thereafter.

Of a much more interesting nature was a patrol in the East China Sea of forty-seven days. The timing was most fortunate as it coincided with a major Chinese submarine exercise. While at that time we would consider the exercise modest in intensity and scope, it was complicated enough to foretell of things to come. When I briefed the mission at the Pentagon, the newly appointed OP-095 brushed off my evaluation. But I think time has proven me correct.

Perhaps one of the more memorable events of my last submarine deployment was seeing Mary Martin and cast performing *Hello, Dolly!* for the troops in Okinawa. The field house was packed and all were on their feet cheering as Martin sang the title song. I invited Martin and cast to visit *Seafox*, but time was too limited. Later I received a note of thanks and I responded by making her an honorary crew member of the sub. The relationship culminated when Lonnie and I attended a performance of *I Do, I Do* with Mary Martin and Robert Preston in New York City and were invited backstage to meet with Martin. She could not have been warmer or more cordial. We were greeted like family. An autographed record of hers hangs proudly in my den.

So what is the essence of diesel submarining? People. The commanding officer, exec, junior officers, chief of the boat, telephone talker, seaman first class. The relationship that brings together a crew in a united purpose. Where an offhand compliment can change a person's life. While our lives were unique, the lessons learned last a lifetime. Thank you, Dusty Dornin, for showing me the way.

Alpha Strike on Hanoi Rail Yard

Jerry Zacharias

CDR Lowell F. "Gus" Eggert, USN, Commander Carrier, Air Wing Nine, embarked in USS *Constellation* (CV 64) (Official U.S. Navy Photo)

Operation Linebacker was the name of a U.S. Seventh Air Force and U.S. Navy Task Force 77 air interdiction campaign conducted against North Vietnam from 9 May to 23 October 1972, during the Vietnam War. Linebacker was different from the previous operation against North Vietnam, Rolling Thunder, in that Linebacker would be a maximum effort to destroy major target complexes in the Hanoi and Haiphong areas and isolate North Vietnam from its outside sources of supply by destroying railroad bridges and rolling stock in and around Hanoi and northeastward toward the Chinese frontier. High on the priority list were primary storage areas, rail marshaling yards, and transshipment points. On the first day of Linebacker, the Navy shifted its attention from targets in South Vietnam to strikes in the Haiphong and Hanoi areas.

On 10 May 1972, classmate CDR Lowell F. "Gus" Eggert, USN, led a major strike near the capital city of Hanoi. As commander, Carrier Air Wing 9 in USS *Constellation* (CV 64), Gus briefed and led an alpha strike of thirty-five fighter and attack aircraft to the railroad switching yards at Yen Vien, northeast of Hanoi. In the face of intense antiaircraft and SAM missile firing, Gus led the strike group in dive bombing runs that destroyed a major enemy railway center. Exiting the target area, Commander Eggert's strike group was attacked by approximately sixteen enemy MiG aircraft. In the ensuing dogfight of less than twenty minutes, five enemy planes were shot down. As strike leader, it was Gus's job to get the attack aircraft out and vector the fighters in to intercept the MiGs, and he did it with superb skill. Later, Eggert had the additional chore of directing the rescue combat air patrol (RCAP), which successfully retrieved a pilot from waters of the Tonkin Gulf. It was subsequently determined that this was the largest air-to-air engagement of the entire Vietnam War. Eggert contributed immeasurably to the success of this mission and was awarded the Navy Cross for his heroic and successful leadership.

Gus Eggert served on active duty from 6 June 1952 until 1 September 1984, retiring in the rank of rear admiral. During that time, he accumulated 6,280 hours of flight time and 876 carrier landings. His aviation commands include the following:

- CO, VA-192 "Golden Dragons" flying the A4F
- Commander, Carrier Air Group 9, embarked in USS *Constellation* (as the CAG, Gus flew every type aircraft in the air group from the ship—A7, F4, A6, RA5, SH60, E2 and EA6)
- CO, USS *Denver* (LPD 9)
- CO, USS *Constellation* (CV 64)
- Commander, Fleet Air WESTPAC

Gus Eggert is the most highly decorated member of the Naval Academy Class of 1952. His combat awards include the following:

- Navy Cross
- Silver Star
- Two Legion of Merit medals with combat "V"
- Two Distinguished Flying Crosses
- Bronze Star
- Twenty-five flight/strike mission Air Medals
- Presidential Unit Citation

Some Naval Vignettes

Paul J. Mulloy

I was ensign/lieutenant (jg) on board USS *Wasp* (CV 18) until May 1954. Cruised the North Atlantic, Caribbean, and Mediterranean and was in the Korean War. CIC and finally officer of the deck. First OOD watch: starboard cat launch, jet limped off, landed in sea. I ordered all engines stop, rudder amidships. The command duty officer wanted to shift the rudder. I didn't. The brow hit the pilot's inboard thigh, bounced him off bow wave and alongside. The angel helo picked him up. Fast forward twenty some years. Outside the office of the vice chief of naval operations, I, a captain, hear this stentorian cry: "Hey you son of a bitch, you ran over me with a carrier." Doors opened as all hands watched. This tall rear admiral picked me up and said, "You saved my life, Paul, by not shifting the rudder."

Flight school. VF/VA-172 flying the beautiful F2H2 Banshee. Collapsed a lung. Transferred to VP-18, fast-tracked to patrol plane commander. Split deployment to Sigonella as the detachment's operations officer. A Soviet sub was reported somewhere near USS *Des Moines* with President Eisenhower embarked. I launched and descended to below one hundred feet, radar off. Went behind an island, came out other side, and turned on radar. Snorkel sighted. Dropped buoys and alerted *Des Moines*, which took off at flank speed.

I taught P2-V pilots how to use the two Banshee jets attached to the P2-V7 wings. Caused a flap at NAS Roosevelt Roads using jets and then applying full prop power at takeoff. Tower hit crash alarm and the CO had a "word" with me. By the way, it worked well, if you needed it. It was patrol plane standard operating procedure to have them on for all takeoffs and landings.

Aide duty. Naval Postgraduate School, master of science (management) degree. BuPers detailer and placement assignments for almost all shore duties. Aircraft and ships for operational duties.

Next was VP-44 as operations officer. Screened for command. I reported to Utapao, Thailand, as an officer in tactical command and prospective XO of VP-26 just as the Tet offensive was starting. Our force

168

consisted of five crews and three P-3As, in company with some fifty-two hundred USAF folks operating B-52s and tankers. We were the "nit noi" (Thai for "little") navy. Within six weeks we lost two aircraft and crews. One known enemy shoot down and another suspected. Much shock in squadron and around VP world and especially families. Patrol planes don't get shot down. Our great carrier shipmates up on Yankee Station do. I flew to Cam Ranh and requested a complete change to the rules of engagement. Commodore "Swift Boat Fame" Hoffman agreed. No more losses and detected two enemy supply vessels. An alpha strike took out one and a Coast Guard cutter off Cambodia blew the other away. Commander in chief, Pacific Fleet signaled "greatest naval surface victory of the war."

Incidentally, we used to put B-52 guys on our P-3 flights to Bangkok. A B-52 was too conspicuous. As a friend of the Air Force general commanding the B-52s at Utapao, I was allowed to fly in a B-52 to Khe Sanh and pickled the 150-bomb load on the North Vietnamese army divisions. The pilot was our classmate, a great guy named Bruce Morrin. B-52s are an awesome bird and weapon. The battle damage assessment photos looked like huge lawn mowers had crisscrossed the enemy positions. Marines indicated that the North Vietnamese panicked and ran into their machine-gun emplacements trying to get out from under.

Next I split deployment between Keflavik and Lajes. As CO, I was directed by CINCLANTFLT to be the OTC of four VP squadrons and an SSN and track a homebound Soviet ballistic missile submarine from Bermuda to the Iceland gap, the Navy's version of *The Hunt for Red October*. Tracked him for several weeks, expending thousands of sonobuoys and flight hours. Once, both our P-3s and the SSN lost him. A chief and I were reviewing sonograms and acoustics. I heard a strange sound. "What's that?" The chief replied, "Porpoise." I said, "Back down about ten hours."

My piano training came into play. There it was again. "Hit the chart," I said. "Chief, porpoises don't do 010 degrees, twelve knots." I told the on-station P-3 where to drop a sonobuoy barricade, and there the boomer was, churning away. With the president being briefed daily to see, if pressed, we could do the job, this had been a cranial compression! The operation was of top national importance and interest. Off Bermuda, estimated missile flight time to the United States was about seven minutes. The sub skipper received a Distinguished Service Medal. As OTC, I received a Legion of Merit, VP-26, and the sub and crew received Navy Unit Commendations.

Selected early for captain, I was offered a VP wing command. I asked about a ship and was assigned command of USS *Ponce* (LPD 15), one of the newest. I didn't know the pointy end from the blunt end. *[Editor's note: U.S. submaRIners will tell you that subMARiners are naval aviators trying to drive a ship.]* The *Wasp* experience and teachings by the chiefs were superb tutorials. I truly enjoyed the challenges and pleasures of ship command. The nukes and aviators have the edge on officer and enlisted personnel. The weapons and nuclear reactor on the nukes mandate it. In aviation, wrapping the rubber bands the wrong way can be fatal—and certainly with carrier ops. So our beloved black-shoe brethren get the rest. Properly motivated, I found them to be superb and wonderful shipmates. It was a mutually enjoyable tour.

Ponce could only make sixteen knots. She hadn't fired her guns in three years. Her safety and combat readiness were unsatisfactory. However, with some selective training and one hour a day for education, realistic drills, liberty at 0800 vice 1600, and reduction of captain's masts from every week with many to once a quarter with few, she shaped up beautifully. Guns fired frequently—including letting Marines have a mount to share. Gear lockers were complete, including ammo types. And the best Navy chow. She eventually reached twenty-two knots. Many of the engineering improvements were adapted by Surface Force Atlantic. She met some challenges. That included the first LPD of either fleet to pass the engineering board exam. Also, she was the favorite "gator" of the USMC.

Some other *Ponce* notes:

At sea in the Med. Shadowed by a Soviet frigate for over a week. One night at 2:00 a.m., he crossed our bow and blasted his searchlight onto our bridge. I came on the bridge, ordered all engines ahead flank. Signalmen manned the two twenty-four-inch searchlights and stood by for my command to hit his bridge with both. I came across his bow about one hundred yards distance. "Sigs! Now!" His ship was bathed with light. Then the bow wave rocked him like a cork and drenched his topside. He reversed course and disappeared.

Off Crete, a Russian cruiser and *Ponce* were anchored for several days, both at an advanced state of readiness condition. We were alerted to events in Lebanon. We held a swim call and cookout on the flight deck. Lowered the gig and, with an ace enlisted Florida water skier towed aft, circled the cruiser. We returned the CO's salute with raised glasses of wine while clad in bathing suits and ball caps and accompanied by a couple of our officers and chiefs (Navy and USMC). Skier had raised a ski in a salute . . . or was it an obscene gesture? They had sailors chipping away and others with machine guns. But when we came down the opposite side, they had secured all hands from topside. I don't think they could take the implications of our confidence and relaxation while obviously ready with or without the CO embarked.

Next was Bremerhaven. We were berthed supporting our embarked 3rd Battalion, 6th Marines. They engaged the German army in battle exercises for over a week. After an all-night forced march, our grunts were hungry, cold, rain-soaked, and furious. At 5:00 a.m., screaming and cursing, they ran through and over the German tents and literally routed their troops. The next day the German general and I called on the mayor. I was provided an interpreter as the entire exchange was in German. Afterward, the general marched down the steep steps expecting his vehicle there with corporal and open door. My vehicle and driver were available, so I offered the embarrassed General a ride. "Ja, danke," he said.

About five minutes down the road, he exploded in English: "I'm going to crush that SOB driver!" I remarked how convenient the English. "UCLA, two years," he replied. He also stated that the TV carried quite a bit about our "Leidernicken" Marines who wear the loop of the Croix de Guerre awarded to the Marines in World War I. He also stated they never expected the Marines to hit them that night. They had moved their troops by truck and couldn't believe the Marines would force march such a distance in such weather. He was sincerely impressed with the Marine warrior spirit. Semper fidelis!

Command of Amphibious Squadron 6 followed, with enjoyable experiences at sea and in port in the first Spanish-American amphibious exercise ever conducted. Midway through, I transferred command to the Spanish admiral for the landing. That was deeply appreciated. All went well, and again friendships were bonded. By the way, the Spanish are real sailors.

I thoroughly enjoyed going to sea on ships and pushed the talented VP officers to follow. Many did and were recognized for their performances and potential; several are now flag officers and most recently one was promoted to four stars and is the commander, Pacific Fleet, ADM Harry Harris. A Tufts Fletcher School of Diplomacy postgrad, he is very bright and personable, a multi-experienced flag.

Commander, Patrol Wings Atlantic Fleet. Back with my beloved P-3s and their talented officers and men. I was concerned about the accident rate and malaise. Asked Lockheed to reinstate Jay Beasley, the Lockheed master pilot trainer of all. He noted the same bit of arrogance and complacency. I instituted unannounced Naval Air Training and Operating Procedures Standardization full flight and written exams. Mandated procedures for airborne check rides. None in the simulator. Brought back happy hours with a proviso to include the brides after 5:30 p.m. Connubial tranquility. Expanded junior officer mini-deployments for leadership experience and opening some new diversion fields. One was a trip to Martinique with the SACLANT French admiral on board. Swapped a reconnaissance sweep around the general's island for occasional visits by the P-3. He concurred. On the return flight, a petty officer second class up for reenlistment asked if he could get back to Martinique. While the Dutch guarded the aircraft at the other end of the island, the crew wandered down the beach and ran into a Club Med, where the ladies in birthday suits invited them in for toddies and snacks. I said if you ship over now on this flight, I'll get you back in two weeks. He did. I did. During that tour, the accident rate was zeroed, 100 percent combat readiness for all deploying squadrons, and top reenlistments, and so on. Loved those lads and brides.

Final tour as assistant chief of naval operations (human resources) (OP15/Pers6.). Upon arrival, CNO Tom Hayward tasked me with cleaning up the drug mess of the eighteen- to twenty-four-year-olds—the Navy and USMC were 48 percent positive (Army, 40 percent; USAF, 20 percent). We initiated a ten-point program I called a "War on Drugs," a name that made the media and alerted the ACLU. President Reagan wanted it in all services and in the government after we demonstrated unusual success. Drug usage dropped to 8 percent on my watch, and for the past twenty-five years it has been about 0.015 percent. It is probably the Navy's most successful people program in terms of combat readiness, morale, retention, and advancement in rate. Indeed, the Navy's program was the world paradigm. I made good on "Get rid of the drugs, not the people." Less than 1 percent of the service members were discharged. We gained their trust and system credibility, and they responded. For example, we expanded people programs from seven to seventeen, including Family Service Centers.

F/A-18 Hornet

The Early Years

Corky Lenox

I t is rather rare for a major procurement program of military significance to be forced on one of the nation's military services, particularly
a service that, at the time, was engaged in the early phases of a similar program. Serendipity reigns when the unwanted program emerges in
later years as a principal asset in that nation's arsenal. This is the story of the
beginning of such a program.

A Breech Birth

The United States Air Force began an air combat fighter (ACF) program in
the early 1970s. Shortly thereafter, the Navy was directed by the Office of
the Secretary of Defense (OSD) to initiate its own naval air combat fighter
(NACF) program. At that time the Air Force was already in the early years
of the production of the F-15 fighter, and the Navy was just starting the
production run of the F-14 Tomcat. The Air Force soon became a strong
proponent of their new "lightweight fighter" program while the Navy was
quite satisfied with the ongoing F-14 aircraft program and not enthusiastic
about starting another fighter program.

The Navy response to the OSD direction was to look at a derivative design of the F-14 that would not have the Phoenix long-range missile. Upon submitting this idea to OSD, the Navy was directed to return
to the drawing board. The second Naval Air Systems Command offering
was another derivative of the F-14A but with more weight removal and less
complexity. This offering also was not well received by OSD. At this time, I
was the head of the Carrier Aircraft Branch in NAVAIR, the technical lead
for all carrier-based aircraft programs.

Subsequent direction from OSD to the Navy was to start a NACF program concurrent with the Air Force Lightweight Fighter Program. Neither
of the competing contractors on the Air Force program, General Dynamics
in Fort Worth, Texas, and Northrop in Hawthorne, California, had designed
and produced a carrier capable aircraft for the Navy during the jet age.
Consequently, they each were directed by OSD to team with a contractor

with Navy carrier–based aircraft experience. General Dynamics (GD) then teamed with Texas' Ling Temco Vought (LTV) and Northrop teamed with McDonnell Aircraft (MACAIR) of St. Louis. This teaming was followed by OSD direction to the Navy to continue with the NACF program, contracting with one of the two teams to develop the Naval Air Combat fighter.

Observing the progress of the Air Force Lightweight Fighter Program made it clear that the Air Force heavily favored the GD aircraft over the Northrop aircraft. When I visited the Air Force's program office and met the test pilots for both the GD YF-16 and the Northrop YF-17, it was clear that the YF-16 was the favored program and aircraft.

There may have been several factors at work regarding the ultimate selection of the GD entry in the Air Force competition. First, the F-15 was having serious problems at the time with the F-100 engine. Since the F-16 entry would use the F-100, any additional development funding could be of significant assistance in the engine program. A second point of interest was that the Air Force had not selected a Northrop aircraft in any tactical aircraft competition since the Air Force had become a separate organization. Additionally, while the Air Force and the Navy could benefit from a smaller, cheaper tactical aircraft, the Texas influence could not be ignored. The deputy secretary of defense who issued the direction to initiate the two lightweight fighter programs was a former governor of Texas. The chairman of one of the powerful committees of Congress was also a Texan. And other strong Texas politicians were expected to be weighing in on the best solution for the Navy.

There were strong opinions held by certain Air Force senior officers at that time, supported by a few influential former Air Force officers, who maintained that the nation needed a superior air combat fighter, one that could defeat any other aircraft in a daytime fighter-to-fighter dogfight (still remembering Vietnam). To that end, the initial design of the ultimate winning entry in the ACF program, the General Dynamics F-16, was focused on high maneuverability, light weight, and superior overall aerodynamic performance, but it had no night or all-weather capability. In fact, Gen Alton Slay, commander of Air Force Systems Command, in later testimony supporting the selected F-16 design before a congressional committee, said, "Not a pound for air-to-ground." I know that is a fact, for I was there, supporting the Navy's selection of the McDonnell/Northrop aircraft for the Navy.

From the beginning of the NACF program, the Navy's interest was to ensure that the new aircraft would add significant capability to the air wing deployed on Navy carriers. The Navy then decided to include both air-to-air and air-to-ground capabilities, coupled with all weather capability, in this new aircraft program. Thus there was an early departure from the apparent OSD intent to create two similar versions of one multiservice, lightweight tactical fighter. We continued to advance the theory that carrier aviation at sea gets involved in "come as you are" conflicts and is unable to call for specialized support, whereas the Air Force can always sense a change in the operational environment that may cause them to "send more fighters" or "send more bombers" to the combat area.

Request for Proposals and Proposal Evaluations

Jack Linden (director, NAVAIR Proposal Evaluation Division) and I (Air 5102, Aircraft Branch) wrote the technical portion of the request for proposals (RFP) for the Naval Air Combat Fighter based on the requirements in the unpublished Navy Fighter Study IV. This RFP established the performance, reliability and maintainability (R&M), and logistics support requirements for the development of the F-18. The rationale for these requirements was to challenge industry to reach the peaks of the then realistic and attainable quality and performance levels of the various technologies without asking for the invention of high-risk features. Thus the objective was to optimize capability while allowing for growth. The main exception to this approach was the establishment of very difficult-to-reach levels of R&M. While earlier tactical aircraft procurement programs focused on aerodynamic performance, this program held R&M requirements equal with aerodynamic performance requirements. We knew that contractor pride would deliver the specified aerodynamics, while industry had to be convinced that the Navy was serious about R&M.

The Navy specified reliability in mean flight hours between failures (MTBF) and maintainability in mean man hours per flight hour (MMH/FH) to be significantly better than the single mission A-7E, the tactical aircraft with the best R&M in the fleet at that time. The good news was that the selected F-18 met these very difficult challenges. Further, the forecast number of squadron maintenance personnel for the F-18 was less than for the A-7E and significantly less than the F-14. These parameters would, and later did, lead to lower operating and maintenance costs in the fleet.

The Navy strongly suspected that the OSD leadership, the Air Force, and certain members of Congress were trying to influence, if not force, the Navy into selecting the preferred Air Force (and Texas) solution. Language in the congressional appropriations bill, for example, directed the Navy to use the Air Force Lightweight Fighter Program "hardware and technology to the maximum extent" in its new aircraft program. It could hardly be any clearer. However, senior levels of the Navy specifically directed the Proposal Evaluation Team to ignore politics and to select the best proposal for the Navy.

While the various parts of NAVAIR worked the programmatic and design problems from initial design ideas through the evaluation of contractor proposals, the senior Navy leadership dealt with high-level officials in OSD and in the Congress, educating them on the unique capabilities required in naval systems in at-sea conflicts as distinct from the daylight fighter concepts in the Air Force program. They explained the needs of the Navy and the way this new aircraft could be cost effective as well as combat effective for our fleet forces.

The contractor teams assigned the Navy-experienced contractor as the prime for the Navy program. Thus LTV and MACAIR were the prime contractors for the Navy F-18. Those two contractors, therefore, designed and submitted proposals to the Navy for this new aircraft. (We learned later that Northrop gave broad freedom to MACAIR to use any portion of their F-17 design and to be in complete charge of their team's proposal for the Navy program. On the other hand, it appeared that General Dynamics maintained a strong oversight of LTV's design for the Navy aircraft and the proposal to the Navy.)

After the detailed evaluation of the contractor proposals, both were considered to be unsatisfactory in meeting the overall requirements established by the Navy request for proposal. A procedure was approved wherein we would invite each contractor to send a two-man team to listen to a summary of the NAVAIR evaluation of their proposal. Any specific requirements the contractor did not meet, based on the NAVAIR analysis, would be highlighted. There would be no exchange of views; this was strictly a "one way" meeting where the Navy would talk and the contractor would listen. Meeting with a contractor during proposal evaluation was a most unusual procedure. However, detailed rules for the meetings approved by the legal specialists were established. Each meeting was scheduled for, and took about, half a day. We cited the requirement, the contractor's proposed solution or number, and the Navy's evaluated number and, if appropriate, how our number was derived. The contractors were given a couple of months to revise and resubmit their final proposals.

Jack Linden and I represented the technical disciplines on both the Proposal Evaluation Committee and the Source Selection Board. The final evaluation was summarized with a list of requirements and how well each proposal met those requirements. The MACAIR proposal was clearly the better overall response to the RFP. Among other items, the carrier suitability design for the LTV proposal was deficient, high risk, and clearly unsatisfactory.

Configuration Evolution

Initially, there were two distinct configurations to be developed: fighter and attack. The F-18 fighter variant had fewer external stores stations, a lower maximum weight, and a different, lighter landing gear. The A-18 attack variant was slightly heavier than the fighter and was expected to have ground-attack radar and the external stores stations and delivery systems that would differ from those in the fighter. Internal systems and cockpit configurations and displays, as well as some of the ground support equipment, would necessarily be different.

As the detail designs of the various aircraft systems were being examined and alternatives considered following the source selection, the radar design requirements and capabilities were being refined for both the fighter and attack designs. There was some external pressure for the Navy program to select and use a modification of the analog type radar that had been selected by the Air Force for the F-16. Such a selection would necessarily require an upgraded design of that radar to add in the required air-to-ground capabilities. In the meantime, Hughes Aircraft had been working on a digital-based radar design. When the Navy radar engineers examined the Hughes program, they found that with a digital-based design, as opposed to analog, it would be possible to include software for both air-to-air modes and air-to-ground modes in the same hardware. The possibility that all F-18 and A-18 aircraft could have the same radar and be equally capable in fighter and attack missions was very appealing.

Careful study by the NAVAIR engineers showed that installing the Hughes radar would be the first use of a digital radar in a tactical aircraft and would be higher risk as compared to a more mature analog design, but the overall mission versatility would be worth that risk. It proved later to be a wise decision as the reliability of digital designs improved along with increased mission capabilities. Once the decision was made for a digital radar, other systems were examined. Ultimately we ended with digital based designs in almost all of the electronic systems. There was a significant payoff with increased overall reliability and the transition to just one aircraft configuration. Thus, detail specifications were upgraded and all aircraft produced for the flight test and development program and those later rolling off the production line for fleet fighter and attack squadrons were identical in both hardware and software. Significantly, there would now be only one set of ground support equipment.

The increased combat capability provided by this multimission aircraft in the air wing at sea, as compared to the original plan to have separate and specific designs of an F-18 and an A-18, would be difficult to calculate. The financial savings of having only one aircraft configuration, one set of ground support and test equipment, one logistics support system, and one training system were never calculated, but the savings are considered to have been very significant. Tactical aircraft in later years have been designed to skillfully perform both air-to-air and air-to-ground missions. But the Hornet program was the first Navy program to realize those benefits.

As the design and development of the various subsystems progressed, we formed working groups (WOGs) composed of pilots and maintenance personnel from both fighter and attack squadrons in Navy and Marine units. For example, we formed an "Electrical WOG" of eight or ten officers and enlisted maintainers from fleet units who had electrical systems experience with various types of aircraft and were dedicated to making aircraft maintenance easy and understandable. The WOGs met periodically with the contractor to review designs, subsystem test procedures, and other factors, depending on the design or manufacturing phase the program was in at the time. Likewise, there was an engine WOG that reviewed all aspects of engine installation and maintenance, whether on aircraft, in the shop, or being installed. Other WOGs addressed the fuel system, lighting, hydraulics, ground support equipment, and so on.

One of the most active WOGs and one with the most variety in pilot experience was the cockpit WOG. These pilots came from various Navy and Marine backgrounds, including F-4, A-4, A-6, A-7, and F-8 aircraft. Cockpit displays and switches were different among these aircraft. We wanted pilots who were to fly the F-18 series to be able to take advantage of the best kinds of displays, including lighting, and the most logical arrangement of instruments and switches. User friendly. As one might imagine, there were some intense discussions on "switchology." For example, should it be on when moved up or left or on when moved down or to the right? Is it a black indication on a yellow background or the reverse? How about radar controls for this multicapable air-to-air and air-to-ground radar? Needless to say, there were strong opinions. But we would not let them finish the visit and debate until they argued it out and there was agreement among all. The design was then finalized regarding cockpit design, symbology, and arrangement. And the contractor produced what the fleet wanted rather than the usual process of producing what the contractor's engineers thought best or easiest.

All of the working groups were well aware of the challenging reliability and maintainability requirements for the aircraft, and they made valuable contributions toward achieving those requirements. The formal cockpit design review some months later was completed with almost no critical comments or recommendations. The overall benefit of the use of fleet pilots and maintainers to review and comment during all phases of development was that the first several aircraft produced for the flight test program were relatively mature from an overall configuration standpoint and there were very few changes recommended or incorporated during the development and early production phases of the aircraft.

The Hornet

In late 1976, several months after the full-scale development contract was signed with McDonnell Aircraft and the establishment of PMA-265, discussions began regarding the popular name of the aircraft. Concurrently, the effort to merge the two designs and produce a single configuration capable of both fighter and attack missions was already under way. As the discussions continued, several names were bounced around. Finally, in a lengthy conversation with a highly respected Navy test pilot, the name "Hornet" was suggested. We agreed that this name not only was a well-known name in naval history but also represented advances in both maneuver and striking power.

The name Hornet was then proposed to and approved by the commander, Naval Air Systems Command. Later discussions confirmed that OPNAV would recommend to the Chief of Naval Operations that the new multimission aircraft be named Hornet. The CNO submitted his recommendation to the secretary of the navy in February 1977, and the latter approved the name Hornet on 1 March 1977.

The policies under which the Hornet was designed and developed emphasized the importance of reliability and maintainability as equal with performance. At the same time, detailed quality inspections down to the piece-part level ensured that reliable parts were used in subsystems development and manufacturing. Overall, the Hornet design was one that required clever advances in technology but refrained from loading the initial design with numerous requirements that brought high risk to both the cost and schedule of development. The careful incorporation of "doable" technology along the way provided a steady improvement in overall aircraft performance.

The design and manufacture of the R&D aircraft in the development phase of the program followed standard practices, with certain aircraft designated for examining specific aircraft configuration requirements and others focused on evaluating flying qualities, structural integrity, performance, and carrier suitability. Reliability and maintainability, as mentioned earlier, were qualities of specific interest and challenging requirements. Thus maintenance practices and logistics support details became highly visible during both development and early production phases, as all factors related to keeping the aircraft flying interacted.

The arena of reliability and maintainability turned out to be one requiring both attention to detail and innovation. As one example, early in the development phase certain electronic subsystems had a higher than acceptable failure rate. After considerable investigation, we found that the normal practices were to subject the "black boxes" to a range of vibration testing but at normal ambient temperatures, and then separately test in a range of temperatures while sitting statically in the temperature chamber. We found that there were no manufacturing standards for testing various vibration requirements through a range of temperatures. In other words, there were no shake tables within an oven or freezer. We then required the suppliers to develop more comprehensive testing capabilities. This same attention to detail was required of all subcontractors in the development of subsystem components.

A second illustration of component testing that revealed reliability problems in electronics systems involved very small piece parts from suppliers, some of foreign origin. In many cases, the cause of a failure during component testing of certain subsystems was the failure of a capacitor, resistor, or an integrated circuit component. As an element of our pursuit of reliability, one of the subsystem suppliers examined some of the small failed parts by taking them apart. They found that some of them were incomplete, with a small piece part with leads or connectors sticking out of each end but empty inside. These parts revealed what appeared to be a clear intent to manufacture and deliver incomplete parts, but an intent that could not be proven. As a result of this experience, we required all suppliers to test down to the piece-part level. Mysteriously, both the major subcontractors and the component suppliers on the F/A-18 program found that subsequent to that requirement they seldom received counterfeit or failed component parts. Wonder where they went?

A lesson learned: reliability must be designed in, beginning at the lowest piece-part level, continuing through subsystems, and measured carefully in operations of the entire aircraft. Aircraft reliability is an inherent characteristic that is created at the design point; it cannot be "grown in" successfully at later stages of development. Desired levels of maintainability are likewise designed in. There must be easy access to parts that can be replaced, a minimum variety of special tools, accurate on-board testing of subsystems, well-defined procedures for all maintenance actions and record keeping, and clear, understandable training for each discipline.

The ground and flight test programs for the Hornet included eleven aircraft, two of which were two-seat versions. During this period the design qualities, structure, performance characteristics, and all systems were thoroughly tested using standard development procedures for the airframe, installed systems, and the engine. Many of the expected types of problems were found, and as in most development programs, several surprises and mysteries were also encountered along the way. Successful development test programs encounter many problems. And that is a good thing, for there are many unknowns in complicated systems in addition to the features that are well designed and problem free. Thorough testing reveals weaknesses, confirms systems meeting design requirements, and helps to define certain limits for the operational employment of a system. As more complex systems are designed, the probability is high for more unknowns to be found. Thus planning that is more detailed and testing that is more thorough will find more of the unusual or mysterious failures. The designers, testers, and leaders who are dedicated to fixing problems encountered along the way, rather than finding excuses for them, will produce a more successful end product.

Special recognition must be given to the General Electric Engine organization for the outstanding development program for the F404 engine. General Electric was, from the beginning, highly dedicated to producing a reliable engine. They took no shortcuts, accepted no excuses, and refused to believe they could not find the cause and solution for any problem, no matter how deep they had to dig to find it. They were very open about problems and solutions and had the total confidence of the Navy's program management.

Much of the success of a military system engaged in the stresses and surprises of the operational environment will depend on the disciplines under which it is developed. The Hornet program contractors, prime and sub, were dedicated to meeting the very high level of the R&M requirements for their multimission aircraft. And the record shows that they met the challenge.

The Naval Strike Fighter

Once we were well under way with the development program of this tactical aircraft, which would be employed in both fighter and attack roles on the Navy's aircraft carriers, it became clear that we must have some kind of term or name for the aircraft that would succinctly relate to its multimission capabilities. During a discussion with a friend about this dilemma of how to quietly inform the public about the significant combat capabilities of the Hornet, we arrived at the term "strike fighter," representing both air-to-ground strikes and air-to-air combat. The challenge then was how to get this nickname approved. I decided not to publicize or ask for approval but to simply begin to use the term. We began with the cover sheet of a monthly report to Congress. Where we normally had used just the name "F-18" on the coversheet, we began to show it as "F-18 Naval Strike Fighter." Nobody asked about this name, but we then slowly began to use it in correspondence and titles of briefing sheets. Use of the name spread, and "strike fighter" is now a universal term.

Opposing Forces

There is always opposition to new ideas and products. Usually it is low level and short lived. In some cases, however, the opposition can be extremely strong and long lasting. The Hornet program had full experience of the latter. It was a program initiated at the Defense Department level, not initially requested by or endorsed by the Navy, and it was in direct competition with ongoing aviation programs within the Navy. Naturally, the operating elements of naval aviation were slow to accept this new program. There was doubt that the lower costs and specified higher levels of R&M would be achieved in this new aircraft while it absorbed valuable R&D and procurement funds that would be better used in ongoing aircraft programs. It took years for the Hornet to gain broad support and become generally accepted within naval aviation. In later years, however, it has become a model program of on-time/on-cost production with steady improvements in combat capability. Years later, through three decades, the Hornet has remained an "on cost, on schedule" program. There appears to be no other major defense program that can make that statement.

The strong opposition to the Hornet, led by certain elements of the aerospace industry and within naval aviation, was active for all of the development phase and through the early production phases of the program. While criticisms were sometimes accurate, they generally were inaccurate or even false. There was no shortage of active opposition within the naval aviation community, but that is not surprising as we remember slogans in the past such as "When you're out of F-8s, you're out of fighters" and "A-4s forever."

A senior writer for *Aviation Week Magazine* called one day, giving me a "heads-up" that he would send, for my information and prior to publication, an article he had written on the Hornet program. Years earlier we were friends when he was a Navy lieutenant and we were in the same air wing. Upon reading the article, I found that it had numerous errors, most of which were damaging to the Hornet program. I called him to inform and complain, giving specifics. He paused for a lengthy moment and then told me the article would be published as written. I wondered who wanted the misinformation to be published and had sufficient influence to see that it was.

The U.S. Naval Institute *Proceedings* magazine published an article, with author credits to a Navy lieutenant, that was critical of the F-18 and contained misinformation and numerous errors. The lieutenant turned out to be a radar operator in a Grumman E-2C early warning aircraft. He probably had some help in writing an article about the aerodynamic performance and combat capability of the Hornet.

About two years into the development program, I received from the Government Accountability Office, for review and comment, a draft copy of a lengthy report on the F-18 program that was classified secret. It had numerous errors related to the features and capabilities of the F-18 Hornet. Three days later, a copy of the same draft report, with the "Secret" stamps covered over, was used by the CEO of a U.S. aerospace company in a briefing for the defense minister of Canada. I wonder how he obtained his copy.

The above comments illustrate the broad range of misinformation that can be used to discredit a program. For continuing success of the program, every publication of misinformation must be challenged immediately with the true facts. A significant amount of a program manager's time can be spent putting out fires set by bad news bears.

Early Production

There were several iterations of procurement planning and funding for the initial production lot of two, four, or six Hornets. The Office of the Secretary of the Navy finally approved a plan for procuring four preproduction aircraft. While we would have preferred a larger number of aircraft, the approval of an even small amount of production funding was a significant milestone that gave us assurance that the program was probably well past any point where it might have been canceled. And it gave us adequate time to resolve any leftover issues. With that milestone accomplished, my tour as program manager was ended.

Postscript

Not mentioned in the above comments, but an essential factor in the success of the Hornet program, was the presence and influence of VADM Forrest (Pete) Petersen. Admiral Petersen was the commander of the Naval Air Systems Command and my immediate boss during the last three-plus years of my tour as the program manager for PMA-265. He was a very bright individual, a tough taskmaster, and a strong supporter of the Hornet program. I enjoyed having his confidence. We first met when I was the air wing commander on board USS *Enterprise* (CVN 65) on a combat tour during the Vietnam War while he was captain of the ship. Beyond some of the less pleasant calls to report to the bridge, we had many discussions about leadership, including his relationship with Admiral Rickover and his experiences with the admiral while CO of *Enterprise*. Needless to say, that was a graduate education in followership.

Having had that experience with him on board *Enterprise* gave me a big head start in working for him five years later as PMA-265. He was always open to discussion about any problems or challenges we had in the program. He gave me a long rope, not a close tether. The result was that we took chances, challenged opponents, managed to the smallest detail, admitted problems when they occurred, and sought help when needed. Pete Petersen was the best leader I ever worked for. He mentored me, taught me a lot, backed me through some important challenges, and deserves great credit for the success of the Hornet program.

[Editor's note: The F/A-18 has been the U.S. Navy's first-line combat aircraft for the past thirty years or so, evidence of the superior planning and efforts of Rear Admiral Lenox, a model for all acquisition programs.]

The Sixth Fleet, June 1981–July 1983

Bill Rowden

I took command of the Sixth Fleet in June 1981. We were preparing for an August live-fire exercise for surface-to-air and air-to-air missiles against drone targets. The south-central air space in the Mediterranean being the least congested with air travel, it was chosen for the exercise. The exercise was well planned and had been briefed throughout the chain of command in Europe as well as Washington, including the president, and was set for mid-August.

The southern edge of the exercise area was inside the northern boundary of the Gulf of Sidra but well clear of the six-mile internationally recognized territorial water boundary of Libya. However, Libya disagreed on the grounds that the Gulf of Sidra constituted a "closed territorial bay" and therefore was Libyan territorial water, and Libya would not permit the United States to operate there.

The Sixth Fleet force included two aircraft carriers, antiair-capable surface ships, several support ships, nuclear submarines, and overhead air surveillance aircraft. Five Combat Air Patrol stations were each manned by two Navy fighters during daylight hours. All required safety notices had been filed well in advance. A number of firing runs of surface-to-air and air-to-air missiles were made on the first day of the exercise with little to no response from Libya.

The next morning, as the force was readying for the second day of live firing, two Fitter aircraft were noted in the air near Tripoli, heading north into the exercise area. Two southern CAP station F-14s were vectored to intercept and warn them off if necessary. Near intercept, the Fitter radar was noted to change from search to acquisition. Almost immediately, the Libyan aircraft both fired on the approaching F-14s. This was certainly an overt hostile action, deadly in intent, and the F-14 flight leader properly responded by firing Sidewinder heat-seeking missiles that shot down both Fitters. On subsequent review, the action taken by our aircraft was confirmed to be well within the U.S. rules of engagement. The episode effectively ended the exercise, and the Sixth Fleet assumed a defensive posture. I advised the Soviet Mediterranean force commander of the situation, on a special circuit established for such situations, and recommended he have his AGI clear the area, which he did. There being no further action by Libya, the exercise was disbanded and the units returned to their regularly scheduled operations.

I knew that generally, in any operation of the fleet, one's concern is with what may not go well, the application of Murphy's Law. In the Libyan exercise, the potential for not going well appeared quickly.

I overheard a conversation among some aviators who were rehashing the Libyan affair when one stated, "We sure were lucky with that A-6 that was jumped by a Libyan aircraft." I asked for particulars and was told that on the first day of the exercise, an A-6 was flying alone toward Benghazi when the pilot discovered he had a Libyan fighter on his tail. The A-6 dove for the sea surface and immediately turned in the direction of our carrier. The Libyan broke off and nothing further occurred. My immediate question was how did the A-6 get into the air when it was clear to all that the live-fire exercise did not include any need for bombers. A crowd had gathered by this time, and there was a lot of mumbling and shuffling of feet until someone said, "We just wanted the attack guys to have some of the action." I said something about stupidity and headed for the aviation leadership. In a lengthy discussion, I emphasized that that incident, had it turned out any other way, would have completely wrecked the fleet's performance in the recent exercise and would have discredited the Navy. The response was gratifying as was the lesson learned.

The remainder of 1981 was generally routine, which gave me the opportunity to understand better the territory within which the fleet operated and how we were expected to interact. Our presence was a significant positive influence among our friends and supporters in the Mediterranean Sea and Black Sea. It was clear that our NATO allies welcomed and supported us, and from Italy to Gibraltar, there was peace and stability. It was the eastern Mediterranean that was the hot spot during the tenure of my command.

The small country of Lebanon borders Syria to the north and east and Israel to the south. Populated by Christians and Muslims, Lebanon had a stable government until the growth of the Muslim population began to create an imbalance that led to unrest and contention. This situation, coupled with the resurgence of militant Islam throughout the Muslim countries, caused southern Lebanon in particular to become a state within a state, occupied by the Palestine Liberation Organization, which had fled from Palestine into Lebanon. When rocket barrages fired from southern Lebanon became intolerable for the people of northern Israel, the Israeli government sent Israeli forces across the border on 6 June 1982. The goal was the destruction of the Palestine Liberation Army (PLA), which controlled most of southern Lebanon. The invasion was swift and effective, and in several days, the PLA was decimated, its remnants fleeing to Beirut with the Israelis in pursuit.

The Sixth Fleet was directed to station its amphibious force off the Lebanese coast near Beirut. The force comprised four or five amphibious ships commanded by a captain and a heavy battalion of Marines embarked commanded by a colonel. Although this area was outside the NATO area, both France and Italy provided forces in and around Beirut as the operation progressed. Their involvement fit comfortably with that of the U.S. forces.

The American embassy at Beirut became heavily involved in negotiations to end the violence, get the withdrawal of Israeli forces, and restore order. The level of involvement quickly ratcheted up to Secretary of State George Schultz and Secretary of Defense Casper Weinberger, who visited Beirut several times. I was in Beirut frequently and certainly when either of these officials arrived. I was kept fully informed and abreast of developments there.

A significant portion of the PLA had taken refuge in Beirut, and it was agreed that their removal from the area was in the best interests of all. About half were to be sea lifted by ferry to other receptive Mediterranean countries, while the remainder were to be taken by land over the mountains east of Beirut into Syria, starting in mid-July.

At this same time, I was directed to "land eight hundred Marines" to reinforce and "stand behind the Lebanese army" as the PLA were removed. Because we were committing forces ashore in a situation of near or actual armed conflict, we needed to establish rules of engagement for the troops involved. Several issues required clarification. First and foremost was the objective of the operation. Marines are organized and trained to "take and hold" ground. But the general thrust of this operation, according to guidance from Washington, was to establish and maintain a "presence" in the area. Lacking a precise definition of presence in military terms, we then had to consider whether Marines should be armed with personal weapons and, if so, should they carry ammunition for the weapons. An overarching directive from Washington was "not to start World War III." After considerable wrestling with the subject, we produced acceptable rules of engagement. We briefed the troops on the mission and sent about a company of Marines ashore in July.

Bivouacked near the Beirut Airport, the Marines had no mess facilities and ate cold C-rations for breakfast and lunch. One of the amphibious ships prepared hot meals for dinner, which were loaded into a truck. The truck was then ferried ashore and the troops had a hot meal for their evening repast.

I observed one of the PLA evacuations by ferries. Marines with side arms stood behind each Lebanese soldier guarding the departure route. Truck loads of PLA arrived, and as they dismounted, some of them fired their weapons into the air as if celebrating their departure. There was little discipline among them. It was a miracle that no hostilities occurred during these rather dangerous operations.

The evacuation occurred near what was called the green line, which passed down the center of Beirut from the port south, separating Muslim eastern Beirut from Christian western Beirut. Many of the buildings near the port were marked with numerous bullet holes from earlier conflicts; many had broken windows and other wreckage of war. One Marine commented that the area looked like films of World War II. How true an observation.

Secretary Weinberger was present when the PLA evacuation was completed. He asked when we would be able to take the Marines back to the ships; we told him about one week hence. He departed Lebanon, and upon arrival in Washington, he ordered the troop withdrawal. They were back on board by early September 1982.

Negotiations seemed to be progressing, but any progress was short lived. Shortly after the Marines were withdrawn, the Israelis invaded western Beirut and brought in Christian militiamen from southern Lebanon whose homes and families had been ravaged by Palestinian militiamen several years before. The Christian militiamen were turned loose in the south of western Beirut, where two refugee camps, Sabra and Shatila, were located. They rampaged through the camps looking for any Palestinian militiamen to attack, and finding none, they turned their rage upon the hapless refugees residing there, with savage results. French, Italian, and U.S. forces were again brought in to restore order, and the Marines returned to their previous encampment near the airport.

The Marine landing was unopposed. Causeways were installed, and ships were unloaded on the causeways and beyond. The hot meal routine was reestablished, and the area took on the aura of a secured beachhead.

The rules of engagement had to accommodate the "presence" directive from on high. A perimeter was set and guard posts were manned, but orders came that prescribed that weapons were to be carried unloaded. The Marines did the best they could to establish a properly outfitted camp. Eventually, mess and medical facilities went ashore, as well as artillery, but there was doubt about placing tanks ashore. So for thirty days, the colonel placed a note at the end of his daily report to Washington of his intention to take the tank platoon ashore at the end of the thirty days. There was no reaction to the note, so the tanks went ashore on schedule. Then Washington erupted with "whys and what fors," but when we reminded them of the daily note, the questions subsided and the tanks remained a part of the force ashore.

As time went on, the Sixth Fleet ships carried on with their deployment schedules and we were careful not to neglect the rest of the Mediterranean. I moved the flagship, a destroyer tender, into the eastern Med to assist the ships permanently stationed there with maintenance. I also ordered the destroyers to keep well trained in the art of gunfire support, although they could not actually fire any projectiles. We were not allowed to interact with Israeli forces in any manner without permission from the embassy, a change from earlier operations when we frequently visited Israeli ports.

The situation in Beirut seemed to be improving, with some tension remaining, but negotiations appeared to be in earnest by all parties. Not being involved in the negotiations, I directed my attention mostly to the structure of our forces, their care and performance. Fall temperatures reminded us that winter was approaching and we needed to arrange better shelter for the troops. The Marine colonel in command mentioned that he had examined an abandoned two-story concrete building in the airport area, so after gaining permission to occupy the building, the Marines moved in. It was early fall of 1982, and I attended the Marine Corps birthday celebration in that building on 11 November 1982.

On 18 April 1983, the American embassy in Beirut was attacked by a truck loaded with explosives; the truck penetrated the front of the building and exploded. The entire building, less its rear wall, was completely demolished, killing seventy-three people, including seventeen Americans. In an area where such attacks were not new, this was considered another terrorist incident. It should have been a bellwether for our defense at the building near the airport.

Accompanied by my wife, Sally, I made my last visit to Beirut in June. We stayed with the deputy chief of mission at his home in western Beirut. I recall visiting a Marine artillery site and was briefed by the young Marine in charge on how his battery operated. He was a fine example of the caliber of Marines we deployed to Beirut.

I was relieved of command of the Sixth Fleet in July 1983. I left the fleet with a measure of confidence and satisfaction in what I had learned and had put into practice for a forward-deployed fleet. This satisfaction was shattered on 23 October 1983 by the destruction of the "Marine barracks" in Beirut by a suicide bomb truck causing hundreds of casualties. How should I have provided for better defense measures for those exceptional troops as we prepared for winter quarters? Why didn't we wring more appropriate protective action from the embassy bombing incident? I'll never really know the answers to these and many other questions, but their absence will haunt me for the rest of my life.

Dame Fortune, the Mistress of Us All

Bill Ryan

I believe that people who have led successful lives imagine that their success was the product of intelligent decisions based on a thoughtful evaluation of available options—the universally accepted concept of how to lead a successful life. In other words, if you make good choices, you should receive good outcomes. I also think that in the afterglow of success, they fail to notice "dame fortune" sitting in the corner with a look that resembles a mixture of smirk and smile. You see, she knows the real source of success. So here is my honest analysis of my professional career. Most of it was based on good fortune. Some people just seem to have been born lucky, and I seem to have been one of them.

Unlike many of my classmates who had to work hard to obtain an appointment to the Naval Academy, all I had to do was travel thirty miles to a small town, meet my congressman on his front porch, and promise not to leave the Academy before I graduated (apparently this is what his last appointee had done). I wrote no letters, took no competitive tests. All I had to do was say yes.

When I arrived at the Academy, I was shocked at the number of intelligent, well-educated young men who were my classmates. I found the scholastic requirements manageable and the regimentation did not trouble me, but I knew that I wasn't going to set any performance records. My overall approach was characterized by acceptance rather than enthusiasm. I continued to be an unenthusiastic member of the Brigade throughout the rest of my four years at the Academy. I still have a letter I received from the commandant of midshipmen during my first-class year warning me of the "precarious nature of my conduct status."

After graduation and an aircraft carrier deployment to the western Pacific during the Korean conflict, I was ordered to Pensacola for flight training (the career preference I had chosen before graduation, principally because it was the choice of "hot-shots"). Although my ground school and flying were supposedly excellent, some incidents during formation and cross-country training, together with my earlier experiences on board the carrier, convinced me that aviation was not the best life for me. I decided to DOR (drop on request) from flight school, a major, high-risk decision. It called into question a number of issues regarding motivation, competence, and so on. Since my record was good, I had to defend my decision before an aviation admiral who, I'm sure, thought I was a total military misfit. The thought also entered my mind.

I was sent back to Korean waters on board a beat-up World War II destroyer. There was plenty of room for advancement when many of the officers departed the ship after the end of the Korean conflict. As a consequence, I rose to department head status quickly. I also qualified as officer of the deck, senior watch officer, and command duty officer.

The material condition of the ship was terrible. The more competent members of the crew were discharged or transferred, and the number of officers was reduced from twenty-three to fourteen. The next western Pacific deployment was hot and hard. By the time the deployment was over, I had decided that I did not want to spend the rest of my life pretending to be a naval officer. Then one day I met a young supply officer, a recent graduate from the Academy, and we discussed his career plans for the future. I was surprised to learn that he had already had two meetings with "Supply Corps officer personnel" and his detailer, and he was still an ensign! He then showed me the standard career path for a Supply Corps officer. All I could see were intervals for graduate school studies and shore duty. I began to wonder if yet another change in my already checkered career would be a good move. Shortly thereafter, BuPers decided that there was a shortage of supply officers and asked for volunteers to transfer from the regular line to the Supply Corps. I applied with the idea that if not accepted I would resign and enter the civilian world. Lucky me . . . I was accepted, along with three other line officers (two became flag officers, the other two retired as captains).

A year at school, a second child, and two years of shore duty followed. And then a bend in the road emerged—orders to a new construction destroyer in Pascagoula (and another child). The idea was exciting to me. Good people, a good job, and I would be the senior officer present (actually, the only officer present). I had confidence borne of experience. I knew destroyer life and organization, and I assumed "command" with enthusiasm.

About six months later, the real commanding officer flew in and I met him at the airport. I was apprehensive because the man himself was preceded by a massive reputation. He had been a company officer during my tenure at the Academy, and while I had never suffered under his well-known lash, many of my classmates had. He was "Key Largo," the "Ghost

Who Walked," the baddest of them all. Then John DeLargy smiled, shook my hand, and greeted me as a fellow officer. Thus began a partnership of mutual respect that continued through my retirement and his death.

I had never met an officer like John DeLargy. He was a consummate professional. Under his command, the ship won every "E" and was the envy of the destroyer force in San Diego. One night, anchored in a heavy fog off Coronado, John decided to risk his ship and reputation by entering port to give his crew long-awaited liberty ashore. His was the only ship to do so, and every man in the crew knew this. What a proud group we were. But this story is not about John DeLargy, it is about how he nudged me into the beginning of my true professional life.

One day, he sent for me in his in-port cabin. He gave me a friendly greeting, asked me to sit down, and then asked me what I wanted to do with my life. I said that I was unsure. He then surprised me by saying that he believed that while I was a good officer, I needed to make a serious commitment to professionalism. He assured me that if I made that decision, I could be a top-notch officer. This was the first time in my life that anyone had taken the trouble to personally counsel me in that fashion. I cannot tell you how surprised and pleased I was. I thanked him and left his stateroom. I then decided to make a lifelong commitment to professional excellence.

When I returned to San Diego after another WESTPAC tour, my wife and I took a few days off and drove down to Ensenada. While there, the executive officer called and said that I had received an invitation to fly to Washington to be interviewed by Admiral Rickover. When I asked the XO for advice, he said that it would at least give me a chance to visit BuPers and view my personnel jacket. So off I went with no idea of the interview process and the potential outcomes. In the event, two of the five in my group were accepted. Truthfully, I was proud to be selected. No one likes rejection.

No one that I know thought the admiral was a likable man, but we all respected him and learned from him. He was amazingly effective, with an uncanny understanding of the sources and use of power, and I don't mean nuclear power. In my mind, his ability to bridge the gap between science and engineering was well beyond all others in his time. The man was a true Titan. He actually created an industry—by brute force and cleverness, if you wish, but he did it. We think of him as the Father of the Nuclear Navy, forgetting that he was also the Father of Commercial Nuclear Power. The first application of nuclear power for commercial power generation was the Shippingport Plant, and it was designed and developed by Bettis Atomic Power Laboratory under his direction.

So I did the job, "stayed Alive for Five," and became mentally tough. I can't remember being easily cowed by people or events after my tour with Naval Reactors. It was not an easy five years. Our hours were long and hard, and we worked Saturdays. Leave was rare and short, and we never wore a uniform. (I can remember one of my sons picking up my officer's cover and asking me what it was!) While the penalty for unacceptable performance was high (only two of the seven supply officers who entered the program that year survived—the other five were summarily transferred), the rewards were exceptional. Most people don't realize that supply officers were heavily involved in the business side of the Naval Nuclear Propulsion Program. Budgeting, contracting for reactor plant components and nuclear fuel, management of two atomic power laboratories, evaluation of potential sources and source selection—these are the kinds of areas the dozen or so of us were involved in. While the admiral had no organization chart, there were certain individuals who played key roles. Vince Lascara (later one of the very few Supply Corps vice admirals) and Ken Woodfin (another future admiral) were major players in the program's business decision process. I should point out that thirteen Supply Corps flag officers have emerged from that program. No other source that I know of has had that kind of success.

I survived, gained confidence (and some arrogance), and was promoted early. I left the program using the only method acceptable at the time: an assignment to graduate school. When I left school, I went to work for the chief of naval material. I had a fuzzy job and mostly wrote speeches for people. Then a classmate came to my rescue. He somehow managed to get me assigned to a submarine tender deployed to the Holy Loch in Scotland. Now that was a real break. This was the only assignment in the Supply Corps that would permit me to have an accompanied tour overseas because it was foreign sea duty vs. foreign shore duty. After five years in Naval Reactors, I was familiar with the submarine force and many of its officers. The tour was intense but enjoyable. The support for dependents in those days, however, was definitely marginal. We lived "on the economy." Wives and children often came on board to have a good meal, see a movie, and take a hot shower. My wife had to "riddle her Rayburn" (coal-burning cooking stove) each morning. The winter weather was horrible: penetrating wet cold with no central heat. We were stuck with fireplaces, kerosene stoves, and portable electric heaters. High marks, though, for the beer and whiskey and the combination bowling alley–chapel–movie theater–officers' club!

When I returned, I went to the Industrial College of the Armed Forces and then to the Office of the Assistant Secretary of the Navy as the director of procurement for major weapons systems. There was a 1952 cabal in the organization at the time—Red Stein, Gene Avallone, and myself—and the four-year tour I spent in the job was a pleasure in every way. Luckily, this was a "springboard" job for my career specialty, which had historically produced a number of successful occupants (like a supply corps deep-draft command). I was fortunate to become one of them. Almost forgot. The job with the secretariat fell into my lap because its occupant was a good friend who had been selected for flag rank, as was I while there.

Only a very few flag officers manage to evade staff duty for their entire flag existence. Mine started out with a tour in New York as the commander of NEXCOM, responsible for all the Navy exchanges. This was not a job I wanted, but it was a traditional "new boy" assignment and the perks were certainly grand. I was the senior naval officer in the city and lived in massive and beautiful quarters in the Brooklyn Navy Yard. I had a car and driver (almost essential in New York), a worldwide organization, an aide, and a happy wife who loved Broadway theater.

I learned that the Marine general who was commanding the Defense Fuel Supply Center (DFSC) was about to retire. This was a prime job that should rotate to the Navy. Ironically, with a nuclear-power background, I sought the job that managed the entire federal government's fossil fuel program. DFSC was a semiautonomous organization that procured, stored, distributed, and managed the nation's entire requirements for all forms of fuel except rocket fuel: heating oil for camps and bases (including the White House), navy fuel, jet fuel, war reserve fuel stored at worldwide locations in support of war plans, diesel, AVGAS, and even crude oil for the nation's National Petroleum Reserve. In essence, the nation's entire wholesale fuel program. At that time, DFSC also managed the Department of Energy's research program to develop alternative sources for fossil fuels such as those currently being extracted from sand and shale. Although I reported to the three star head of the Defense Logistics Agency, my actual functional boss was a deputy assistant secretary of defense. Ours was a mutually supportive and respectfully maintained relationship for four years, and I would have gladly extended it for four more.

My Marine predecessor had told me that the only difference between DFSC's job in wartime and peacetime was operational pace. He was right. We had a Command Center that could be manned within one hour—and often was. We maintained continual liaison with the State Department and major oil companies, as well as with DOD and the area commanders. We had regional staffs throughout the world, including in London, France, Germany, Italy, the Middle East, Japan, Singapore, Hawaii, and the Philippines. Among other assignments, we were instrumental in supporting British operations in the Falklands and French operations in the Sudan. We managed the logistical support for fuel and heavy cargo for the Aleutians and the North Slope of Alaska. We not only thought "outside the box," we sometimes invented new boxes.

Example: the Sudan job. The only known way to get fuel to Khartoum was a long, nominal, four-inch pipe line that was reduced to a little over two inches in its interior because of fertilizer and sludge flow. The pipeline simply wouldn't cut it. The road that paralleled the pipeline wasn't much better—unpaved, one lane, no "gas stations." Solution: lease fuel trucks through oil companies, ferry them over the Red Sea to Port Said, and get enough jet fuel to Khartoum. Incidentally, solutions such as these were generated by a team of men unlike any others I had previously served with. They knew their territory, they were mature, they were self-reliant, and most of them were graduate petroleum engineers from the Army, Air Force, and the Navy officer corps with extensive experience in their field. Their job was to make sure the fuel that was being received, moved, issued, or stored was "on spec" and to solve problems that arose with quick-reaction capability. My job, frankly, was to settle any disputes, consent to their best recommendations, and otherwise stay out of their way. I am particularly mindful of a lieutenant commander with a German accent (born and raised in Germany) who could go anywhere and do anything, He was definitely not a "parade ground" officer, but he was often my "point man" for difficult situations. The petroleum specialists in the armed services are a treasured hidden asset, smart, experienced, and confident. And very few even know of their existence!

Of all the aspects of the job, the most tension-laden was buying crude oil on the "spot market" for the National Petroleum Reserve. For a period of about two years, DFSC was the biggest buyer of crude on the spot market (competitive bidding for cargoes of crude in ultra large or very large crude carrying vessels rather than buying under contracts based on quantity and term). A team of four (a top-notch lawyer, a crude procurement expert, the head of our worldwide marketing staff—yes, we had one—and I) would form the decision team when a desirable cargo of crude became available. We had very little time to make a decision: buy or pass. The professional stakes were high because the cargoes were large and expensive. A Government Accounting Office team was always on hand to immediately review our decisions because of the unusual nature of the major expenditure and the national and congressional interest in the program. I know of no other program with this level of immediate oversight. Even the GAO praised our work. Needless to say, when the time came, I hated to leave. I had already been extended for a year. An Air Force general relieved me and I was "piped over the side," a happy and genuinely fortunate man.

One last note is in order. RADM John DeLargy attended every one of my change of commands and my retirement ceremony. I attended his funeral as a pall bearer, and the subsequent funeral of his beloved wife, Maggie. As you see, ours truly was a lifelong relationship.

From Land-Locked Norwegian
to Naval Aviator

_____ *W. D. (Bill) Knutson* _____

A North Dakota, land-locked Norwegian, Bill Knutson received an appointment to USNA that would change his life forever. After graduation in 1952, Bill stayed at the Naval Academy to indoctrinate the incoming plebe class before going directly to naval aviation training. He went through the VF pipeline and earned his wings on 3 February 1954 in the same group with Jim Lovell. It was disappointing for Knutson and Lovell to get orders to VC-3, a night fighter squadron at Moffett Field, California. It turned out to be a career enhancing assignment.

VC-3 provided five pilot (four aircraft) detachments for Pacific Fleet carriers to perform night missions. The night fighter teams from 1948 to 1954 were made up of second-tour experienced pilots. In 1954 commander, Naval Air Force Pacific Fleet decided to try newly winged pilots, called "nuggets," from the training command to see if they could handle night missions. In the screening process, it was found that Lovell and Knutson had high flight grades, especially in instrument flying. After fleet all-weather training at Barbers Point, they were assigned to Team "Jig" flying the F2H-3 Banshee. Team Jig made a very successful WESTPAC cruise on the USS *Shangri-La* (CVA 38) in early 1956. While deployed, VC-3 had become VF (AW)-3 and assigned a new mission as the transitional training unit (TTU) for the sacred six of the new swept-wing aircraft that were entering the fleet: the FJ Fury, the F-3H Demon, the A-4 Skyhawk, the F-4D Skyray, the F-7U Cutlass, and the F-8U Crusader.

The TTU was the forerunner of the replacement air group concept, which trained pilots in specific fleet aircraft before they went to their fleet squadron. Initially, the TTU took a cadre of pilots and maintenance personnel from a squadron transitioning to a new aircraft and trained them so they could train the rest of the squadron. Knutson and Lovell were initially assigned to the F-3H Demon training program but were checked out in all the other types of aircraft. It was a tremendously broadening experience to fly all the latest aircraft. The greatest training was given us by being associated and learning from fellow squadron mates like Tom Hayward,

199

Wally Schirra, Don Shelton, and Jig Dog Ramage, our CO. They motivated and inspired us to be professional and encouraged us to become Navy test pilots.

After two years in the TTU, Lovell and Knutson went to Test Pilot School at Patuxent River, Maryland, and graduated with Classes 20 and 21, respectively. Knutson was assigned to the Service Test Division, where he conducted high-altitude performance tests in the F-8 and F-4 aircraft at altitudes of 70,000 to 90,000 feet and flew through hundreds of thunderstorms to determine the effects that heavy, super-cooled water had on jet engines in the F-3H, F-8U, and F-4H aircraft.

Orders back to sea duty seemed, on the surface, a disappointment to Bill Knutson. Orders to CVW-6 as the CAG LSO (air group landing signal officer) was not the fighter squadron duty he had hoped for as a test pilot right out of Patuxent. He had never been an LSO. The Bureau of Naval Personnel said that with the high-performance F4, A6, and RA5 joining the air wings, they wanted test pilots who had flown all of them to bring them on board the carriers safely. CVW-6 was assigned to USS *Enterprise* (CVN 65), the first nuclear carrier, and immediately participated in the Cuban Missile Crisis. For the first ten days of the crisis, attack aircraft were fully loaded and briefed to destroy all the military targets in Cuba. The order to launch never came, and the crisis ended with the SA-2 missiles being shipped back to Russia.

The Vietnam War started in August 1964, and the USS *Independence* (CV 62) was immediately scheduled from the Atlantic Fleet to help fight the war and had the first A6 Intruder squadron (VA-65) in its air wing. Knutson was assigned as the ops officer of VF-84 flying the F-4B Phantom. The Vietnam air war had many restrictions, and for the most part the fighter squadrons were less than pleased to have the secondary air-to-mud mission, dropping bombs and shooting rockets. Ammunition and missiles were in short supply, and every one of them had to be used to maximum advantage. In particular, the heat-seeking Sidewinder missile that had accounted for all MiG kills so far in the war was a scarce item.

On 18 September 1965, there was a report that enemy PT (patrol torpedo) boats had gathered at a small harbor on Hainan Island and were prepared to make a high-speed run at the carriers to try to sink them. A night strike was quickly planned, with A6s doing the bombing. The F-4Bs were along as flack suppressors to drop flares and provide combat air patrols. We dropped flares over the bay and the island harbor and the attack commenced. My F-4B division rolled in firing Zuni 5-inch rockets at the antiaircraft gun sites that had opened fire on the A-6s. There were several waves of flares and attacks. Finally, our F-4s were out of rockets and the A-6s were getting hit hard by the antiaircraft. I felt helpless, but I did have two Sidewinder missiles. In desperation, I rolled in on an AAA site, got a missile tone, and fired my Sidewinders. I don't know if they hit, but the AAA site stopped firing. One of my best friends, CDR L. F. "Mike" Vogt, was shot down and killed in his A-6. The raid had destroyed and damaged some of the PT boats, and the rest sped back to mainland Vietnam. I got chewed out for expending air-to-air missiles at ground targets, but it was well worth helping my comrades.

Selected for command, I joined VF-33 in 1966 as XO to classmate John Mitchell, who was the CO. VF-33 deployed in 1967 on board USS *America* (CV 66) for a Mediterranean cruise with Sixth Fleet. When the Arab-Israeli Six-Day War broke out, *America* was called to the eastern Mediterranean on high alert. On 8 June 1967, *America* was anchored in Suda Bay off Crete doing a nuclear weapons loading exercise when a flash message reported that Rockstar (USS *Liberty* [AGTR 5]) was under attack. I was standing the five-minute alert in *America* in an F-4B. We were immediately launched and given a vector to Rockstar but without real information of what the attack was about or how far away the battle was. We started at max speed, but when we found out that Rockstar was off the Sinai coast, we throttled back to max range power. Before we had traveled a hundred miles, we were recalled with no explanation. *America* steamed south all night and I flew a CAP mission over *Liberty* the next morning. It was a sad sight to see a ship listing and with a huge hole amidships. *Liberty* had been attacked by Israeli aircraft, gun helicopters, and torpedo boats. The rumor was that President Johnson sent an order down through Secretary of Defense McNamara to commander, Sixth Fleet Admiral Kidd that the whole incident was not to be discussed, and it essentially was covered up.

VF-33 returned from Sixth Fleet in July 1967 and were immediately told they would get the first F-4J aircraft with a new fire control/radar system, the AWG-10. It would be a short turnaround as the Navy wanted to get the F-4J into combat to try out the new systems. It was my second tour to Vietnam. From the previous tour, I had gained a great appreciation of how the pilots and squadron had to be trained. USS *America* deployed to Vietnam in the spring of 1968, and VF-33 and the F-4J conducted a most successful cruise, with the F4J scoring a MiG kill.

Surprise orders in June 1968 sent me to CCD-9 staff as the strike ops officer on board USS *Hancock*, which was starting her Vietnam cruise. My third Vietnam cruise on the staff was not as much fun or challenging as flying combat missions. Next orders were to the National War College, where I graduated with the class of 1970.

I was selected for Air Wing Command and returned to COMNAVAIRLANT for a short period before taking command of CVW-7 in USS *Independence* in January 1971. *Independence* was deployed to the Sixth Fleet. Chief of Naval Operations Admiral Zumwalt had just instituted the program of lowering the rank of commanding officers, unofficially called the "Bobby Socks program." VADM James Watkins, chief of naval personnel, called and advised Captain O'Rourke, commanding officer, *Independence*, and myself that USS *Independence*/CVW-7 would have the first Bobby Socks air wing. Upon return to CONUS, all the commanders in every squadron were ordered out and replaced with lieutenant commanders. As the first Bobby Socks CAG, I had my hands full administratively. The pilots were all good, but they didn't understand the chain of command. By sending messages bypassing the chain of command, they caused headaches for both the carrier CO and me. All in all it was a successful program, but it didn't last past its first two years.

Naval aviation was going through a big reorganization and was placing all similar type aircraft under a new functional wing commander at the same base. I was chosen to be the first fighter wing commander for the Atlantic Fleet at NAS Oceana. All fighter squadrons were assigned to a fighter wing (FITWING) during their shore duty cycle. FITWING was responsible for manning, training, and equipping the squadrons during their turnaround cycle before rejoining their carrier air wing and ship for the next deployment. The F-14 Tomcat was ready for fleet introduction in 1972 to replace the F-4 Phantom. Fleet introduction of the first four Tomcat squadrons to the Atlantic Fleet was a major evolution and a most successful project.

In 1974, I moved from commander, Fighter Wing 1 to become CO of NAS Oceana and retired from active duty in September 1976. I joined Hughes Aircraft and was assigned to San Diego to coordinate with the Navy all Phoenix missile and AWG-9 radar training and utilization on the F-14 Tomcat. While in San Diego, I was elected chairman of the Tailhook Association in 1990. In 1991, the now infamous Tailhook convention debacle occurred. Tailhook 1991 occurred after two significant events. The first was that American forces, with major help from Naval Air Forces, had completed the Gulf War, defeating Saddam Hussein in the "Mother of all Wars." The returning naval aviators were in a mood to celebrate. Second, Clarence Thomas had just had his hearing for confirmation to the Supreme Court and Anita Hill had accused him of sexual harassment. Over the objection of Congresswoman Pat Schroeder and the National Organization for Women, Thomas was confirmed. Schroeder publically stated that sexual harassment would be a national issue before the end of the year. The Tailhook convention was the next month. LT Paula Coughlin, an admiral's aide who met with Schroeder before the convention, was the "whistle blower."

It was interesting to note that the Secretary of the Navy and Chief of Naval Operations were both at the convention, and I received personal letters from them the next week telling me how professional and informative the reunion was. Three weeks later this same event was the biggest sexual harassment story in the nation. For naval aviators it became an inquisition process. Any active duty officer who attended was under investigation. Some five hundred active duty officers were not promoted and literally forced to resign simply because they were there. As the chairman, I also had to assume the office of president of the organization. As such, I spent five years preparing for and going through the fourteen lawsuits against Hilton Hotels and Tailhook. There were late-night/early-morning parties that got out of hand involving a few young naval officers in the hotel. However, everyone at the convention was painted with the same broad brush of guilt. It was a media frenzy.

All the alleged sexual harassment occurred in areas of the hotel not under Tailhook control. Counter to our desires in the case, our insurance carrier settled out of court with all parties. The Tailhook Association never had a chance to exonerate itself at trial.

The incident was the impetus for Tailhook to institute better administrative and security measures. The association has regained its position as the premier professional naval aviation organization and is again fully supported by the Navy.

Clear the Deck, Bird Dog on Final

Larry Chambers

O n 31 March 1975, just four days after I had assumed command of USS *Midway* (CV 41), she and her escorts got under way from Yokosuka, Japan. Commander, Carrier Group 7 RADM W. L. Harris, a former commanding officer of *Midway*, embarked just prior to sailing as CTG 77.4. I had been looking forward to this moment ever since that day in March 1954 when I made my first carrier landing. I had finally gotten the job that all naval aviators aspire to during their careers. I was CO of an aircraft carrier and I was elated!

We had just arrived in the operating area east-southeast of Honshu late on the morning of 31 March when our team was put to its first test. We had commenced refresher landings for Air Wing 5 pilots who needed to get back in the air after a lengthy in-port period. With light winds out of the east, we steadied up on a heading of 135 degrees to get the wind down the angle deck for the recovery of aircraft.

On the horizon, the lookouts reported visual contact with a surface combatant on a relative bearing of 340 degrees. This contact correlated with a "skunk" that had been previously reported by the Combat Information Center. The CIC had picked up this contact at 30,000 yards and had been tracking it on a collision course with *Midway*. The pulse quickened on the navigation bridge when the signal bridge reported an ID for our "skunk": a Russian man-of-war. I had always firmly believed that the Russians kept book on our ships and their COs. Ever since their trawlers had been harassing our ships on the high seas, I had observed that those COs who gave way were continually harassed while those who held firm were seldom confronted by the Russians.

I ordered the signal bridge to inform the contact that we were a U.S. Navy carrier conducting flight operations and that site should remain clear. Under international law, since a vessel launching and recovering aircraft is restricted in maneuvering, all other vessels should remain clear. Because of light surface winds, we were steaming at twenty-eight knots to get wind over the deck for flight operations. Needless to say, the Russian frigate did not acknowledge my signal, but she appeared to pick up speed and the bearing started to drift to the right. At a range of 10,000 yards, the OOD computed that the contact had a closest point of approach of 1,500 yards. At 7,000 yards range from *Midway*, when it appeared that the frigate could cross my bow safely, she commenced a hard turn to her starboard. After completing a 180-degree turn, she appeared to go dead in the water (DIW) just as she was recrossing my bow. She ran up the international signal that indicated that she had experienced a breakdown and was not under command. (Under international law, other vessels are required to remain clear of a vessel not under command.) I thought to myself that those SOBs were out to test me and I'd cut them in two before I gave way.

Simultaneously with the Russian going DIW, the air boss informed me that an F-4 Phantom was in trouble and wanted to land immediately. He alerted the flight-deck crew that he had an emergency in progress. The immediate recovery of the Phantom became my first priority. I had no time to play games with a Russian man-of-war. The tension on the bridge continued to build, but there was a sigh of relief when I informed the OOD that I had the conn. The relief, however, was short-lived. The tension returned instantly when I ordered the helmsman to steer nothing to the right of 135 degrees and proceeded to bear down on the Russian frigate, which was now dead ahead. When it became obvious to the Russian that I had no intention of altering course, he immediately hauled down the breakdown signal and cleared my bow, emitting black smoke with screws churning and a big swath of foam and green water. He was passing abeam to port at less than three hundred yards when the Phantom with the hydraulic system failure landed on board. The Russian fell astern, and the OOD asked as I returned the conn to him, "Skipper, at what range did you intend to alter course to avoid a collision?" While I did not answer his question, it was never my intention to give way to a Russian man-of-war.

In early April 1975, the situation in Cambodia and Vietnam worsened. Violations of the cease-fire agreement increased in frequency and the South Vietnamese government was on the verge of collapse. As the military and political situation continued to deteriorate, we received a heads-up from commander, Task Force 77 that our battle group might be needed in the South China Sea or the Gulf of Thailand to augment the U.S. forces that were already on station and that we should make preparations to return to Vietnam.

En route to Subic Bay, *Midway* was ordered to embark two Marine Corps helicopter squadrons that were based on the island of Okinawa for further transfer to USS *Hancock* (CV 19) and the helicopter carrier USS *Okinawa* (LPH 3). *Hancock* was just west of Guam and had entered Seventh Fleet's area of control. She had received orders to proceed to the South China Sea at best speed, and we understood that when *Hancock* arrived in the vicinity of the Philippines, she would offload her tactical air wing and embark the Marine helicopter squadrons, two of which we were assigned to ferry from Okinawa to the Philippines. To make room in *Midway* for the Marines, Air Wing 5 assets had to be positioned ashore at NAS Cubi Point.

On the morning of 5 April 1975, we anchored east of Okinawa in Buckner Bay and loaded on board the aircraft and personnel from HML-367 and HMA-369. After the pickup, we departed Okinawa at high speed of advance for a rendezvous with *Hancock* in San Bernardino Strait. On 13 April 1975, we transferred the Marines to *Hancock* in the mouth of San Bernardino Strait. Upon completion of the transfer, *Hancock*, under the operational control of commander, Task Force 76, RADM D. B. Whitmire, proceeded to Southeast Asia to stand by for Operation Eagle Pull along with other ships of Task Force 76. (Eagle Pull was the code name assigned to the operation that evacuated Phnom Penh, Cambodia.) After we exited the strait, we resumed our attack carrier posture and headed for Subic Bay. I thought at the time that we were only hours away from receiving orders to proceed to the Gulf of Thailand or the South China Sea to join the carrier groups already on station off the coast of Vietnam, and I was glad that it was *Hancock* that was becoming a helicopter carrier and not *Midway*. I wanted to get into the action, but I wanted to be there as part of Seventh Fleet's Carrier Striking Force.

Even though the situation in Southeast Asia was tenuous, *Midway* was allowed to enter Subic Bay on 15 April 1975 for a scheduled ten-day upkeep, but we were instructed to maintain a four-hour readiness posture for getting under way. We did not like what we were seeing in the intelligence summaries, but we had a list of emergency repairs that needed attention. We envisioned that we could get many of them done while maintaining the readiness posture. In spite of our optimism, the military and political situation in Southeast Asia was not getting any better. Eagle Pull was executed, and on 18 April, just three days into our scheduled ten-day upkeep, *Midway* was ordered to get under way immediately and proceed at maximum speed to the coast of Vietnam.

Prior to leaving Subic Bay, we stacked the hangar deck with as many Air Wing 5 aircraft as it would hold and offloaded the rest of our tactical aircraft plus several hundred crew members to make room on board for our upcoming mission. After we departed Subic Bay, my immediate problem was to get the fire rooms and the main machinery spaces put back together as rapidly as possible in order to get the old girl up to speed. The engineers did a fantastic job, but it seemed like forever before all four shafts were making turns in excess of thirty-one knots.

After our full-power run, we arrived off of the southern tip of Vietnam on 20 April, and were joined by ten U.S. Air Force HH-53 helicopters from the 56th Special Operations Wing. With the arrival of the HH-53s, *Midway* changed to CTF-76's operational control. When I was assigned to Admiral Whitmire's group, I joined *Hancock* as the other attack carrier that had assumed the duties of an LPH (amphibious assault ship [helicopter]). Like all good naval officers, we knew how to execute orders, but speaking for myself, I had hoped to participate in these operations under CTF-77's operational control as one of the attack carriers, not as an LPH. I was disappointed at first; however, my disappointment was short-lived. I should have anticipated that with Admiral Whitmire, a former All-American football hero from Alabama and Navy, as my new leader, life in the fast lane certainly was not going to be dull, routine, or boring.

The Air Force helicopters that came on board *Midway* were part of the 21st Special Operations Squadron and the 40th Aerospace Rescue and Recovery Squadron. Together we spent the next eight days preparing for Operation Frequent Wind, the evacuation of Saigon. Although *Midway* was not called on to support Eagle Pull, we all had hoped that neither Frequent Wind nor Eagle Pull would be executed. On the other hand, during the next eight days, we spent all of our time making preparations to execute Frequent Wind. We increased the frequency of all emergency drills and conducted thorough briefings of all hands as to what each of our roles would be. We rehearsed every possible drill that we thought would enhance our readiness in the event that we received orders to execute. In our preparations, we handpicked a group of our sailors and Marines and trained them to process evacuees, should any arrive on board *Midway*.

As the intelligence reports were predicting, the military and political resistance in South Vietnam collapsed. On the morning of 29 April, while we watched and waited, a South Vietnamese Air Force UH-1 helicopter landed on board *Midway*, and with deep sorrow I recognized the vice president of South Vietnam, Gen. Nguyen Cao Ky, when he disembarked on my flight deck. At that moment, I knew it was all over, but it was not until 3:30 that afternoon that we received orders from CTF-76 to execute Operation Frequent Wind. *Midway* launched nine HH-53s for the landing zones in Saigon. These helicopters shuttled back and forth from Saigon to *Midway* all that afternoon and on through the night until early morning of 30 April, often staying on board only long enough to offload evacuees, refuel, and switch crews. None of these Air Force helicopter pilots had ever made a night carrier landing, and I was deeply concerned for the safety of the air crews, the evacuees, and my own flight-deck crew. I had hoped that the evacuation order would come early enough in the day that we could complete the job before nightfall; but as the hours ticked by, I was cursing my luck that we had not had enough time to train the Air Force pilots in night carrier operations. My worries were all for naught—the U.S. Air Force pilots really came through when the chips were down. Not only did they get to make their first night carrier landings, but before the night had ended, they had also shuttled hundreds of evacuees from Saigon to *Midway*. Their performance under these circumstances was magnificent.

During the course of the evening, *Hancock*, which was also participating in Frequent Wind, had an emergency. There was a mishap on her flight deck, causing her to suspend helicopter operations temporarily. At that moment, eight of her helicopters were returning from Saigon and were running low on fuel. Six of them reported fewer than ten minutes of fuel remaining to splash, and the other two had only fifteen minutes. The quick thinking by *Midway*'s Air Department saved all eight of these helicopters from going in the drink. Our flight deck was jammed with evacuees and helicopters, but we did have open spots where we could land the *Hancock*'s helicopters three at a time. Because of this limited space on *Midway*'s flight deck, the air boss, CDR Pete Theodorelos, instructed the landing crews to service the first helicopters that landed, giving them just enough fuel for fifteen minutes of flight time before launching them again. The second group of three to land was given twenty minutes of fuel. This bootstrap operation was repeated until all of the airborne fuel states were eventually raised to thirty minutes to splash. By this time the helicopters could be held on deck long enough to be topped off without the risk of any of them running out of fuel while in the air. This was no small feat in the midst of the chaos on *Midway*'s flight deck, which was jam-packed with a large number of evacuees. It was a miracle that during all of these operations no one was injured. The flight-deck crew performed amazing feats keeping the landing zones clear by expeditiously moving the aged, the sick, and the young—as well as the able-bodied—out of the danger areas at the same time that they were hot refueling and turning the helicopters around for another sortie.

Once the evacuees arrived on deck, *Midway* sailors and Marines moved them quickly and safely, identifying and processing all who came on board. Many of the evacuees arrived on board *Midway* in possession of small arms and grenades. In the interest of preserving good order and discipline on board, I ordered our Marines to confiscate all weapons, and since we did not have adequate space in our magazines to store them for safe keeping, I then ordered them to throw them overboard.

After receiving the refugees, our immediate concern was to move them on to other ships in company so that we could make room in *Midway* for more refugees from Saigon. The H-3 helicopters from HC-1 Det 2 worked around the clock to transport the evacuees from *Midway* to the other Navy ships in company. Despite their Herculean efforts, over fifteen hundred remained on board *Midway* overnight.

Prior to departing Subic Bay, we had emptied several crew's berthing spaces and officers' staterooms. By doubling up and filling all empty bunks in the remaining occupied compartments and staterooms, we managed to free up berthing space for five hundred personnel. These empty berthing spaces and staterooms were quickly jammed with people, and the overflow crowd bedded down on mats that were placed on the forecastle and under the aircraft and equipment that packed the hangar bays. Even my in-port cabin was crammed full of people. There were seven or eight Air Force, Army, and Navy general and flag officers sleeping in the captain's mess, and the ambassador and his wife occupied the in-port cabin. Those on board included the rich, the poor, the anonymous, and the famous. Although most were found to be in good physical health, *Midway*'s medical team treated nearly three hundred evacuees for minor illnesses and injuries.

While on board, all of the evacuees were treated as guests. Our sailors made toys for the youngsters and donated their own clothes to some of the needy adults. More than six thousand meals were served to the refugees during the course of Operation Frequent Wind. The warmth with which our sailors greeted the evacuees, providing compassion and assurance at a time when these people surely needed it, was a source of particular pride for me.

With the arrival of the American ambassador, his wife, and the embassy staff early on the morning of 30 April 1975, the last of the Americans had been lifted to safety from the embassy in Saigon. I was thankful that we were able to evacuate the embassy before it was overrun by the North Vietnamese because our ambassador was hanging tough and waited until the last possible moment before he would be evacuated. Regarding the withdrawal, I felt awful that after all the military had done in this war, our country had given up at a time when we were winning. The military had done one hell of a job, but the politicians didn't have the will to win. In the end, we had abandoned South Vietnam to the North Vietnamese. We had sacrificed our comrades, our classmates, our sons . . . for what?

We continued to receive evacuees, however, as thousands of Vietnamese fled their homeland on their own. The sky was full of helicopters, many carrying entire families searching for refuge. Fifty-five UH-1 Huey and five CH-47 Chinook helicopters landed on board *Midway*. Included in the UH-1s were a number of Air America helicopters that shuttled back and forth to Vietnam until they were out of gas. We were astounded to discover that some of the Hueys carried as many as fifty people. This was extraordinary for an aircraft designed to carry only ten combat-ready troops. No matter how they arrived, all evacuees received the same hospitable treatment on board *Midway* as those who had been picked up in Saigon by the Air Force HH-53s.

It was in the midst of these hectic operations that one of the most significant events of the cruise began to unfold. About 11:00 a.m. on 30 April 1975, the lookouts reported a Cessna OE-1 Bird Dog observation aircraft approaching *Midway*. The flight deck at the time was extremely crowded with people and helicopters. Most of the helicopters had shut down and the crews had already departed *Midway* with the other evacuees. Without flight crews and maintenance personnel, those helicopters were just so many obstacles fouling the landing area. In addition, the Hueys were equipped with skids, and we did not have the wheels (which could be attached to the skids) to make it easier to move the helicopters out of the landing area quickly. And, of course, these helicopters had landed on board without the required support equipment to service them for further flight. My initial efforts were to try to communicate with the Bird Dog's pilot to try to get him to return to Vietnam. The odds were that he had never made a carrier landing, and with no tail hook, I would need very high wind over the deck to keep him from running off the flight deck and going over the side. That is, provided that he somehow managed to get over the ramp in the first place. Hell, I thought, this is no place for a novice who has never seen the blunt end of a boat. How am I going to get out of this one?

As the Bird Dog approached the ship, I was hoping that once the pilot saw the condition of my deck, he would either go somewhere else or would ditch alongside the carrier. In fact, the flag officer embarked suggested that we let him ditch and rescue him from the water. I wondered if the Bird Dog had realized that there was not enough room on deck to move all of the helicopters that were parked in the landing area. I knew he would not be aware that we did not have the proper yellow gear (handling equipment) to remove the helicopters from the flight deck expeditiously. I instructed Commander Theodorelos to try to communicate with the Bird Dog on all emergency frequencies with the hope that the pilot spoke enough English to understand us. I had but one thought in mind: Go away! I can't do a damn thing for you! While attempting to communicate, we quickly screened the evacuees for an interpreter, thinking that even if he spoke good English, he might be so pumped up that we needed to talk to him in his native language. We found a Vietnamese woman who spoke excellent English and we rushed her to the control tower where we continued our attempts to communicate with the pilot on all emergency frequencies.

The Bird Dog circled the ship several times with his landing lights on, which indicated that he wanted to land on board. While he was circling, we noticed that there were more than two people in this two-place aircraft. We counted four heads in the cockpit. Since there were only two seats, it was obvious that not everyone was strapped in and thus would not have any chance of survival in the event of a ditching or crash landing. We observed what appeared to be a woman in the rear seat and concluded that there was a distinct possibility that untrained people were on board the Bird Dog. This would further complicate any rescue attempts in a ditching or a crash landing on *Midway*'s flight deck. Likewise, our experience had shown that aircraft that ditched with wheels down almost always flipped over to an inverted position upon impact with the water. This was not a pleasant thought for me. I did not relish the idea that I would be a witness to an escape attempt by an untrained crew from an upside-down aircraft in the water.

With this scenario developing, the embarked flag officer who had been, and who would again be, my immediate superior surveyed the situation.

Again he suggested that I let the Bird Dog ditch alongside since I had such a clobbered deck, but by now I knew that idea was not going to work. I tried to put myself in the pilot's position and realized how desperate I would have been under the circumstances. Worse yet, I now firmly believed that he would crash it on deck before he would attempt to ditch it. I knew if it were I, that I would rather take my chances that the crash crew would be better able to rescue me from an on-deck crash than from a ditching at sea. My present worries also were for all of the people and equipment that would be involved in a crash on board, not to mention the possibility of a disastrous fire on the flight deck. By now, I had convinced myself that if the pilot did not return to the beach, I would have to give him a shot at the deck. I thought to myself, Why me, Lord?

Meanwhile, the circling Bird Dog flew low over the flight deck and attempted to drop a note on the deck. On the first two tries, he was unsuccessful and the notes went over the side. But on the third attempt, he succeeded, dropping a note that remained on deck. The yellow shirt (flight-deck supervisor) who picked it up rushed the note to the bridge. It read: "Can you move the helicopters to the other side, I can land on your runway, I can fly one hour more, we have enough time to move. Please rescue me! Major Bung (Ly), wife and 5 child."

In reality, I did not need his note to convince me to clear the landing area and give him a chance to come on board. We had already counted four heads, confirming our suspicions that he had his family on board. He was not going to ditch. In one sense, I was relieved to learn that he had an hour of fuel remaining, and I now knew that he would not return to Vietnam. *Midway* was far enough out to sea that he simply did not have enough fuel remaining to go feet dry (reach the Vietnamese coast). However, I did have enough time to oversee orderly chaos on the flight deck. I directed Commander Theodorelos to make a ready deck and he screamed back that it would take a miracle, that he could not easily move the Hueys because of their skids and the high friction caused by the non-skid coating on the flight deck. As an old former air boss, I knew the task would not be easy, but I also knew that we were going to have to shove a few of the helicopters over the side to make room since we neither had the time nor the space to park all of them clear of the landing area and over the foul line. Theodorelos and I together concluded that the cross-deck pendants (arresting wires) might be a hindrance and had them removed from the flight deck. Likewise, we ruled out a barricade arrestment since the aircraft was not designed to take the stress. We were afraid that the wings might pull off and the fuselage would continue through the barricade.

To get additional manpower on the flight deck, I got on the ship's intercom, explained the situation to all hands, and requested that all flight-deck personnel report to the flight deck on the double. The results were unbelievable. There were yellow, brown, green, blue, and red shirts coming from everywhere. Even I was surprised at the number of volunteers who showed up. Every single air wing and Air Department man on the ship appeared on the flight deck, as did pilots, deckhands, and most of the Marines who were not on guard duty. It truly was an all-hands evolution. You would have thought I had just authorized a demolition derby. In making final preparations for the landing, Commander Theodorelos and I felt that if we could get forty knots of wind down the flight deck, there would be no danger of the Bird Dog overshooting, landing long, and going off the angle end of the flight deck. However, we knew that high winds down the deck produced a significant downdraft up to a quarter of a mile aft of the ship. We decided that the lesser of the evils was to have the wind with accompanying downdraft, and to hope that the pilot would carry enough power to maintain altitude and airspeed as he rode through the turbulence. The weather was generally good. The visibility was over five miles in light rain, the ceiling was more than five hundred feet, and the surface winds were holding steady at fifteen knots.

Because we had not needed high winds over the deck for helicopter operations, we had only six of the twelve boilers on line, and there was not enough time to bring on additional boiler power, so I ordered the chief engineer to strip all nonessential electrical loads to make more steam available for the main engines. We secured two of the four ship service generators and lit off both emergency diesels. I wanted to be sure that we could get at least twenty-five knots out of the old lady, and that would be fast enough to have forty knots down the angle deck.

When Theodorelos had cleared the landing area, I ordered the chief engineer to give us all the steam that he could make and commenced a turn into the wind. We were still attempting to contact the pilot on the off chance that he had a receiver and no transmitter. We transmitted instructions to him in the blind, including a warning about the downdraft aft of the ship. These transmissions were made in English and Vietnamese.

To complicate the situation further, another flight of helicopters arrived in our area as we steadied up into the wind. We attempted to communicate with the helicopters to remain clear until after the Bird Dog had landed, but it turned out that they were low on fuel and did not respond to our attempts to communicate with them. Five more Hueys landed without signal and fouled the landing area. I ordered Commander Theodorelos to push them over the side to make a ready deck for the Bird Dog again. What's a few more helicopters? I thought. We were already committed. Whatever the number, I knew I would be the one accountable for this action, and it passed through my mind that I could have the shortest career ever of a CO of an aircraft carrier. But at least I could not be accused of letting women and children drown without an attempt to save their lives.

"Bird Dog" touching down (Official U.S. Navy Photo)

By now, everyone who was not on watch was in vultures' row to watch the show, and I prayed, "Please God, let the Bird Dog make it." I had done everything that I could do to prepare the ship, and now if he would only carry enough power to get through the turbulence in the groove. When we steadied up again, we had forty-three knots of wind over the deck, and I felt that if he got over the ramp, he would have it made, even though the deck was rain soaked. The Bird Dog rolled out on final approach. So far, he looked pretty good. We were all praying, "Don't take the 'cut' [take power off] too soon!" The aircraft cleared the ramp and touched down on center-line at the normal touchdown point. Had it been equipped with a tailhook, the pilot could have bagged a number 3 wire. He bounced once and came to a stop abeam of the island, amid a wildly cheering, arms waving, flight-deck crew. Upon exiting the aircraft, he and his family were immediately surrounded by well-wishers. I issued a well done to all hands. A fantastic feat! I had the pilot, Maj Bung Ly, escorted to the bridge, and I congratulated him on his extraordinary display of airmanship. He had more guts than anyone I had ever known. He went beyond the point of no return with his wife and five children on board, and with no assurance that he would find a place to land! It would be another ten years, in a face-to-face meeting with Major Ly at the National Museum of Naval Aviation in Pensacola, Florida, before I could confirm that we had both been thinking the same thing. Major Ly had no intentions of returning to Vietnam. He said, "I was going to crash land on board, had you not cleared the runway."

For *Midway's* crew, the dramatic landing was the most memorable story of Operation Frequent Wind. Our crewmen were so moved by the courage of Major Ly and his family that we established a fund to help them start their new life, wherever they chose to settle.

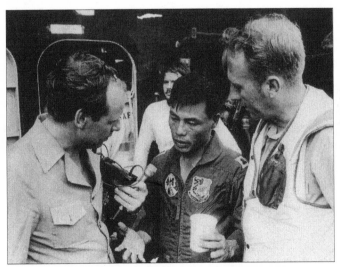

Major Bung Ly, "Bird Dog's" pilot (Official U.S. Navy Photo)

[This article is adapted from an article that appeared in FOUNDATION, *Fall 1993, the periodical of the Naval Aviation Museum Foundation, Inc., with permission of the editor and of the author, RADM Larry Chambers, USN (Ret.).]*

The Golden Eagles

Compiled by Jerry Zacharias

T he Early and Pioneer Naval Aviation Association, better known as
the Golden Eagles, was founded in 1956 and is limited to two hundred living members. Selection for membership is made from those
who are pioneers in some new aspect of naval aviation or are respected by
their peers as leaders because of their outstanding skills as a pilot, wide
experience, good judgment, personal character, and dedication to flying,
with an emphasis on strong performance in the cockpit. Fifty-six Naval
Academy graduates, twelve of whom are members of the Class of 1952,
have been selected as Golden Eagles:

CAPT Roger C. Bos, USN
RADM Lowell F. Eggert, USN
Col Paul K. German Jr., USMC
RADM Paul T. Gillcrist, USN
CAPT W. Scott Gray III, USN
ADM Huntington Hardisty, USN
CAPT William D. Knutson, USN
RADM Glen W. Lenox, USN
CAPT James A. Lovell Jr., USN
MajGen Kenneth W. Weir, USMCR
VADM Joseph B. Wilkinson Jr., USN
CAPT Jerrold M. Zacharias, USN

Courtesy of Dave Davison, Class of 1952

VI

SOME BECAME CIVILIANS

What is often overlooked by the taxpaying public is that many of those Naval Academy graduates who leave the service after completing their "payback" service obligation go on to contribute to the greater good as captains of industry, in civic service, and so on. The Class of 1952 was certainly no exception.

The Navy, the Academy, and Me

Robert J. Courtney

Dhe Naval Academy offers a profound and exciting educational experience. For four years, midshipmen are in a "demanding environment" of performance and learning. Most "stay the course" and become career officers. Some leave to enter the civilian business world. Does the Annapolis man fit or blend into civilian business life? My answer is, he not only fits and blends, but he most often makes life on the outside a success. The Navy's mission is to defend our country against all enemies. Medicine's mission is to care for the health of our citizens. Both professions require strong discipline and extensive study. I am a retired medical doctor and surgeon. This is my story.

I enlisted in the Navy after my junior year at Princeton High School in New Jersey. World War II was to end six weeks later, following the two A-bomb attacks on Japan. Following boot camp and Hospital Corpsman School, I was ordered to the Naval Hospital at Bethesda, Maryland, where I was assigned to a ward for the neurologically injured veterans. It was an instantly sobering and maturing experience. Most of the patients who were there when I arrived were still there when I left four months later. Treatment was demanding, as was care, and recovery was slow, if at all.

Jack Bowen was the "ward favorite." He was about twenty-five years old, a strong, proud, and fiercely independent Marine—paralyzed from the waist down. He never asked for help. One day, knowing that I would make liberty that night, he asked if I would bring him a pint of whiskey. I was eighteen, and in the District of Columbia it was legal for me to buy alcohol. But it was not legal to bring it to the patients. Jack got his whiskey.

A surgical technician training slot opened, and I got it. Some of us worked shoulder to shoulder with the surgeons. There were only two RNs. They were in charge. We did it all, from orderly to first assistant—a dynamic experience.

Pre-operation shaving was required of all patients. Enlisted men were shaved in the prep room of the OR (operating room), while officers were prepped in their rooms. Hearing this from me during his shave, one officer said he wished he had been taken to the OR, just to see the inside of the OR suite. I told the head RN, and the officer must have made some contacts, because soon, all were shaved in the OR prep room, which was obviously more efficient in time and energy. The Navy really does make changes.

Duty transfer orders came after eighteen months at Bethesda. Having won the coin toss to choose a duty that was available, I wanted "sea duty," so I chose the USS *Reina Mercedes* at Annapolis. When I first saw her, I was dumbfounded. The *Reina Mercedes* was a relic from the Spanish-American War, raised from the mud of Havana Harbor and secured to the seawall at Annapolis by heavy beams and concrete. It was used as an office and a barracks for enlisted. Up a gangplank to the reporting desk I went, to find that they had no idea I was coming. "Pick a bunk and take a walk until we find out where to send you," I was told.

As I was walking, I heard a shout, "Courtney, what are you doing here?" It was Mac, a pharmacist's mate second class from Bethesda. He took control, and in less than an hour, I was in the Midshipman Dispensary inside Bancroft Hall. Bethesda had been wonderful and exciting as well as educational. This facility was also a beautiful one, fully equipped and immaculate. It was to become the singularly most pivotal experience of my career.

Duty at the dispensary was a breeze. Beautiful girls—midshipmen's dates—were all over the yard. Some were not happy with their dates, and I met one of those the afternoon before a spring hop. Instant crush! I said I would figure a way to get into the dance. My solution: be an officer. I borrowed a uniform from one of the dentists, a lieutenant (jg), and we walked right in. Afterward, we exchanged letters for awhile, but I never saw her again. It's a wonder I didn't land in the brig.

In the spring of 1947, sailors from the Naval Academy Preparatory School (NAPS) came through the dispensary for physicals. NAPS is the school for those enlisted men chosen from a fleet-wide competitive exam. I was eligible, but before I received orders to NAPS, orders came through for duty on board the light cruiser USS *Duluth* (CL 87), home ported in California. I was an independent duty OR tech on a ship headed for an eight-to ten-month cruise in the Western Pacific. So for seven to eight weeks, I had my sea duty before being transferred to NAPS at Bainbridge, Maryland.

After nine months of study and successfully passing the Academy entrance exam, I received a fleet appointment and entered the Naval Academy with the Class of 1952. And Princeton High School awarded me my diploma. Talk about irony. Here I was a midshipman, following the very group from NAPS whom I had given physical exams the year before, the

Class of 1951. Our curriculum combined liberal arts with engineering, as well as professional subjects such as navigation and gunnery. The standard was twenty-plus credit hours per semester as compared with the civilian maximum of sixteen hours.

In conforming to the discipline imposed by rules and regulations, the midshipman becomes responsible to self, his unit, and the Navy. He must be honest, considerate, cooperative, and conduct himself with dignity and decorum, all traits expected of professionals throughout the world, civilian or military. Above all, he has been taught to think, analyze, and act.

At the end of plebe year, I had passed the most difficult year at the Academy, a year of demanding studies and demanding tasks imposed by upper classmen. I decided to pursue my instincts: medicine. Pre-med was not offered at the Academy, so I resigned, taking with me an experience that enhanced every day of my social life and my career as a physician and surgeon. We expect from doctors the same traits taught to midshipmen; we expect a confident and trustworthy expert whose demeanor is one of quiet dignity and decorum.

My naval experience gave me the ability to innovate and to lead. I was the first to introduce to the Tampa surgical community the computer-guided core needle biopsy of the breast for diagnosis without surgical intervention. I did the same for the laparoscopic technique to remove the gall bladder through the umbilicus. Both required confidence and trust in my ability to do the procedures. My operating room ran with the efficiency of a well-trained crew because all of my team knew their jobs. Teamwork. Had I not been molded to think and be responsible at the Naval Academy, I doubt I would have tried either procedure on my own. There is no room for "casual" in the professions of the Navy and medicine.

The Barrett Story

Bob Barrett

Unplanned happenings have a way of changing one's life. I give you my story as an example. I enlisted in the Marine Corps in 1945, and in 1947 I arrived at the Naval Academy Preparatory School at Bainbridge, Maryland, along with several hundred other Marines and sailors. After nine months of studies, we took the entrance exam for the Academy, and in June of 1948, a group of Napsters, including me, were sworn in as midshipmen.

I fully intended to be a career Marine officer, but I met a girl from Baltimore after one of the home football games, and after we became engaged, I didn't think the Corps was the best choice for me, so I resigned. Meeting Betty was the first unplanned happening.

After we were married, we lived in York, Nebraska, the town where I grew up. I worked in my father's blacksmith and welding shop. After a short while, we moved to Baltimore. I job hopped for awhile, but at the same time, I attended Johns Hopkins University at night and graduated with a degree in mechanical engineering, an event that was a second unplanned happening since I had originally planned to graduate from the Naval Academy.

I went to work for Western Electric as an associate engineer, and I retired as a senior engineer. Although the work at Western Electric paid much better than any other job, it was not my favorite. I had worked several years in a small production machine shop, starting as a welder, followed by machinist, working foreman, and, ultimately, a combination tool designer and tool maker. I can't explain it, but if I had been wealthy, I would have bought the company. I would even have been willing to pay them to let me work there.

I never was far from the Marine Corps. I introduced my sister-in-law to John Kyle, one of my former Marine classmates at the Academy. It was during his second year. They were married a week after the Class of 1952 graduated, their meeting and marrying being another of those unforeseen happenings. Kyle, Garnett Bailey, and I met at NAPS, and I saw them when they were at Basic School at Quantico. Later on, John was teaching electricity at the Academy, and the two of us got together and drank beer at my home on many weekends. I had not advanced enough as a mid to take electricity, but on one visit, John said he wanted to tell me the same thing he had told the people in all the sections he was teaching. Then he gave me the same two circuit drawings he had used to test them in calculating several resistances. To me, it was just two sets of algebra problems. I got 4.0 on the test. He said I was the only who had passed that test. The next weekend, John told me what he had told his classes: "I gave that same test to a drunk up in Baltimore and he got 4.0 on it, but none of you even got a passing grade." He said they just laughed and said they didn't believe him.

When John retired, I was living in Phoenix, and John and his family stayed with me until he bought a house. I was transferred back to Baltimore, but I returned to Phoenix several times on vacation. Four of us who had been together at the Academy would gather in the White Mountains to go trout fishing. The two beside John and myself were Cy Blanton and Ned King. One of those times, Cy and I were in the boat on the far side of the lake when the engine quit. We couldn't get it started, so we had to row across the lake against the wind. Both of us had previously been operated on with bypass surgery. When we reached the other side of the lake, we both just flopped onto the grass and reclined there until we recovered. We both are still hanging in there, but we almost cashed in our chips that day. That would have been a very unplanned happening.

So ends the Barrett story, with best wishes to all the Class of 1952.

Tales from the Marshall Islands

Al Enderle

It was at a bar in Majuro, in the Marshall Islands, that I met CAPT Dewey Huffer. As we downed a few, he told me that he had been a Marine prior to World War II. However, when the war started, he joined the Navy. He stayed in Micronesia after the war, marrying a Chamorro woman. Their home was in Pettie on Guam.

Dewey was an expert at celestial navigation as well as ship handling in general. He had skippered many ships in Micronesia and had taught most of the native skippers how to navigate. At the time we met, he was captain of the *Ralik Ratak*, which means "West East" in Marshallese. It was a single-screw, diesel-powered, interisland trading ship of about 110 feet in length.

Dewey asked me if I would like to go on a field trip with him, and of course I accepted. We stopped first at Arno Atoll, eleven miles away by air but twice that distance by sea since Majuro exits to the east and Arno is to the west of Majuro. Next stop was Ebon, and then Jaluit, where Japanese headquarters had been. Jaluit was followed by Ailinglapalap Atoll, Namu Atoll, Lae Atoll, Aur Atoll, Kili Island, Ebeye Island, Namorik Atoll, Mili Atoll, and, lastly, Kwajalein Atoll. The inhabitants of Bikini had been evacuated to Kili for the atomic bomb tests and longed to return to their home atoll.

A major benefit of my weeks on the *Ralik Ratak* was being able to swim in the lagoons in total isolation, nobody else around, as if I was in my own private pool. The average water temperature was eighty-three degrees, and the water was unbelievably crystal clear.

Besides Dewey, I became close friends with a second-generation Japanese-American couple, born in Hawaii, named Bob and Harumi Nii. With visions of owning a fishing fleet, Bob had bought two fishing sampans in Japan and had arranged their shipment to Majuro by ship. Unfortunately, the ship carrying the sampans had to unload one in Saipan to get access to a hold, and the crane that lifted it off almost toppled over, so the *Narita Maru* was not reloaded.

When the freighter arrived at Guam, the larger shore crane there offloaded the *Ginzu Maru* and left it there. In a letter to Bob, the shipping company accused Bob of lying about the weight of each sampan and informed him that they had impounded both sampans until an additional two thousand dollars was paid. In addition, they would not ship them the remaining two thousand miles. The Japanese crews were with the sampans, living in hotels at Bob's expense. When Bob asked Dewey and me if we would bring both ships to Majuro, I jumped at the chance for an adventure in a sampan, sailing two thousand miles across the Pacific.

Dewey signed on as navigator, the Japanese crews not being able to navigate by the stars. I was first mate and radioman, although *Ginzu Maru*, at Guam, had no radio. So off we went to Guam on Air Micronesia. At Guam, we went to the harbor master's office at Apra Harbor. Dewey was not having much success in trying to persuade the harbor master to let us take the *Ginzu Maru*, so I started taking pictures with my large, professional looking camera. The harbor master suddenly realized that his picture was being taken, and asked what I was doing.

"I am doing a story on the delivery of the two sampans from Japan to Majuro," I replied. "By the way, I used to deal in heavy equipment. Good crane operators know if something they are lifting is heavier or lighter than what is on the invoice. Bob Nii knows nothing about cranes or ships. All he did was buy two sampans, get two invoices that showed the weight as told him by the sellers, and gave the invoices to the shipping line. When the shipper's crane operators started the loading process, they would have known immediately that the sampans were over the invoice weight. Mr. Nii had no way of knowing that. The shipping line is taking advantage of Nii's ignorance. I plan to write a story about it."

The harbor master made a quick phone call and then turned to Dewey and said that he had obtained the releases of both sampans and no further payment was required. Since the *Ginzu Maru* was sitting on the dock, the harbor master generously had the yard crane lift it into the harbor at no cost. He seemed glad to be rid of it and to be free of playing the villain in my "story."

After collecting the three non-English-speaking Japanese crewmen, Dewey and I bought some supplies and boarded *Ginzu Maru*. She was forty-five feet long with a nine-foot beam. There were no cabins, no bunks, no galley, and no head. The only navigation device was a compass, but she did have a depth finder used to locate schools of fish. The engine was a four-cylinder, 40-horsepower Yanmar diesel. The bridge had neither sides nor an overhead. A large lectern-like bulkhead faced forward. A long, horizontal rod with a handle on it was mounted on the lectern. Pushing it forward shifted the engine transmission into reverse. Pulling it back half way was neutral, and pulling it all the way back was ahead. A round hole in the stern deck overhang substituted for the head. It had two raised boards about ten inches high on either side so that when one was relieving himself, one could hold himself up with his hands. I got used to it, but Dewey never used it, probably due to his massive weight. Instead, he would hang from the radio antenna over the side of the ship, trying to time himself with the roll of the ship to avoid fouling the ship's side.

Dewey slept in an enclosed space just above the engine room. There was just enough room for his mat and the Japanese skipper's. They had no problem with the ship rolling, the tight fit holding them in place. The engineer slept alongside the engine, and the deckhand slept in the forward storage locker in the bow on top of some coiled lines. My "stateroom" was a four-by-five-foot locker under the lectern console. My upper body was sheltered, but my lower half was exposed to the weather and was right under the feet of the man on the helm. The helm was a long wooden tiller near which we built a bench so the helmsman could sit down. We also rigged an awning over the bridge with some canvas, giving us shelter from the sun.

We sailed for Saipan, where we joined the *Narita Maru*. We also obtained a brand-new military-issue shortwave radio, courtesy of a friend of Dewey. When I tested the radio on the emergency frequency, there was no response. Dewey's friend walked over to a nearby warehouse and made a phone call. When he returned, he told me to try it again, and this time I got a response from the Saipan radio operator. Dewey's friend had called them and told them to turn up the volume on the emergency frequency.

I subsequently learned that every station in the islands kept the volume down because the static on the emergency frequency made it hard for the operators to sleep. If there had been an emergency on our voyage across that lonely part of the Pacific . . .

On to Truk, where we were tying up at the dock on Moen Island when the district administrator arrived and informed us that we would have to anchor in the lagoon. He was curt and impolite toward our Japanese skipper, who did not understand English. I took out my camera and started to take pictures just as I had done at Guam. He asked what I was doing, and I told him the same story I had used at Guam, with the same amazing results. His attitude changed completely! He graciously permitted us to tie up at the dock as long as we were on Moen. I later learned he was from a town in California just five miles from where I live.

A day short of Ponape, our next stop, *Narita Maru*'s engine lost a rod, meaning we would have to tow her into port. Towing a ship has its own unique problems. Swells can put heavy stress on the towing line, requiring careful planning of the line and harness, as well as continuous monitoring of the towing line to ensure it is not being excessively strained. By the time we were approaching Ponape, the *Narita* engineer had removed the broken rod and was able to operate the engine on three cylinders. Innovative! We didn't have to tow *Narita* into the harbor. But *Narita*'s skipper failed to follow our lead and ran aground on the side of the narrow channel. The tide was out at the time, so *Narita* was able to float off at high tide.

Ponape is a beautiful island with high mountains and plentiful water from the high rain fall (about one hundred inches a year). We tied up at Kolonia, the capital, a town with dirt streets, poorly built houses, and twenty-one bars on the main street—not a very attractive place. Drinking and smoking were big time on all the main Micronesian islands. It was great traveling with Dewey Huffer due to the fact that he seemed to know everybody.

The *Narita Maru* had to be repaired before we could continue our voyage, so Dewey wired Japan for a replacement rod. A German freighter, MV *Taipoohsek*, had arrived and was scheduled to drop off some passengers at Kusaie. Dewey suggested that I take passage on it with eight fifty-five-gallon drums of diesel fuel so that, when the sampans arrived at Kusaie, they would be assured of fuel to finish the trip from there to Majuro, our destination in the Marshall Islands.

In addition to the captain and the crew, the freighter, of some four hundred feet in length, carried a number of Peace Corps members on leave. One of them and I became friends. Dick had been stationed on Kusaie, so he was able to tell me about Lelu, where his hut was, and some of the history of the island. He added that I could use his hut since he was being transferred. The second night out, while we were having a couple of beers, he mentioned a lost temple on Kusaie. That really caught my attention. One of my nicknames is "Indiana Al" because my adventures, although not on the scale of Indiana Jones, remind people of the Indiana Jones movie series, one of which has the Temple of Doom in it.

When we entered Lelu Harbor at Kusaie, the tide had just turned and was ebbing. The skipper told everyone who was to disembark to get off immediately because he would not be able to anchor. Instead, he would do a slow turn in the harbor and leave. I asked him about the drums of diesel fuel. He said that was my problem—he was not the friendly sort.

The drums were on the main deck, and with the help of my Peace Corps friends, we rolled them over the side, where they remained afloat although very low in the water. After getting the attention of a native paddling by in his outrigger canoe, I asked him to corral the drums with a line that I tossed to him. I jumped into another outrigger waiting for me at the bottom of the accommodation ladder.

Looking back at my Micronesian experiences, as well as my travels alone to other parts of the world, it seems almost scary to me how easily I made friends and felt at home wherever I happened to be. Making friends paid dividends for me at Kusaie. The town of Lelu boasted a two-room native "hotel," if one could call it that. But even at the bargain price of three dollars a night, it was out of my reach, my funds in hand amounting to seven dollars. So it was that the hut that my Peace Corps friend offered me was a windfall, a blessing, because the alternative would have been sleeping in some native dwelling in the jungle, never a good thing.

The hut was about fifteen feet from front to rear, and about twenty feet from side to side, fairly roomy for a hut. It had folding, woven palm leaf sides on the front and the side facing Lelu. A log with three steps cut in it sufficed as stairs at the entrance. Inside, at the right rear, was a small sink with a water faucet that controlled any water in the catchment on the back side of the thatch roof. The water tank was the wing tank from a World War II aircraft, installed so that most of the water that ran off the roof drained into it.

To the left of the kitchen, a wall bookshelf held over two hundred paperback books ranging from Plato to adventure and romance novels. Not a bad little library, all things considered. A two-person swing was suspended in the middle of the hut, and when the front side was opened, one could swing out and see the beautiful harbor entrance. The hut had two windows, one directly behind the sink and one in the wall to the right of the sink. The windows could be shuttered should the heavy rain and wind start to come through. A sleeping platform above the main floor covered half the downstairs and was accessed by a ladder that could be pulled up for security while sleeping. Not surprising, there was no bed, but I was used to sleeping on a mat I carried with me.

About noon on my third day in the hut, there was a knock on the post next to the front door. There stood a native man who luckily spoke English.

He told me his name was Raymond Aliksa. After chatting for a few minutes, Raymond asked me if I would like some Kusaian soup. "You bet I would!" I responded. He stuck his head out the door and called to his wife who had been patiently waiting just out of sight of the doorway. She ran back to their home in Lelu and returned very quickly with a large wooden bowl of the best soup I have ever tasted. It was almost solid with little shrimp, sort of like a Cajun gumbo filled solid with small shrimp. Just think what small shrimp could do for Campbell's Chicken Gumbo.

Out of curiosity, I asked Raymond if he had ever heard of a "lost temple." Surprisingly, he said he had.

"Have you ever seen it?"

"No."

"How do you know about it?"

"My father told me about it."

"Why haven't you seen it?"

"It is in a forbidden area."

To an adventurer such as I, the words "forbidden area" caused my heart rate to jump. I thought if there was even only one chance in a hundred that it actually existed, I had to look for it.

The next morning at sunrise I was on my way to search for the temple. I was wearing my usual safari shorts and white short-sleeved hand washable shirt, but I had replaced my Zoris with light hiking boots. I strapped on my short-bladed Marine combination machete and throwing knife, and one hundred feet of five-hundred-pound nylon test line. I carried my camera in its waterproof aluminum Halliburton case.

One thing I foolishly failed to take was water. Kusaie has an annual rainfall of over two hundred inches, and it rains virtually every day. I figured I could either catch all the water I needed or get it from the streams the rain always formed. From my hut, I visualized the route I thought I should take, because once in the jungle, I would not be able to see any landmarks.

I had to cross Lelu Harbor to reach the place where I intended to enter the jungle, so I hired a native with his outrigger who took me across for a dime. There was a native hut where I landed, near my entry point into the jungle. I waved to the owner and said, "Kasalalia," the equivalent of "Good morning" or "Aloha," "Yakwa yuk" in Mashallese, "Hafa dai" in Chamorro, or "Roninem" in Trukese. What with my Halliburton case, he probably thought I was a government inspector of some kind.

As I worked my way up the ridges, I blazed my path so that on the way back I would be able to retrace my steps. Although the growth under the canopy of trees was not thick due to the lack of sunlight, there were a lot of vines that cut my arms, legs, and shirt. After climbing for a while, I came to a sort of open area where gigantic ferns were growing. I decided that the best way to get through them was to hold my Halliburton case over my head and fall forward, flattening the ferns in front of me, repeating that process until reaching the jungle on the far side. About the third time I flattened the ferns, I happened to look down through them to my left, and I found myself looking over a cliff that dropped straight down for what appeared to be about a thousand feet (but likely was several hundred feet). Regardless, if I had flattened those ferns just a few feet to the left, I would not be telling this story.

I eventually broke out of the jungle to find myself on the peak of one of the mountains of Kusaie. I noticed that none of the other mountains were as high, meaning that I had accidentally climbed to the top of Mount Crozer (now called Mount Finkol), the highest mountain on Kusaie at 2,061 feet above sea level. I took an empty plastic film container, placed a piece of paper in it with my name, address, and the date, and buried it beneath a small monument of rocks. I then took 360 degrees of pictures to establish that I had actually been on the top.

I noticed that the *Tunga Maru* had anchored in Lelu Harbor. Tony, the skipper, was a friend, a great cook, and good with a guitar. He always had a stock of cold beer, so I looked forward to seeing him when I retraced my steps down the mountain. I realized that where I supposed the temple to be could not be reached from where I was. I would have to return to where I started and make some major adjustments in how I would reach the valley between the two pointed mountain peaks.

By that time I had become very thirsty. It had not rained, which was unusual, but I could hear the sound of a small stream to my left. I slipped and slid down the muddy hillside to get to it. After having my fill of water, I tried to climb back up, but the roots I tried to use to pull myself up were all rotten and broke off when I pulled on them. I regretted that I had not tied on my nylon line before going down.

I decided, as if I had a choice, to follow the stream down a ways until I could climb out and find my blaze markings. When I finally climbed out, there were no markings to be found. Thinking that the stream obviously had to go to the bottom of the mountain, I resolved to follow it down. The farther I went down, however, the steeper it got, and now I was unable to climb out either side or even return up stream.

As I went around a bend in the stream, there in front of me was a wall of mud. Apparently the sides of the stream had collapsed and caved in, making an almost vertical wall about ten feet high, far too high for me to climb over. But the wall had not dammed the stream. Bending over, I saw that the water had made a hole through the wall, through which I could see light. Since it had not rained that day, the stream was shallow enough to permit me to lie down in it. Shoving the Halliburton into the hole, I saw that it just fit, although a bit snugly.

It seemed to take me forever to work my way through that hole, and as I crawled, I tried not to think what would happen if the rain started and the hole collapsed, burying me alive where no one would ever find me. It was a tremendous relief when I finally emerged on the other side, no worse for the experience other than being covered with mud.

Finally I came to the edge of the jungle and found that I was exiting about ten feet from where I had entered it that morning. It was now getting dark. The same native I had seen that morning was standing next to his hut near a bunch of bananas. When he saw me, his mouth fell open. I must have been a real sight—muddy, with my shirt cut almost to shreds from the vines, and with a muddy camera case. All he could say was "Banana?" I said, "You bet!" He gave me one, which I ravenously ate.

Crossing Lelu Harbor with another native in his outrigger, I noticed that both sampans had arrived. When I reached the sampans, the crew told me that Dewey had borrowed a jeep and was looking for me. No one knew where I was since I had not told a soul that I was going into "forbidden territory." I told them to find Dewey and tell him I would be on the *Ginzu Maru*.

It had started to rain as I walked to Raymond Aliksa's house. He let me jump into a fifty-five-gallon drum he used to catch water, and I jumped in fully clothed. Afterward, I got my gear from the hut and went on board the *Ginzu Maru*, where I fell asleep. When I awoke the next morning, Kusaie was out of sight. I wondered if I would ever be able to return there one day to continue my search or even perhaps see if I could find the treasure from Bully Haye's sunken pirate vessel at Utwa.

By now I had been on the *Ginzu Maru* for almost a month, less the several days on Kusaie, and the diet of raw fish and rice was really getting old. Dewey had brought a bunch of candy bars and a gallon container of pickled eggs for his meals. He kept the pickled eggs where I slept, and although I can still remember the smell of those eggs, I never ate one, nor did I touch a candy bar. I wanted to eat what the crew ate. Suzuki, the skipper, had no concept of what standing a watch meant. The usual shipboard watch is four hours on and eight off, but Suzuki would take the helm for as long as he felt like it, which might be eight hours. He would then yell at a crew member to relieve him.

The day after we left Kusaie, the wind grew and the sea became very rough. When Suzuki got tired, he kicked me to awaken me since I was sleeping halfway under the lectern style console. Whoever had the helm had to straddle my legs. Suzuki went below where Dewey was, the engineer was down with the engine, and our one deckhand was asleep in the rope locker up in the bow.

I started to get tired, but there was no way for me to get anyone to take my place. I dared not let go the tiller in such a rough sea. The noise of the wind and the sea drowned any shouts from me. My "watch" lasted eighteen hours into the next day. When I was at last relieved, I was so tired I just dropped to my knees and fell forward into my "cabin" and passed out. I have no idea how long I slept, but no one asked me to relieve them the rest of the three hundred or so miles to Majuro.

Bob and Harumi Nii met us at the pier at Uliga on Majuro, and we presented them the first fish caught from the first boats of their planned fishing fleet. Dewey and I then went to the Mieco Hotel for a shower and some sleep.

Thus ended my adventure in the Marshall Islands.

Courtesy of Dave Davison, Class of 1952

VII

OUR FAMILIES

A life in the sea services includes the pain of family separation and the joy of homecoming. Sea service families must contend with challenges and experiences that would be wholly unfamiliar to those in other walks of life. Few sayings have more resonance among those who have "gone down to the sea in ships" than these words: "Home is the sailor, home from the sea."

My USS *Maddox* Experience

Mary-lin Jackson Ryan
(Navy Junior–Navy Wife)

Thereare two sayings that often come to mind when I think of my days as a Navy wife. The first is the old adage regarding military wives: "If the Navy had wanted you to have a wife, they would have issued you one." The second is by poet John Milton: "They also serve who only stand and wait." Milton's quote may have no relation to the Navy per se, but it sums up what is a truism: what happens on a ship impacts and involves the wives in many ways. The following two stories provide a good illustration of my involvements throughout Dempster M. "Demp" Jackson's Navy career. As you will read, the first was a bit of a warm-up or practice for what followed in the far more serious and complicated *Maddox* incident.

Before describing my experiences in what became the *Maddox* Incident, I should tell you that Demp had been commanding officer of an LST (landing ship, tank) back in 1958. During one deployment, I was awakened by the doorbell and my mother wanting me to hear the news from her as she handed me the front page of the *San Diego Union* bearing the headline "San Diego Ship Lost in Storm!" It was *Sumner County* (LST 1148), his ship. By then my very small children were up and wanted breakfast. The phone started ringing, the first call being from a Navy office telling me not to believe the article, that the ship had been located and I should calm any distraught wives I might hear from. The senior chief's wife was also being notified so that she could pass the word, and I was asked to notify all of the wardroom wives. Demp later wrote (no e-mail in those days) that they had never been lost. As instructed, they had headed out to sea to ride out the storm. I start with this incident to illustrate that Demp already had experience as a commanding officer, as did I, the wife of same.

Nineteen sixty-four found us living in Long Beach, California. Demp was executive officer of *Maddox* (DD 731). Our son David was in second grade, Dennis was in the first, and I still had Riley *before* ombudsmen programs, and there was really little organized for the wives other than whatever each individual ship wardroom wanted to do and the squadron luncheons, and so on, from time to time. I had met many of the wardroom officers and many of their wives. The commanding officer of *Maddox* was married to a woman of French descent, and they had two daughters. I had not met them and knew nothing other than she worked at night as a French singer in a local nightclub. We had little in common!

The ship left for a six- to eight-month deployment, and the wardroom wives had expressed a desire to get together for "coffee" every month. Nothing formal was planned at all. Several of the wives worked, some weren't interested, and others had returned to their homes of origin during the deployment.

Maddox deployed about June 1964 as part of Patrol Force, Taiwan Defense Command, a branch of the U.S. Seventh Fleet guarding the waters between Japan and Taiwan and attached to Destroyer Division 192. The commodore was now on board *Maddox*. He was to take her into the Tonkin Gulf for collection of information, an activity called the DeSoto Patrol. The previous DeSoto Patrol had been uneventful, and this one didn't promise to be any different. As Mike McLaughlin wrote in the U.S. Naval Institute *Proceedings*, Captain Ogier, the commanding officer, briefed the crew via the ship's public-address system: "The ship is proceeding into the Gulf of Tonkin in order to collect hydrographic and oceanographic information. To the west is the coast of North Vietnam, and to the east is the island of Hainan, belonging to Communist China. We have a right to enter the Gulf since at all times we will be in international waters. We will leave the Gulf around 9 August. Keep alert and conserve fresh water. The ship's daily routine will be carried out."

On 2 August, the television, radio, and newspapers exploded with news of an attack by Vietnamese PT boats on an American destroyer. Yes . . . once again it was Demp's ship. I started getting calls from the other wives and then friends, calling long-distance: "Isn't *Maddox* the ship Demp is on?" In those days there was no caller ID to know who was calling, so I did my level best to keep the calls very brief and hoped that I would hear soon from *some* official about the news that was being reported! I was also doing what I could to keep from indicating to the four children my worry as well as trying to run all as normally as possible while the phone rang continuously! I recall that before the first twenty-four-hour period passed, I did receive an official call, telling me that there had been no injuries and wanting to know if I knew how to get hold of the CO's wife. I gave the caller the only number I had, and he said he had not been able to reach her. I explained that I thought he could reach her after school as her girls would be returning from school. According to iBiblio's Online Library of Selected Images, U.S. Navy Ships,

> On the afternoon of 2 August 1964, while steaming well offshore in international waters, *Maddox* was attacked by three North Vietnamese motor torpedo boats. The destroyer maneuvered to avoid torpedoes and used her guns against her fast-moving opponents, hitting them all. In turn, she was struck in the after gun director by a single 14.5-millimeter machine gun bullet. *Maddox* called for air support from the carrier *Ticonderoga*, whose planes strafed the three boats, leaving one dead in the water and burning. Both sides then separated. (http://www.ibiblio .org/hyperwar/OnlineLibrary/photos/sh-usn/usnsh-m/dd731-k.htm)

No further events occurred in the next day and a half. All was beginning to get back to normal again in our home. I had even turned my thoughts toward David's eighth birthday, which was the fifth of August. Since the news first broke, I had dutifully been clipping all of the articles that were being printed by the likes of *Time* and *Newsweek* magazines, as well as various clippings friends had been sending and the local papers, of course. As had been my habit, I always kept an ongoing scrapbook. This time Demp would be more interested than usual in seeing what I had saved in his absence.

Then the next day arrived and it started all over again: "*Maddox* was soon ordered to resume her patrol, this time accompanied by the larger and newer destroyer Turner Joy. On 3 August, the South Vietnamese conducted another coastal raid. Intelligence indicated that the North Vietnamese were planning to again attack the U.S. ships operating off their shores, although this interpretation was incorrect. During the night of 4 August, while they were underway in the middle of the Tonkin Gulf, *Maddox* and Turner Joy detected speedy craft closing in. For some two hours the ships fired on radar targets" (http://www.ibiblio.org/hyperwar/OnlineLibrary/photos/sh-usn/usn sh-m/dd731-k.htm).

Now I was furious! We had just begun to live normally again and our husbands were out there like sitting ducks. This time I heard much sooner, and when I voiced my concern, the Navy officer informed me he understood but that I should not be alarmed and I should be assured that all would be well and not believe all that the media was putting out. He also asked me to assure the others. I then methodically called all of the wardroom wives. Some made it very easy for me, and others required more time, energy, and patience. The calls had to be worked around other calls and the things I was dealing with at the time to try to keep things running as smoothly as I could at home. After I had finally completed calling everyone, I vowed that if I had to make such calls again, I would break up the duty into a "telephone tree" kind of thing.

LCDR Dempster Jackson, executive officer, USS *Maddox*, showing bullet from North Vietnamese patrol craft lodged in the after gun director. (Official U.S. Navy Photo)

From iBiblio's Online Library: "Though information obtained well after the fact indicates that there was actually no North Vietnamese attack that night, U.S. authorities were convinced at the time that one had taken place, and reacted by sending planes from the carriers Ticonderoga and Constellation to hit North Vietnamese torpedo boat bases and fuel facilities. A few days later, the U.S. Congress passed the Tonkin Gulf Resolution, which gave the Government authorization for what eventually became a full-scale war in Southeast Asia" (ibid.).

Several more months passed before the cruise finally ended and *Maddox* and her men returned home. Thus began much speculation, back and forth, expert and amateur, about what actually had transpired. The ship and her crew were under the stamp "Top Secret." Even my own husband could not, or would not, divulge to me, our family, friends, or fellow officers the facts.

In our case, Demp had injured his back pulling an air conditioner away from the bulkhead at the same time the ship rolled. He hobbled off to strict bed rest and eventually was turned into Balboa Naval Hospital in San Diego for surgery. For at least a month, I would drive down every weekend after school was out to spend the weekends visiting him. The children were not allowed to visit in the hospital, which was most upsetting to them after waiting for so long to see their dad. San Diego was Demp's hometown, and his parents were there as well as his brother and sister and their families. He underwent a back surgery called a laminectomy. Enough time had elapsed since his injury with the air conditioner, and with simultaneous ship rolling and the surgery, his legs were fairly useless; he had a lot of rehabilitation to go through, so the children and I continued our trips and weekends visiting. It was far from an ideal way to live, and it was a time of great rejoicing when he was finally discharged from the hospital and we were allowed to bring him home.

For many years following, he would turn away all inquiries about the *Maddox* Incident with a cat-mouse response that read, "That's top secret and you don't have the need to know!"

Many years later, in the 1980s, after he had been retired from the Navy, he received a call from the BBC. They wanted to schedule a series of interviews at our home about the *Maddox* Incident. After all this time! I was in and out of their sessions and after he had given his standard need-to-know reply for the umpteenth time, it dawned on me that they might like to look at my scrapbook of those years. I went to the closet where I kept the volumes of scrapbooks I had kept for all of our married life. I knew exactly what that particular book looked like, and it simply was not there. I have moved several times since then and find its loss very mysterious. I often wonder if the BBC ever did anything from what little they got from those interviews!

[Editor's note: RADM Dempster M. Jackson, Class of 1952, died on 3 April 2001.]

Three Weeks!

Geri Madigan

My husband, Jim Madigan, was in the Gulf of Tonkin in USS *Arlington* (AGMR 2), the World War II carrier that had been converted to a floating communications station, and the children and I were in Marina Point in Chesapeake getting ready to leave for Mass when the phone rang. It was someone from Naval Operating Base (NOB) Norfolk with a message from Jim. He was being transferred from *Arlington* to *Providence* (CLG 2), the Seventh Fleet flagship based in Japan, and we had to get there before the end of the year or we'd end up having to pay our own way. That was 10 December 1967. I asked if Jim had said when we would get a copy of his orders, and Jim hadn't mentioned that except to say I'd know what to do. Great.

After church, we were talking to some Navy friends, telling them about the call. I knew Jack was in the Navy but didn't know exactly what he did. It turned out he was the commanding officer of the Naval Supply Center, and he told me, "We'll get this done!" First he said we had to go to D.C. and get our passports. We took care of that the next day, and by offering to hand carry the forms to State Department, as Jack had suggested, we were able to drive back home the same day. The biggest obstacle was, of course, getting transportation and putting the furniture in storage—with *no orders*. Jack had a plan. I was to be in the office at NOB the next morning at exactly 9:30 to tell them I wanted to make arrangements to go to Japan, and when I was asked for my husband's orders, I was to hem and haw and somehow stall them. In the midst of my ad lib tirade, the phone rang and the man helping me answered it, saying, "Yes, sir! . . . Yes, sir! . . . I'm not sure I can. Yes, sir!" All I know is I walked out of there with transportation to Japan and a date to pick up and store our furniture as well as send a small shipment going with us.

Next we had to go to the Portsmouth Naval Hospital and start getting our shots. I don't know if that is still a requirement, but we had to get six weeks' worth of shots in two and a half weeks, each one making us sicker and weaker than the previous one.

Fast forward to Midnight Mass on Christmas Eve. Jimmy was serving as altar boy, his face a shade of minus gray and his head swirling in circles from all the shots. He made it, though, and Christmas morning found us boarding a plane from Norfolk Airport to Travis Air Force Base. When we arrived at Travis, it was late at night, but we went straightaway to check on flights to Tachikawa Air Base. The man there said for us to come back the next day between 5:00 and 7:00 a.m., which seemed odd, but we had no other choice. We got there at 5:30 only to be told the flight was filled. Good ol' Jack had warned me that might happen, and I had been given instructions if anywhere along the way I had a problem that seemed insurmountable, to say something I didn't think I could pull off, but, I said very firmly, "In that case, I must speak with your commanding officer." And it worked. He said, "Never mind. I'll take care of it. You go over to the food bar and get some breakfast. I'll send somebody to get you when the plane is ready for takeoff. How many bags do you have?" When I told him thirteen, he rolled his eyes and just looked up in total frustration. As we were in line for something to eat, four sailors in front of us were talking about some lady with three kids and how they, the sailors, could stay in the airport overnight better than they could. We didn't say a word, but quietly I prayed, "God, bless these men—forever." Reorganizing the baggage area on the plane took a while, but we were finally on our way.

A Japanese man got on the plane in Hawaii and sat next to me. He asked where we were going when we got to Japan, and when I said I wasn't exactly sure, and no, I didn't have any reservations, he was very disturbed. "Ahh!" (a very gaspy inhale I thought of as "hiss"). No reservation? (hiss). Bad! (hiss). Whereupon for the first chance I had to do nothing but sit and worry about what was going to happen when we got to Japan, I did just that. From Wake, we stopped at Tokyo Airport, where my friend got off and then on to Tachikawa Air Base. When we arrived, we decided to wait until the line was shorter to pick up our luggage when in a matter of minutes, my eyes beheld the most *glorious* sight: an American sailor who got down in front of me, looked me straight in the face and said, "Mrs. Madigan?" *I knew at that moment we'd be all right.* That was his third straight day of driving there because Jim had no idea when we would arrive. I told him we hadn't picked up our luggage, and he said it was already in the truck, "all thirteen pieces of it."

We went directly to the Navy Exchange Hotel in Yokosuka, where our sponsor had left snacks and drinks with a note saying that at some ungodly time of the night we would wake up hungry. It was 28 December, Jimmy's birthday. He was relieved because the girls had teased him that when we crossed the international date line, he would miss his birthday. The next morning, *Arlington* arrived, and we began what was a wonderful tour in Japan. The girls went to a DOD high school in Yokohama and won beaucoup medals at swim meets in Tokyo, and Jimmy was in *Stars and Stripes* for making an unassisted triple play in Little League. In the seventh inning, with runners on first and second, and no outs, he snagged a line drive, tagged the runner coming from first, and stepped on second base—retiring the side. While *Providence* was in Vietnam, the XO's wife and I did a three-week tour of the Far East. We had great quarters on base—overlooking the water, even though we had to climb ninety-seven steps to get up there.

Jim had told me at the Ring Dance that we would be traveling the globe, and we did. Our favorite tour was four years in London. We had many excursions all over the continent, and I even went to Russia. Because of his clearances, Jim had to sign a waiver saying he wouldn't come get me for five years if anything happened to me. Jim retired in March 1980, and in August 1980, he passed away in the middle of the night with a heart attack. In 2009, soon after I moved to Falcons Landing, I was having dinner with Bill and Mary-lin Ryan one night, and when Bill asked and found I was not getting DIC (dependency and indemnity compensation), he gave me the name and number of someone in D.C. to ask about my eligibility. Jim had been commanding officer at Naval Communications Station in Cam Ranh Bay from May 1969 to August 1970 while Agent Orange was running rampant, and there was never a doubt that the difficulty he had breathing for ten years when that tour was over had taken a final toll on his overworked heart. Bill's inquiry resulted in my receiving DIC benefits, with over half of my SBP (Survivor Benefit Plan) being nontaxable.

Jim had only twenty-eight years with us, but they were filled with wonderful memories. I hope this chapter confirms what I say with firsthand knowledge: the Navy looks out for its own, especially 52ers in looking out for the widows. Thanks, guys!

VIII

REMEMBERED

Day is done, gone the sun
From the lakes, from the hills, from the sky
All is well, safely rest
God is nigh.

Fading light dims the sight
And a star gems the sky, gleaming bright
From afar, drawing near
Falls the night.

Thanks and praise for our days
'Neath the sun, 'neath the stars, 'neath the sky
As we go, this we know
God is nigh.

Taps

Friends Indeed

Dick Denfeld

I'm sure all of us remember people who have contributed greatly to the vital process of our gaining maturity, choosing and attaining appropriate goals, and developing the strength to confront the challenges we face during all phases of our lives. Certainly family members, teachers, coaches, friends, and acquaintances fall in that category. How many can name *two people* who were most influential? I can.

At a critical time during the long winter of our youngster year (Dark Ages), when two and a half more years at the Academy seemed endless, I began doubting my resolve to remain. In fact, I actually prepared a resignation letter and had it ready to turn in to our company officer. I'm convinced that's when my Lord and Savior, Jesus, stepped in and put me back on the path toward the success and happiness I have enjoyed since that time. My 4th Company roommate, Dick Dietz, and 13th Company football teammate, Bill Bryson, were the instruments through which God got me back on track.

First, Dick saw my resignation papers sitting on the corner of my desk, and while I was out of the room, he disposed of them. When I got back to the room I asked Dick what had happened to the papers. He casually said, "I tore them up." Dick's action was likely a simple expression of the respect we had for each other. He knew what I needed better than I did myself, and staying in the Academy was foremost.

For the most part, Bill Bryson and I had little contact with each other except during the football season, but we became very good friends. During our four seasons of football, in games and many practices, we lined up side by side countless times in the offensive line, he as center and I as left guard. Probably sensing my frustration and unease during our youngster year, Bill invited me to join a Bible study group he chaired that met every day after evening meal. Through Bible study and with Bill's help and guidance, following my aborted resignation incident, I was able to establish a foundation of faith that has had a profound, positive, and lasting impact on my life.

I have always suspected that others felt as I do that Bill Bryson was a positive influence in their lives. So I asked Earl Chinn, classmate and 13th

Company mate. Earl's response: "The first word that comes to mind when I think of Bill Bryson is 'good.' He was a good friend, a good midshipman, a totally good person, and yes, his Christian message did extend to his company mates. It was always a pleasure to be around Bill Bryson."

Maj Gen William Burdette Maxson, USAF (Ret.)

—— *Nancy Maxson (and daughter Suzie and son Bob)* ——

Bill Maxson always wanted to fly, as his dad was a pilot and air balloon racer whose flying license was signed by Orville Wright. So Bill chose the Air Force, going to pilot training immediately, as the Navy required one year at sea before going to Pensacola. The Air Force commissioned Annapolis and West Point graduates on 3 June, so when Bill graduated from the Naval Academy, he was already a second lieutenant in the Air Force, which prevented the Navy from delaying graduation of his class for leaving their shoes on the field during the color parade. I stood right behind Bill's company, the 17th, and saw the whole show!

After graduation, we were married in July, in Lakewood, Ohio, and what followed were thirty-five moves in thirty-two years. Bill had several commands but he always said his favorite was being a SAC wing commander of B-52s and KC-135s, even though he had to answer the brick for commander availability checks in thirty seconds, 24/7.

Little known fact: all of Bill's 283 combat missions in Southeast Asia were in the B-57—one pilot and one navigator (who had no flying controls). And his navigator, for most of those missions, was Col David M. Hammett, USAF (Ret.), also a USNA grad, Class of 1955. What a team!

While Bill was commander at Eglin Air Force Base, another rewarding assignment, classmate RADM Dempster Jackson called to see if the Navy could move the Explosive Ordnance Disposal School from Indian Head, Maryland, to Eglin. After talking to the chief scientist, Howard Deming, Bill called Demps right back and said sure! Then they informed the Department of the Navy and the Department of the Air Force of their decision.

When Bill retired in 1984, he served on the board of Cypress International in Alexandria, Virginia. While there he was so honored to be elected president of the Class of 1952. Classmates and their wives have always meant so much to us both. We'd go anytime, anywhere to be with our buddies—and I still do. After all these years they continue to be my sisters and brothers. We always cheer for Navy even when they play Air Force. USNA was Bill's school.

Bill was actively involved with the community—especially the Salvation Army and the Red Cross—which he continued to serve after retirement. When we retired in Destin, Florida, Bill was asked by the president of Northwest Florida State College, Niceville, Florida, in 1991 to form an organization of retired senior professionals interested in contributing their skills, talents, expertise, and experience in meaningful ways. Today the Northwest Florida State College Institute for Senior Professionals continues to be "a service organization committed to providing opportunities for retired professionals to make contributions to the community and the college through participation in problem solving and economic development of the college district."

We "retired retired" in 2012, after moving to Fleet Landing, a CCRC in Atlantic Beach, Florida, from Destin. Ten months later, on 3 January 2013, Bill died after having heart surgery. Bill and I chose to be buried in Clyde, Ohio, at McPherson Cemetery, named for GEN James McPherson (West Point), the youngest Union general killed in the Civil War.

Despite the U.S. government sequester, which denied Bill an Air Force flyover, our family had a meaningful and soulful train whistle toward the end of the beautiful military service, which was attended by many dear friends of the Class of 1952.

CAPT John Robert Cummings Mitchell, USN (Ret.)

Bill Knutson

John Cummings was a gifted, unique man of many talents. He possessed a strong sense of purpose of what he wanted to do in life and in the Navy. Some say John lived a charmed life, but in reality he was a driven perfectionist who created his own good fortune. He became addicted to aviation at the age of thirteen, when, for his birthday, he was given two flights in private aircraft, one a Stearman N2S.

John joined the Marine Corps after high school and was appointed to the Naval Academy in 1948, graduating with the Class of 1952. He stayed at the Academy as an instructor for the incoming class of midshipmen before rushing to Pensacola to get into aviation training ahead of his USNA classmates. John earned his wings on 18 December 1953 and selected the VF pipeline to the fleet. After jet transition, he was assigned to VF-193 at Naval Air Station Moffett Field in California, flying the F-2H3 Banshee. The squadron was deployed at the time, so John was sent to Fleet All-Weather Training Unit Pacific at NAS Barbers Point, Hawaii, for instrument, radar, and night intercept training.

John's tour of duty with VF-193 was both legendary and infamous. Alan Shepard, later of astronaut fame, was the operations officer. Alan was frustrated for not being picked for the Blue Angels and formed his own acrobatic team within the squadron called the Mangy Angels. Although just a Nugget pilot, John was a superb aviator and flew wing in their stepped up formations.

The squadron deployed on USS *Oriskany* (CV 3) in 1955, and John's most unbelievable and infamous incident occurred on 22 June 1955. John had completed a night Combat Air Patrol mission in the Sea of Japan and was making his night carrier landing. In the last moments of the approach, just before landing, the Banshee started losing power. John tried to turn to miss the landing signal officer's platform and clear the stern of the carrier. The Banshee was too low and too slow, and it flew into the fantail of the carrier just below the flight deck. There was a large explosion and fire, and the aft section of the Banshee fell into the water. The cockpit area, with canopy gone, was wedged forward toward the hangar deck. Miraculously, except for a couple cuts and bruises, John was not hurt. He unbuckled his harness and scrambled out onto the hangar deck. Five sailors sleeping on the fantail at the time of the accident were injured, and John helped carry one of them to sickbay for treatment. The flight surgeon checked John out and said he was OK. John asked if it would be all right for him to call the ready room to let them know that he was uninjured.

Meanwhile those on the bridge and flight deck who had witnessed the crash and explosion reckoned there was no way that John could have survived. It was a considerable shock when someone claiming to be Mitchell called the ready room to say, "I'm OK." The duty officer who took the call told him in outrage that he was a sick person, and another officer grabbed the phone and delivered a tirade of profanity before Mitchell was able to convince them that he had actually survived the crash. The next day John was shown the remains of his Banshee, the cockpit section wedged between a large vertical flight deck support and two massive cylinders. The ample dimensions between the two objects had permitted the nose of the fighter to pass between them and stop just short of the hangar bay. If John had hit the stern anywhere but in perfect alignment with the flight deck support and the cylinder, he would have perished. It was a miracle.

John finished the cruise in USS *Oriskany* and made a second cruise with VF-163 in the USS *Yorktown* (CVS 10) before detaching with orders to U.S. Naval Test Pilot School in Patuxent River, Maryland. He was the first member of the Class of 1952 to enter TPS and graduated with TPS Class 19 in February 1958. John was ordered to the Flight Test Division, where he was assigned to the Carrier Suitability Branch as the F-8 Crusader project pilot.

In 1959 John was a candidate in the astronaut selection process but was not selected. NASA announced that it would accept applications for a second group of astronauts in April 1962. John again applied but again was not chosen. NASA sent him another invitation to apply for the fifth group of astronauts in 1965, but John declined as he had just joined VF-33 for his command tour. He returned to sea duty with VF-74, flying F-4D Skyrays in 1960. VF-74 was chosen to be the first fighter squadron to transition to the new F4 Phantom and made the first Phantom deployment on board USS *Forrestal* (CV 59). John was selected early for promotion to lieutenant commander and finished his tour at VF-101, Detachment A, at NAS Oceana.

John's early training as a Marine and at the Naval Academy made him sharp looking and neat in appearance. Those traits, coupled with his articulate speech and command of the English language, made him a prime candidate to be an admiral's aide. In February 1964, he was picked to be the flag lieutenant and aide to VADM Paul H. Ramsey, commander, Naval Air Forces, Atlantic Fleet. John admired the man and said, "He was one of the last World War II Navy Cross winners: cigar-smoking, good-natured, hard-drinking fighter pilots, with three stars."

John screened early for squadron command and joined VF-33 (Tarsiers) as executive officer in 1965 and became commanding officer in 1966. One might say that he was a model commanding officer. He was not full of fire and brimstone. His method was to control the situation and not show his emotions. He was quick to praise and support his men and the squadron when they performed and a master at taking those who needed a reprimand or correction aside in private. John led by example in the air and around the squadron. He used the experience he acquired during his tour at Patuxent River as a test pilot to teach the aircrews how to aggressively fly the Phantom and do it safely. The squadron won the safety award both years John was in the squadron and those principles carried forward for many years. He was great on challenging every officer and sailor to live up to their full potential.

VF-33 were the Tarsiers, and the squadron patch looked terrible. The Tarsier was reported to be pound for pound the most ferocious animal on earth—usually referred to by others as the "bug eating monkey." John completely redesigned the patch with the face of a fierce, dynamic animal. His leadership in VF-33 resulted in the squadron winning the Battle "E" for the best fighter squadron in the Atlantic Fleet.

John graduated from the U.S. Army War College in 1968 and reported to CTF-77 for a one-year tour in the Gulf of Tonkin as the staff antiair-warfare officer. After a year at a desk, at sea John was selected to be a carrier air wing commander and in 1969 took command of CVW-2 assigned to USS *Ranger*. During the CVW-2 work up, John was given new orders to take command of CVW-9 destined to deploy in USS *America* in the Atlantic Fleet. A series of mishaps that were not John's fault, like the F-8 crashing into the hangar at Miramar, killing men and destroying F-4Js, posed significant management and leadership challenges. However, CVW-9 met the schedule and deployed onboard USS *America* for a nine-month combat cruise to Vietnam in 1970.

John's post-CAG tour was air wing training officer at commander, Naval Air Force, Pacific Fleet. After selection to captain, he returned to the Pentagon as the F-14A/AWG-9 program coordinator for the deputy chief of naval operations (air warfare). He helped shepherd the Tomcat through its final phases of procurement before taking command of his deep draft, USS *Sylvania* (AFS 2) in 1974.

John was given swift orders to take over command of the carrier USS *John F. Kennedy* (CV 67) after the *Kennedy* had collided with the USS *Belknap* (CG 26) off the coast of Sicily. John finished the Mediterranean cruise with Sixth Fleet and returned to complete repairs to the carrier in the spring of 1976. While John was CO, *Kennedy* was involved with another collision off Scotland on 14 September 1976. During night underway replenishment, the destroyer USS *Bordelon* (DD 881) experienced steering difficulties and collided with *Kennedy*. *Kennedy* had minor damage, but *Bordelon* had to be towed to Plymouth, England.

During 1977 and 1978, John was in the Carrier Programs Office fighting the battle to keep the nuclear carrier program alive. President Carter's effort to cancel production of a second nuclear-powered carrier was the focal point. In the end the supercarriers *Theodore Roosevelt* (CVN 71), *Abraham Lincoln* (CVN 72), and *George Washington* (CVN 73) survived, and much credit was given to the efforts of John Mitchell.

John was not selected for flag officer. Some said it was John's opposition to President Carter's efforts to cancel more nuclear carriers, some thought it was his divorce from his first wife, an action not condoned at that time, and some felt the collision with *Bordelon* played a role. But one thing is clear—the Navy passed over a very charismatic, dedicated, and focused leader who always stuck by his beliefs and did what he thought was right, no matter what the personal consequences.

The Honorable John E. Sheehan

Jerry Zacharias

I am writing this brief history of classmate Jack Sheehan because his health did not permit his writing it. I have been a friend of Jack and his family for more than sixty-two years. Jack had a magnificent career, and I thought his story should be documented.

When the words "character," "duty," "honor," and "integrity" are spoken, the name of John E. Sheehan comes to my mind. Jack Sheehan is living proof that a midshipman, naval officer, public servant, and businessman can do it all in one career: serve his nation in the military and as a civilian, serve his fellow man through philanthropy and humanitarianism, and distinguish himself in the world of business and management.

Active Duty

Upon graduation from the Naval Academy in June 1952, Jack went to Pensacola, where he completed basic flight training in the SNJ aircraft, which included formation flying, aerobatics, aerial gunnery, navigation, night flying, and carrier landing practice at a local field. The final hurdle was completing six arrested landings on a carrier. During his first approach to the ship, the engine of his SNJ quit and he crash-landed in the water in the wake of the carrier. He sustained a concussion that rendered him unconscious. As the aircraft slowly sank, the cold water roused him. He exited the aircraft, popped the Mae West CO2 bottles, and began swimming furiously to the surface. The plane-guard destroyer was right there when he surfaced and plucked Jack out of the water. Two days later, Jack returned to the USS *Monterey* (CVL 26) and completed his six arrested landings, a really gutsy performance. He received his Navy wings of gold on 17 December 1953 and headed for advanced flight training in Corpus Christi, Texas.

Following two months of instrument flying (blind under the hood), Jack reported to ATU-101 at Naval Air Station Corpus Christi to learn to fly the powerful F-6F Hellcat fighter. The aircraft had a 2,800-horsepower engine. Compared to the SNJ trainer, when you added throttle for takeoff, the F6F was like "being strapped to a cannonball," and you needed lots of right rudder to keep it headed straight down the runway.

Next it was on to NAS Kingsville in Texas for jet training in the F-9F Panther. While at NAS Kingsville, Jack and I revised a copy of the Naval Academy Regulations for use in training aviation cadets. This extra task enabled us to go anywhere in the fleet that we wanted. We both selected Fighter Squadron 72 at Quonset Point, Rhode Island, to fly the F-9F Panther jet.

LTJG John E. Sheehan and F-9F Panther (Official U.S. Navy Photo)

When we arrived in 1954, the squadron stood last in the Atlantic Fleet competition. One year later, VF-72 won the Navy "E" as best fighter squadron in the Atlantic Fleet. (It must have been the Class of 1952 influences. In weapons training and during competitive evaluations, Jack was the top rocketeer in the squadron.) Eight months after arriving in the squadron, we flew our aircraft to NAS North Island, California, and embarked in USS *Hornet* (CV 12) for an eight-month Western Pacific deployment. Our squadron later introduced the A-4D Skyhawk to the fleet, the first unit to receive that aircraft. The squadron was operating from the USS *Forrestal* when the battle group commander, RADM Don Griffin, Class of

1927, invited Jack to become his aide, which he did. In August 1958, Jack resigned his commission, which involved the most difficult decision he ever made, and decided to enroll in Harvard Business School.

Professional Management Career

Jack earned an MBA at Harvard and was one of twelve in the class of eight hundred recognized as a George F. Baker scholar for academic excellence. Jack said that his experience at the Naval Academy and in the Navy made all the difference.

From Harvard, Jack went to New York City and joined the staff of McKinsey and Company, the top management-consulting firm in the world at that time. In 1963 he became vice president of Martin Marietta's Cement and Lime Division, and in 1966 he became president and CEO of Cohart Refractories, a subsidiary of Corning Glass Works. After five years at Corning, Jack interrupted his promising career as a professional corporate manager to reenter federal service.

Federal Reserve Governor

In 1971 Jack was appointed by President Nixon and confirmed by the U.S. Senate as a member of the Board of Governors of the Federal Reserve System in Washington, D.C. Jack was very well prepared for his Senate confirmation and his questioning by Senator William Proxmire of Wisconsin. In fact, Jack was so well prepared, Senator Proxmire called him on it and said, "Mr. Sheehan, you are reading the answers to my questions."

Jack was the only experienced corporate manager on the board, which consisted of seven PhD economists. Governor Sheehan was assigned the job of reducing the cost by reorganizing the management system of the Federal Reserve (Fed), the nation's central bank. During his nearly four years on the board, Jack implemented an improved check processing system and a substantial payroll reduction program, which netted the Fed over $200 million in improved performance.

During his term at the Fed, there was a break-in at one of the Fed storage facilities. Jack thought that the perpetrators might have also found a copy of the delivery schedule for money at various Fed units. Accordingly, Jack doubled the security at many of the Fed facilities. It was the Fed security detail at the Watergate Hotel in Washington, D.C., that happened upon the burglary of the Democratic National Committee office in the Watergate Hotel. The rest of the story is history.

Jack Sheehan and family with President Nixon in the Oval Office (Official White House Photo)

Congressional Liaison

Jack was an informal advisor to Congressman John P. Murtha, 12th District, Pennsylvania, on a wide variety of matters including the needs of the U.S. Naval Academy. In 1994 Murtha obtained an appropriation of $14.5 million for the modification of Ricketts Hall and the construction of the visitors center. In 2003 Jack requested and received a $50 million budget supplemental to repair damage to the Naval Academy caused by Hurricane Isabel.

Service to the Naval Academy

Jack's sixteen years of service to the USNA Alumni Association and the USNA Foundation is the longest uninterrupted tour of any living graduate. He first served on the Alumni Association Board of Trustees in 1988 and then as vice chairman of the Eastern Region in 1994. In 1995 Jack was elected to chairman of the board, one of only two noncareer graduates ever to hold that position.

On his two-year watch as chairman, Jack made many significant short-term changes and strategic contributions to the association. His most important achievement was to lay the groundwork for, and play a critical role in, establishing the Naval Academy Foundation, the fund-raising arm of the Naval Academy. Jack continued as past chairman of the Alumni Association until 2003.

Private Investor

After Jack's tour of duty on the Fed, he reentered the private sector and embarked on a new career as a private investor. In the future, Jack would acquire eight companies in the metalworking, machinery and steel related industries. Even in his investment career, Jack had an eye toward public service. Four of his buyouts have been closed or nearly closed manufacturing operations, primarily steel plants in economically distressed communities. These restarted operations have resulted in the saving of approximately seven thousand domestic jobs.

Additionally, one of his businesses, Korn's Galvanizing in Johnstown, Pennsylvania, hires ex-convicts to offer them a "second chance" opportunity. The foreman at Korn's is an ex-convict and one of the company's very best workers. Jack believed in second chances. You truly made a difference in this world, Jack. I am proud to have been one of your shipmates, and I send a hearty "Bravo Zulu." God bless you.

Jack made his final flight on 30 October 2014.

Vince and Esther

Vince Manara III

Т he true measure of any group or organization's strength, success, and longevity is represented in the way the individual members support each other and interact, each taking on different roles relative to their inherent abilities, culminating in the body as a whole. As such, the infamous and nearly doomed (color parade episode) Class of 1952 is no exception.

For CAPT Vincent J. Manara Jr., one of his contributions to the greater Class of 1952 was expressed through both his "natural talent, and willingness to lead," exemplified during his tenure as class president. Vince accepted the reins of leadership and thrived in the role, truly leading the class. It's been said that Vince and Navy wife Esther were the "heart and soul of the class during his term of office."

Esther expressed her gifts to the class by becoming a true first lady through her strong support of the Navy wife sisterhood and her endeavors as a gracious hostess. As the "hostess with the mostest," Esther complemented Vince's natural communication talents with a mutual love of entertaining others, be they neighbors, family, friends, or, ultimately, the prestigious Class of 1952 (their Navy family). It was a passion that Vince and Esther developed independently, growing up in neighboring New Jersey towns—one from the city, enjoying Italian cuisine and its traditions, and the other from the country, where a home-cooked German influence was prevalent. Both were devoted to family and to giving caring attention to their children, much of which took place around the dinner table during that "disarming" time of eating and drinking; and as such the day's events were shared and discussed openly. Ultimately, the two honed their collective talents for entertaining and brought it to an art form with their extended family of the Class of 1952.

As evidence of this passion, one can remember various occasions. It is said during Vince and Esther's descent to Cocoa Beach (chosen due to the proximity to other classmates) every winter, where they helped organize the Class of 1952 get-togethers, little was left to chance. Their spreads were fabulous, ranging from pastas (not Esther's favorite, but enthusiastically prepared for Vince) to the local seafood, and more, with no limits except as to the concerns of others' dietary needs. Legend has it that as hostess, Esther even brought oyster forks to one affair! Every evening was an opportunity to exercise their hosting skills, and they thoroughly enjoyed and truly thrived on it.

And who could forget Vince and Esther's previous beach locale and exquisite entertaining events at the "Captain's Choice" in Duck, North Carolina? A "casual spread" there with classmates, friends, and neighbors involved fresh blue crabs, boiled shrimp, and other local cuisine. Wonderful times created great memories, and all took place around picnic tables with Esther's trademark linen "table cloths" and napkins. What a time it was.

Esther and Vince also entertained at the coveted Navy football games. There the hosting duo were considered cofounders of the "'52 tailgate concept of the modern age." Esther turned the affairs from a group gathering to a jubilant session with good food and good spirits.

Per Vince's orders (of course), Esther always brought more than enough food for everyone. What started on a single card table (yes, with Esther's table cloth) and Vince's invitation to get the word out, became a pregame dining tradition. The affair grew with each ensuing game; the menu grew as well, evolving into a reported sighting of lobster tails. All the classmates brought food and celebrated. What wonderful times!

And in later years, as Vince and Esther settled into retirement at Willow Valley in Pennsylvania, they continued their passion for entertaining. They organized the "Class of '52 at 5," an event intended for the classmates in the area to get together for drinks, appetizers, and great conversation once a month, alternating the get-together location among the group, a tradition that still exists today.

Ironically, it was in expressing this love and passion for entertaining others that Vince and Esther last shared Vince's time on earth. They were preparing appetizers for a party for a classmate that was to take place later that night, laughing together in the kitchen one morning and doing what they loved to do together most—preparing for a celebration with friends. Shortly after, as Vince finished cleaning dishes, he passed suddenly. He is truly missed.

Non Sibi Sed Patriae
Our Honored Brothers

Compiled by Jim Sagerholm
and Jerry Zacharias

Killed in Action

CAPT Donald D. Aldern, USN	Vietnam, 1969
Lt Col Charles D. Ballou, USAF	Vietnam, 1968
Maj Robert G. Bell, USAF	Vietnam, 1965
Maj Joseph E. Bower, USAF	Vietnam, 1965
2ndLt Mortimer W. Cox, USMC	Korea, 1953
CAPT John C. Ellison, USN	Vietnam, 1967
CAPT Thomas C. McEwen, USAF	Vietnam, 1965
Col John F. O'Grady, USAF	Vietnam, 1967
Col Charles H. W. Read Jr., USAF	Vietnam, 1968
Maj Raymond L. Tacke, USAF	Vietnam, 1969
CAPT John D. Yamnicky, USN (Ret.)	11 September 2001

Line of Duty

LTJG Robert C. Allison, USN	Aircraft accident, 1955
Capt Warren R. Anderson, USAF	Aircraft accident, 1957
LCDR Charles E. Andrews III, USN	Aircraft accident, 1962
Maj Thomas N. Bakke, USAF	Aircraft accident, 1964
LTJG Timothy D. Bartosh, USN	Aircraft accident, 1954
LTJG Olivier R. Billion, USN	Aircraft accident, 1955
LTJG Lucien P. Borden, USN	Aircraft accident, 1955
LTJG Robert E. Calkins, USN	Aircraft accident, 1956
LT Robert Z. Cornwell, USN	Aircraft accident, 1959
2ndLt Frederic C. Davis, USAF	Aircraft accident, 1953
LTJG Ernest R. Genter Jr., USN	Aircraft accident, 1957
1st Lt Richard Geriak, USAF	Aircraft accident, 1954
LTJG James W. Gooding Jr., USN	Aircraft accident, 1956
LCDR Frederick E. Grammer Jr., USN	Aircraft accident, 1962

2nd Lt Edward F. Greer Jr., USAF	Aircraft accident, 1952
LTJG Robert B. Gulley, USN	Aircraft accident, 1955
LTJG John J. Hackett, USN	Submarine battery explosion, 1955
LCDR Robert F. Hansen, USN	Aircraft accident, 1963
CDR Harold F. Hicks Jr., USN	Aircraft accident, 1966
LTJG William P. Holmes, USN	Aircraft accident, 1956
LTJG Herbert C. Knipple, USN	Aircraft accident, 1955
LT Harry A. Lackey II, USN	Aircraft accident, 1960
1stLt Maurice L. Lallement, USAF	Aircraft accident, 1954
LT Walther G. Langloh, USN	Aircraft accident, 1957
LCDR John P. Manfredi, USN	Aircraft accident, 1965
1stLt Alan M. McAneny, USMC	Aircraft accident, 1955
LCDR Arthur H. Moore, USN	Aircraft accident, 1962
LT George F. Morrow, USN	Aircraft accident, 1959
LTJG Michael C. Moushey, USN	Aircraft accident, 1954
Capt Harry A. Pribble, USMC	Aircraft accident, 1958
LTJG W. Max Riggs, USN	Aircraft accident, 1957
Midshipman 2nd Class Henry R. Sadowski, USN	Aircraft accident, 1950
ENS Ronald R. Swanson, USN	Aircraft accident, 1953
1stLt Charles R. Troppman, USAF	Helicopter accident, 1955
Capt Robert W. Whaling, USMC	Aircraft accident, 1961
CDR Robert R. Wilson, USN	Helicopter accident, 1968
LCDR Michael A. Zibilich, USN	Aircraft accident, 1963

Until we meet again . . .

About the Editor

After enlisting in 1946, **Vice Admiral James Sagerholm** received fleet appointment to the Naval Academy in 1948, graduating in 1952. He served in a cruiser, minesweepers, destroyers, and nuclear submarines, various staff duties, including a year in the White House as executive director of the President's Foreign Intelligence Advisory Board. His final active duty was as Chief of Naval Education and Training. He retired in November 1985.

The Naval Institute Press is the book-publishing arm of the U.S. Naval Institute, a private, nonprofit, membership society for sea service professionals and others who share an interest in naval and maritime affairs. Established in 1873 at the U.S. Naval Academy in Annapolis, Maryland, where its offices remain today, the Naval Institute has members worldwide.

Members of the Naval Institute support the education programs of the society and receive the influential monthly magazine *Proceedings* or the colorful bimonthly magazine *Naval History* and discounts on fine nautical prints and on ship and aircraft photos. They also have access to the transcripts of the Institute's Oral History Program and get discounted admission to any of the Institute-sponsored seminars offered around the country.

The Naval Institute's book-publishing program, begun in 1898 with basic guides to naval practices, has broadened its scope to include books of more general interest. Now the Naval Institute Press publishes about seventy titles each year, ranging from how-to books on boating and navigation to battle histories, biographies, ship and aircraft guides, and novels. Institute members receive significant discounts on the Press's more than eight hundred books in print.

Full-time students are eligible for special half-price membership rates. Life memberships are also available.

For a free catalog describing Naval Institute Press books currently available, and for further information about joining the U.S. Naval Institute, please write to:

Member Services
U.S. Naval Institute
291 Wood Road
Annapolis, MD 21402-5034
Telephone: (800) 233-8764
Fax: (410) 571-1703
Web address: www.usni.org